1993

Happy Ret[ir]

to one fabulous

schoolteacher.

Happy Cooking :)
in Arizona

— Nancy Hasenauer

BHS

BERT GREENE'S KITCHEN

A BOOK OF MEMORIES AND RECIPES

∾

BY BERT GREENE

COMPILED BY
PHILLIP STEPHEN SCHULZ

ILLUSTRATIONS BY ANDREA WISNEWSKI

WORKMAN PUBLISHING•NEW YORK

Bert Greene's Kitchen was originally syndicated by Bert
Greene & Associates. The column made its debut on
September 17, 1980, in the *New York Daily News* and
appeared weekly in major newspapers. The final column
appeared on June 8, 1988.

Library of Congress Cataloging-in-Publication Data
Greene, Bert
    Bert Greene's kitchen : a book of memories and recipes
/ by Bert Greene ; compiled by Phillip Stephen Schulz.
        p.   cm.
    ISBN 0-89480-765-X
    1. Cookery, American.   2. Diet—United States—
Miscellanea.   3. Food habits—United States—
Miscellanea.
    4. Gastronomy—Miscellanea.   I. Schulz, Phillip
Stephen.   II. Title.
TX715.G81158   1993
641.5973—dc20   92-50931
                                                CIP

Cover illustration: Pamela Patrick

Workman Publishing Company, Inc.
708 Broadway
New York, NY 10003

Manufactured in the United States of America

First printing April 1993
10 9 8 7 6 5 4 3 2 1

In memory of Bert Greene
and Myra Greene,
Dude, and Lulu.
This book is dedicated to all those
family, friends, and fans
who were touched by Bert, in or out of his kitchen

Many people were instrumental in Bert's career, but I would like to pay special tribute to Jean Hewitt, Joan Leonard, Nao Hauser, Arthur Schwartz, Suzanne Rafer, Lisa Hollander, Peter and Carolan Workman, Nat Sobel, Judith Weber, Dawn Dahl, and Pam Pettinella. Thanks also to Bert's cousin, Bunny August, and her husband, Jerry, for all their support. And last, but certainly not least, Bert Greene's kitchen could never have functioned without the help and friendship of Judith Blahnik, who somehow managed to keep us all on an even keel—even in the midst of chaos.

—*Phillip Stephen Schulz*

FOREWORD

ert Greene was born in New York City on October 16, 1923. He was a very handsome man with many talents and a great deal of charm. His very first job was as art director and illustrator for Helena Rubenstein—a heady experience for a young man straight out of college. And though he was never totally fulfilled in the world of commercial art, he stayed with it until 1976 when he retired as promotion art director for *Esquire* magazine.

Being a man of enormous energies, Bert moonlighted during his working career. He was co-founder of Theatre 12 in New York City in the 1950s and wrote a collection of one-act plays for that group. His Off-Broadway adaptations of such plays as *The Trial* by Franz Kafka and *Daisy Miller* by Henry James gained him a wide reputation. He was most proud, however, of his adaptation of Colette's *My Mother's House* starring Colleen Dewhurst, which was televised on PBS's NET Playhouse.

In 1966, Bert co-founded The Store in Amagansett, on Long Island. The Store was reputed to be the first gourmet take-out establishment in America. Though others were originally involved in the venture, it was Bert's vision and cooking skills that not only made The Store a success but gained him instant acclaim in the food world. His first cookbook, written with partner Denis Vaughan, was *The Store Cookbook,* published in 1974. He wrote eight more books and published hundreds of magazine articles in the next fourteen years. He also became a familiar face on the television show *Hour Magazine* with host Gary Collins. Nothing, however, gave him more pleasure than writing his weekly newspaper column.

"Bert Greene's Kitchen" first appeared in the New York *Daily News* on September 17, 1980. It was shortly syndicated in various major markets around the country. His column was not merely an outlet for his philosophy of life, it connected him directly with a far larger audience of readers than teaching classes and writing books afforded. Bert's fans were legion and verbal. He received many phone calls and many, many letters. Some were argumentative about errors in the editing room, others downright hostile over his nonconforming Jewish background. Most, however, were just friendly, chatty letters from people he had somehow touched. He answered every letter, even those that wounded his sensibilities. Bert, being Bert, often found himself in the midst of an on-going correspondence.

Bert once jokingly called himself the "Anne Landers" of cooking columnists. He wasn't too far off the mark. For many years, a woman in Michigan wrote to him about her miserable husband in particular and her unhappy life in general. According to her letters, her husband was extremely jealous of Bert. Bert feared for her; his co-workers feared for him. She was childlike in her writing and took great pleasure in sending Bert recipes clipped from newspapers and pasted into spiral notebooks. Though the recipes were often straight from some product's PR release, Bert was always moved by her efforts. She signed her letters "Your recipe nut." The story had a happy ending, or so Bert hoped. She finally left her husband and moved to Florida to be with her daughter and grandchildren. She seemed content with her new life, shopping, baby sitting, visiting with other elderly people. One day the letters just stopped.

Then, too, there was the elderly widow from Brooklyn, with her dog named Rusty. She was obviously not well and always seemed to write just after she was released from the hospital, where she had spent time for one reason or another. She may not have been well, but she certainly was spunky. She could go on and on for pages about the fights she had with her sister-in-law. As it was, she was always fighting with her tenants about late rent payments. Or so she wrote. It was always a drama. Her letters, too, abruptly stopped.

There were many others. These unseen faces became Bert's responsibility in a way, but not one of them asked for more than just a good ear to listen to their woes. And Bert had a very good ear, not just for his letter-writing fans, but for everyone who ever entered his circle of life.

Bert's columns and books had a way of reaching people on the most personal levels. Readers always clipped and saved his columns. He received many requests like the following:

Dear Bert,

We like to read your articles in the *News*. We like how you write about your family and friends. This is not like a cookbook which gives you nothing but a formula—it is more like a chat with friends. May we suggest that you compile *all* your articles in a book—or booklet—and let us have it at the end of the year? It will save us cutting out the articles and paste them in my scrap book. Cooking together with joy and happiness.

J.M.

Unfortunately Bert didn't live to fulfill that request.

SCHULZ MEETS GREENE

I first met Bert at a Boxing Day gathering in 1971. Before I knew it, I was working weekends at The Store in Amagansett. The Store truly was a wonderful place. The walls were covered with blue gingham, the shelves filled with wonderful kitchen antiques interspersed with home-made jams, jellies, relishes, and pickles. The stenciled refrigerator cases were always cram-packed, filled with the freshest of salads, homemade mayonnaise, aïoli, and pesto. It was a place where the daily ham and roast beef were always sliced by hand. Before my four-year stint in The Store's kitchen, the only cooking experience I had was a less-than-tonic (in Bert's words) bout as a cook in the U.S. Army. As I learned about food, I discovered that I had actually learned one thing in the army: how to use a knife—for chopping, that is. I knew little of haute cuisine (and still don't for that matter), but Bert didn't care, for he was not a "fancy" cook. His was a world of just plain good food. What set him apart from his peers was his sense of humor and his impeccable taste—in and out of a frying pan. When The Store was sold in 1976 and Bert devoted his time to writing articles and books, I was drafted as kitchen tester and recipe writer. And while many cookbook authors have professional kitchens to make their lives easier, this was not the case in the Greene establishment.

Bert referred to his kitchen as the size of a Checker cab—or "a mite smaller." It was indeed a mite smaller. Food processors, mixers, and other "gourmet" equipment were hidden away in closets or under the bed. The stove was so old, newcomers to the scene asked (only half jokingly) where the coal was kept. The dining room, crowded with card tables, served as workspace for two, then three when Judith Blahnik joined our crew. Add two cats and one dog to the picture, and you have a scene in a movie that nobody would believe. Yet the three of us, or should I say six, not only survived—we flourished.

Bert loved to teach, and his students responded exuberantly. He was a man who made instant contact with people. On the rare occasion that someone in a class, or for that matter in life, failed to respond to his open, outstretched hands, it upset him immensely. He believed in helping others, both friends and strangers. He had an enormous sense of responsibility in his role as a food-world personality. To this end he was president-elect of the International Association of Culinary Professionals when he died. One of his goals for this organization of food writers, educators, caterers, and chefs was to get the food industry to present a united front in the fight to eradicate world hunger. He also believed that the organization should lobby against the use of chemicals and unhealthy additives in our nation's food supply. He was emotional on these subjects—too emotional for the politics of the day. He was also stubborn, willing to take a chance in a world that has become too complacent with the status quo.

Bert was a special person. He was in good health and always looked twenty years younger than his age. He died in 1988 of complications from a rare form of vasculitis called lymphomatoid granulomatosis— nobody knows how he contracted the disease. It happened relatively quickly, and he did not have to suffer great pain. His death was a loss to all who knew him, whether in person or through his writing.

In selecting columns for this book, I have, for the most part, avoided duplicating his recollections that have appeared in his books, *The Store Cookbook, Bert Greene's Kitchen Bouquets, Honest American Fare, Cooking for Giving, Greene on Greens,* and *The Grains Cookbook.* He had written much about his life and times in those tomes, and I trust they will be kept in print for a long time to come. The introduction that follows is his own, the first column in the series he called "Bert Greene's Kitchen."

PHILLIP STEPHEN SCHULZ

CONTENTS

෯

BERT ON PEOPLE
page 102

BERT ON THE ROAD
page 172

BERT ON BERT
page 238

FROM MY KITCHEN TO YOUR KITCHEN

When viewing my quarters for the very first time, someone inevitably asks: "What's a man of your size doing in this kitchen?" Greene's answer? Doing the best I can, obviously. For though I am over six feet, four inches in height and matchingly well upholstered, my scullery in Manhattan is no larger than a Checker cab! Perhaps, on proper reflection, even a mite smaller. But if the proportions do not exactly dovetail with my amplitude, I have—to paraphrase Alan Jay Lerner—grown accustomed to the space!

Luckier than most, I have a country kitchen as well. The dimensions there are more commodious, but the equipment is similarly antique. Both these galleys (where I have cooked happily for years) doggedly resist the blandishment of modern enterprise.

I do not truly know why, but the mystique of microwaves or Garland ranges embedded in islands of snowy tile has always eluded me. When I had money enough to afford such utility, I frankly hadn't the heart. Instead I bought my kitchens a grandmotherly rocking chair and a marzipan mold or two. The rationalization for not renovating is lame. Since neither dwelling was less than a century old, I claimed unwillingness to disinter the happy shades who chopped and carved there long, long before me. Actually I guess I merely mistrusted the spic and span of the newfangled.

Sensuality is what I love most about cooking. It is the frizzle of bacon on a back burner and the froth of scalded cream whisked into vanilla and sugar until pans, sink, cook, and even the walls are pale and polka-spotted that makes a kitchen kitchenly. Remove the mess, and for me you dispel a measure of the magic.

I got a head start finding my home on the range when I grew up in Queens. A child of the Depression, I was channeled into light cookery early on by working parents who sensibly reasoned that my homework could not possibly suffer more from my duties as "mother's helper" *before* meals than it did from my endless movie-going *after* them. As a result, Greene spent the better part of his formulative years improbably wedged betwixt muses: Garbo, Dietrich, and Fanny Farmer!

First I was merely a kitchen stand-in. Picking up the groceries on my way home from school, I also did a little peeling and slicing. That shortly led to a more important role: watcher of the pots. At five every afternoon, while freer spirits played stickball in the empty lots that crowned most of Jackson Heights in those days, it was my assignment to turn up the gas under those pans my mother had left partially prepared before she went to work. My attention span was slack, however, so periodically I burned something. It was this defect that prompted my debut as a chef.

Attempting to repair some utterly charred stew and dropping spoon after spoonful of peanut butter into the sorry pan (reputedly a cure-all for scorch in those prehistoric times), I remember thinking, "To heck with it. I couldn't possibly cook up anything worse!" I threw out the entire contents and started dinner from scratch.

In retrospect, the act seems signally audacious for a kid of eleven or twelve, but I was a born pragmatist (and an intrepid liar into the bargain). So, after ferreting out a recipe alike enough to the burnt offering and making a quick trip to the corner store for new ingredients, I produced my very first lamb stew.

I remember it well because (on the counsel of *The Settlement Cookbook*) I added a handful of fresh peas to the casserole at the very end. Uncanned vegetables were an unlikely adjunct to any dish in our house, but I defended their alien presence with a myth. I announced that the greengrocer had obviously included a sack by error.

Apparently the ploy worked, for everyone admired the peas in their stew. Until the end of the month, at least. Then, with a terrible jeremiad, my scrupulous mother tallied up the monthly charges from our grocer. Not only did the derelict peas appear on his statement, but a pound or so of stewing lamb came to light as well.

That is the reason I never saw Katharine Hepburn as *Sylvia Scarlet* (at least until the performance was revived on TV in my advancing years). For I was barred from movie attendance for seven terrible days for that misdeed.

It might have been worse. I fully anticipated a month's restriction, but parental consternation was mingled, even then, with grudging pride at my culinary accomplishment. And soon our family kitchen—equipped with Hoosier cabinet and dome-topped Frigidaire—became my uncontested bailiwick.

As a chef, I had a legacy. I acquired my taste buds from my grandmother. A small, feisty lady (less than half my size when I was fourteen), she lived only for house and garden. Whatever her matriarchal frailties, she never erred on the side of homely pleasures. This woman cooked like an angel and her thumb was pure jade. Her greensward was an embarrassment of riches: flowers of staggering proportions and a kitchen garden of herbs that alerted bees for miles around. And why not, when she poured the best of her soup stock on the roots all year long?

My grandmother cooked effortlessly. Omelets were produced in a single gesture. Using a fork to whip the eggs (no wire whisk for her) and the same utensil to scramble the golden froth in a pan, she would fill the runny center with any leftover that was stoveside and turn the delectable whole onto a warmed plate with the very same fork. All in less than five minutes.

We developed a curious rapport, my grandmother and I, over our mutual menus—she the master, and I the acolyte. I lunched in her kitchen during my grammar school days and many times would be late for afternoon class because I lingered too long while she advanced a theory why my soufflé had fallen the night before.

But I never *cooked* in her kitchen. I was not even allowed to wash a dish there. For that room was *her* territory, and any well-meant invasion was kindly but firmly discouraged.

Oddly enough, when I ate in Julia Child's kitchen for the first time, her dominion held the same inviolate if homely air about it.

I started The Store in Amagansett with four enthusiastic partners in the summer of 1966. Before the first autumn leaf had fallen, half the original quartet had decamped and the remaining two had cut a wide swath to escape the seething kitchen airs. I, however, thrived in this thermal arena; it became Bert Greene's battleground. To be utterly candid, cooking at The Store made my reputation, and I loved every arch-shattering, backbreaking moment of its ten-year existence.

Now I chef for friends alone. But if I had not once burned a batch of sacrificial lamb, I might never have acquired the derring-do (or skill) that fed the rich and famous for years. Neither would I have written a best-selling cookbook, nor taught hundreds of students all over the country the pleasures of my small kitchenly accomplishments. Let alone be sharing them with you.

BERT GREENE

BERT GREENE'S KITCHEN

A BOOK OF MEMORIES AND RECIPES

BERT ON FAMILY

CHAPTER ONE

SATURDAYS AT THE TABLE WITH MYRA

t an earlier age than most, perhaps, I discovered that the aroma of melting cheese can whet a man's appetite—but only under the right circumstances.

When I was about ten, my sister, Myra (several years worldlier than I in the ways of gracious living), decided it was time to upgrade my untried palate by exposing it to the savor of *haute cuisine*. This, mind you, in the dead center of the Depression, when epicurean ingredients were simply out of the question in our household.

My sister was an intrepid believer in old-fashioned glamour, and once every week she arranged for us to dine like the magic personae of the society pages she held dear. These collations always took place on Saturday, while the rest of the family were at their various employments. But no luncheon preparations would begin until my mother—who had recently secured a position as a beauty demonstrator, carrying her wares door to door in a handsome leather case—was safely out the door and waiting at the corner bus stop, for our parent maintained a low, low threshold for folly.

My sister was the one who found the recipes for our luncheons, made up the menus, and set the dining room table with my parent's best (unused) china, crystal, and linen. All of the food she prepared was dreadful, but we never admitted the defect, pressing on gamely week after week, hoping for better luck next time. Finally, however, one of these culinary forays was such a bona fide disaster that it ended our quest for the high life.

Stumbling upon a description of Welsh rarebit in some shiny women's magazine, Myra set about acquiring the components for our next party. My mother, however, stubbornly ignored the requested Cheddar cheese on her grocery list and brought home Muenster instead.

It was not an auspicious beginning for our Saturday concoction. My sister bravely set the yellow loaf in a sauté pan, and together we watched, transfixed, as it refused to liquefy. No amount of milk or beer sprinkled into the pan—nor the added increments of cream and butter—would set it flowing. Instead each new ingredient was merely absorbed into the quivering mass. And what we created, for all our stirring, was a kind of mucilaginous spaghetti—long rubbery strands of cheese that we hastily scraped onto "toast fingers" in the kitchen, knowing full well that our dish would never make the transition to the dining room table.

"It's *interesting*," we lied over our ginger ales—but weakly, for the substance had become so congealed on our forks that it could no longer be chewed and had to be swallowed whole.

The death knell for our weekend gourmetry came fast, because no matter how much Old Dutch cleanser was sprinkled on the surface, no matter how many Brillo pads scrubbed away, neither my sister nor I could pry the hardened evidence of Muenster cheese, turned into solid ochre latex, from the bottom of my mother's favorite saucepan.

Eventually those epicurean Saturdays passed into family lore, and the chronicle of my sister's first attempt at Welsh rarebit became an oft-repeated story. But the intensity of my mother's rage when she discovered the evidence was so monumental that I still cannot sniff the scent of scorched cheese without a tremor of guilt!

WELSH RAREBIT

❧

*T*he following formula for Welsh rarebit (or rabbit if purists abound) is my adult revenge on the world of elegant food my sister once hankered after. It was given to me by a proper Welshman, who insisted that a dram of Scotch whisky will turn any self-respecting cheese runny!

2 tablespoons unsalted butter
3 egg yolks
1 teaspoon Dijon mustard
½ teaspoon beef bouillon powder
1 teaspoon soy sauce
Dash of hot pepper sauce
Pinch of ground allspice
¾ cup light beer
10 ounces sharp Cheddar cheese, grated (about 2½ cups)

1 tablespoon heavy or whipping cream
1 teaspoon Scotch whisky
4 slices hot toast, buttered

1. Melt the butter in the top of a double boiler.

2. Beat the egg yolks in a large bowl with the mustard, bouillon powder, soy sauce, hot pepper sauce, and allspice. Stir in the beer, and add the mixture to the melted butter. Stir over simmering water until hot, 5 to 6 minutes.

3. Add the grated cheese, ¼ cup at a time, stirring constantly in one direction with a wooden spoon until the mixture is smooth.

4. Stir in the cream and the whisky. Do not let the mixture stand more than 5 minutes before serving it over hot buttered toast.

Serves 4

PAPAS
CHORREADAS

☙❧

Cheese melted with everything that grows in the garden (potatoes, tomatoes, scallions, peppers, string beans, and garlic too) is the formula for my favorite dish from Colombia. If you balk at this vegetarian precept, think about adding half a cup of diced ham before the cheese.

4 medium-size baking
  potatoes, peeled
4 ounces green beans,
  trimmed
3 tablespoons unsalted butter
1 clove garlic, minced
4 scallions (green onions)
  with their tops, trimmed
  and finely chopped
1 medium-size onion, finely
  chopped
1 can (8 ounces) Italian plum
  tomatoes, drained and
  chopped

¼ teaspoon finely chopped
  dried hot red pepper
½ teaspoon salt
½ teaspoon ground coriander
Pinch of ground cumin
Pinch of dried oregano
½ cup heavy or whipping
  cream
½ cup grated mozzarella
  cheese
2 teaspoons chopped Italian
  (flat-leaf) parsley
Freshly ground black pepper
  to taste

1. Cook the potatoes in boiling salted water to cover until just tender, about 20 minutes. (They should be still slightly crunchy.) Rinse under cold running water, drain, and cut into ½-inch-thick slices.

2. Cook the beans in boiling salted water to cover for 1 minute. Rinse under cold running water, drain, and set aside.

3. Melt the butter in a large, heavy flameproof skillet. Add the garlic, scallions, and onion; sauté until tender, 8 minutes.

4. Add the potatoes to the skillet, and stir over medium heat until the slices are coated with the butter mixture. Add the tomatoes, dried red pepper, salt, coriander, cumin, and oregano; cook until the mixture begins to thicken, 12 to 15 minutes. Then stir in the cream and reduce the heat. Add the beans, and cook 6 to 7 minutes.

5. Meanwhile, preheat the broiler.

6. Sprinkle the cheese over the vegetables, and cook until it has melted, 1 minute. Place the skillet under the broiler to lightly brown the top, 30 seconds.

7. Sprinkle with the parsley and pepper, and serve.

Serves 6

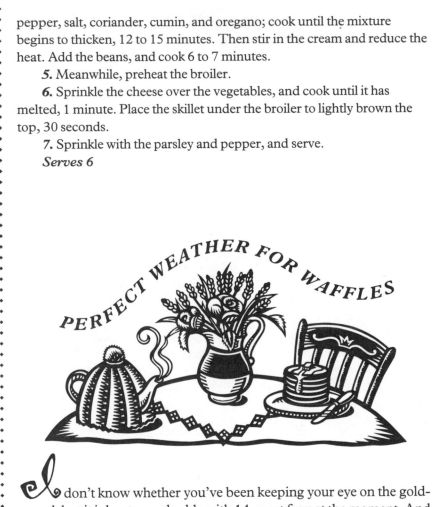

PERFECT WEATHER FOR WAFFLES

don't know whether you've been keeping your eye on the goldenrod, but it is bent over double with 14-carat fuzz at the moment. And the maple leaves (on my tree, at least) are turning scarlet at the seam just as the last tomatoes appear on the vine. Even to a dilettante landsman like me, that means an early winter is decidedly on the way.

My friends at the *Farmer's Almanac* have been sending up trial balloons for some time, predicting that a really cold equinox is probably the forecast for the country at large. I didn't need their admonition because I've been watching the onions. The skins on the last aureate crop are as thick as bookbindings—and that, my sky-watching readers, indicates a drop in the wind chill factor a heck of a lot sooner than usual.

If you are thinking that this climatic preamble is a clarion call to stock up on thermal long johns or new galoshes, you are dead wrong. I am merely counting off the prandial blessings that a frostbitten season brings for a food lover—unrestrained breakfasts, for starters.

Since my usual morning meal is extraordinarily Spartan (nothing more than a banana and a cup of coffee), cold weather provides a fine excuse for a binge of indulgence. To wit: a platter of diaphanous waffles or butter-drenched pancakes.

When I was growing up, such luxurious breakfast options were usually saved for solid gold occasions, like birthdays or Christmas morning. In the first place, it took hours for my mother to rout out such a rarely used appliance as a waffle iron, and longer still for her to scrub it to some semblance of serviceability. And when it shined at last, the problems had only begun.

"I never remember how to make waffles," my parent would muse rue-fully as she cracked eggs into puddles of milk and flour. "I'll just have to play it by ear, I guess."

My mother was a gifted pianist and a moderately acceptable cook, but her talents did not include improvisation—neither at the Steinway nor at the stove. But true to her Scorpian nature (she was born on November 1), she never admitted a misstep once it was made. If a first waffle proved flannel-like, it would be eaten anyway, while she added egg whites to a second batch or cream to a third until she got it right. In the end the waffles were always delectable, but our appetites had very often failed us by the time the right consistency had been achieved.

My mother always ate last, so it never bothered her in the slightest. She also totally resisted writing down the final formula.

"Why?" She would shrug. "These are delicious. So what if it took a little while to get them right? Unlike you—" this last directed at me—"I don't believe in life being so cut and dried!"

That was her philosophy, in a waffle iron and out!

My own is safer and saner. Try the following formula for wonderful cool-weather waffles. I adapted it from James Beard!

C O U N T R Y   W A F F L E S

ↈ

*J*his recipe requires no improvisation—unless you notice, as I just did, that plums are still in season. Adding some to the batter makes a sensational fruited pancake. Try a slosh of homemade plum syrup as topping too!

1¾ cups all-purpose flour
2 teaspoons baking powder
½ teaspoon salt
2 tablespoons sugar
1 cup heavy or whipping
   cream
¾ cup milk
3 extra-large eggs, separated

4 tablespoons (½ stick)
   unsalted butter, melted
1 cup prune plums, pitted
   and chopped (optional)
Plum syrup (see Index),
   maple syrup, or other
   topping

1. Preheat a waffle iron. Grease it if necessary.

2. Combine the flour, baking powder, salt, and sugar in a large bowl. Mix well. Using a wooden spoon, stir in the cream and milk until smooth.

3. Lightly beat the egg yolks in a small bowl; stir them into the batter. Add the melted butter.

4. Beat the egg whites until stiff but not dry. Gently fold them into the batter. Fold in the plums if desired.

5. Spoon about ⅓ cup of the batter onto the center of the waffle iron and cook until golden, about 5 minutes. For best results, serve the waffles straight from the waffle iron. They may be kept warm in a low (250°F) oven, but they will lose some of their crispness.

Serves 4 to 6

SOUTHERN LACE CAKES

*L*ace cakes are a Mason-Dixon bequest, and very toothsome on the first nippy morning of the year. I like them lightly dusted with confectioner's sugar first, then paved with lots of butter and syrup.

2 eggs	*½ teaspoon salt*
2 cups milk (or more as needed)	*6 tablespoons (¾ stick) unsalted butter, melted*
1 cup finely ground yellow cornmeal	*Plum syrup (recipe follows) or maple syrup*
1 teaspoon sugar	

1. Preheat a pancake griddle or a skillet.

2. In a medium-size bowl, beat the eggs with a large whisk until light. Then whisk in the milk, cornmeal, sugar, salt, and butter.

3. Butter the griddle or skillet, and spoon about 3 tablespoons batter for each cake onto it. When the undersides are golden brown and well set,

30 seconds to 1 minute, flip the cakes over and brown lightly on the other side, another 30 seconds.

4. Repeat until the batter is used up, beating the batter well before making each cake (the cornmeal tends to thicken). Add more milk if it becomes too thick. Keep the lace cakes in a 250°F oven until ready to serve.

Serves 4

P L U M   S Y R U P

*P*lum syrup is a natural on waffles, hotcakes, and the like. It is also a treat when spooned over lemon ice, or when drizzled into a glass of white wine for a most unusual version of Kir. This syrup keeps for months in an airtight container in the refrigerator or in a sterilized canning jar.

*1 pound (approximately 2
    cups) blue Italian plums,
    pitted*
1 cup fresh orange juice

1 cup sugar
½ cup water
Pinch of ground cinnamon

1. Combine all the ingredients in a medium-size saucepan, and heat to boiling. Reduce the heat and simmer until the fruit is tender, 15 to 20 minutes. Cool slightly.

2. Transfer the mixture to a food processor or blender, and purée until smooth. (If you are using a blender, take care, as hot liquid will expand.) Strain the syrup if desired, and refrigerate or store in sterilized jars until ready to use.

Makes about 1 quart

TRAVELING FOOD

To a footloose food fancier like me, there is no joy to compare with eating on the open road, tasting America's bounty on the fly.

I developed my wayfaring appetite at a tender age. Both my parents were mettlesome individuals with strong opinions and divergent views about everything under the sun—except driving.

My father was the first car owner in the borough of Queens, and he reputedly courted my mother in a Model T on back roads where even horses feared to tread. Needless to say, shortly after they wed, she followed him to the wheel.

As a couple they used any excuse to drive anywhere, all the while complaining vociferously about each other's skill as a motorist.

When we toured the country prior to World War II, there were practically no superhighways, few cars, and not a single motel. Usually my parents drove in shifts, stopping to eat at roadside rests and bedding down directly after the sun set so they might get an early start the next morning. Most often these stopovers were made at tourist homes rather than plush hotels, lodgings where the tariff for a night's stay always included breakfast—and if the trippers were lucky, a light supper into the bargain.

I will never forget the glories of that early road food tasted at the source: spoonbread and grits in Virginia, blueberry pancakes and maple syrup in Vermont, and my first boiled lobster on some rocky Maine shore.

One aspect of traveling has remained constant for me ever since I was a backseat passenger in my father's sedan. My mother would always pack a full-scale picnic that was to be consumed on the first leg of every journey—not on some shady wayside turnout but while very much in motion! And after years of car-sickness, I still go the very same route.

Mother's hamper never changed: cold chicken and slices of pot roast to be consumed with the fingers, plus deviled eggs and buttered bread. There was never any dessert, but we Greenes never traveled without two containers of liquid refreshment: a generous thermos of iced tea that occasioned many unscheduled road stops (for me) and a small silver flask of whisky that my father kept in his back pocket for "medicinal purposes only."

Times have changed, but as you will see, the menu I am planning for a trip later this month follows a familiar route.

PATE OF POT ROAST EN CROUSTADE

Instead of pot roast, my choice for the road is a pâté composed of seasoned leftovers and butter, stuffed into a loaf of French bread. This delicious lunch will also do double duty as an unusual hors d'oeuvre if the bread is sliced somewhat thinner.

2 cups coarsely chopped
    cooked pot roast,
    chilled
6 canned anchovies, rinsed
    and drained
¾ cup strong homemade
    beef stock or canned
    broth (or more as needed;
    see Note)
8 tablespoons (1 stick)
    unsalted butter, at room
    temperature

1 tablespoon grated onion
1 shallot, minced
1 clove garlic, mashed
Dash of hot pepper sauce
1 teaspoon fresh lemon
    juice
Salt and freshly ground black
    pepper to taste
1 loaf fresh French bread,
    about 3½ by 10 inches

1. Place the pot roast, anchovies, and beef stock in a blender or food processor. Purée until smooth, adding more stock if needed to make a smooth paste.

2. Transfer the meat mixture to a medium-size bowl. Using a heavy wooden spoon, beat in the butter, a few tablespoons at a time. Then beat in the onion, shallot, garlic, hot pepper sauce, lemon juice, and salt and pepper.

3. Slice 2 inches or so off the ends of the bread. Using your fingers and a long thin spoon or knife, remove as much of the soft insides of the bread as possible without breaking the crust. Stand the bread on one end on buttered paper. Spoon the meat mixture into the hollow bread, forcing it in with a spoon. Trim off any unfilled portion of bread. Wrap in waxed paper; chill well.

4. To serve, cut the bread into 1-inch-thick slices.
Serves 4

Note: To make strong stock or broth, simmer 1½ cups until reduced to ¾ cup.

PICNIC EGGS

4 hard-cooked eggs
¼ cup mayonnaise
1½ teaspoons Dijon mustard
3 tablespoons finely chopped
   cooked ham
½ teaspoon capers, rinsed and
   drained

½ teaspoon minced fresh
   parsley
¼ teaspoon finely grated
   lemon zest
1 small shallot, minced
Salt and freshly ground black
   pepper

1. Cut the eggs in half lengthwise. Remove the yolks, and crumble them into a bowl. Reserve the whites.

2. Add the mayonnaise to the egg yolks, and mix well. Then add the mustard, ham, capers, parsley, lemon zest, and shallot. Stir well. If the mixture seems too dry, add another teaspoon or so of mayonnaise. Season to taste with salt and pepper.

3. Mound each egg-white half with stuffing, and dust them lightly with more ground pepper. Chill slightly before serving.

Serves 4

CRUSTY CHICKEN

1 chicken (4 pounds), cut into
   pieces
1 clove garlic, mashed
Juice of 1 lemon
2 teaspoons Dijon mustard
Dash of hot pepper sauce

½ teaspoon soy sauce
3 tablespoons vodka
¼ cup olive oil
¼ cup fine dried bread crumbs
Salt and freshly ground black
   pepper to taste

1. Place the chicken pieces in a large bowl. In a medium-size bowl, combine the garlic, lemon juice, mustard, hot pepper sauce, soy sauce, and vodka. Stir in the olive oil, and then the bread crumbs. Pour the mixture over the chicken, and toss well to coat each piece evenly. Refrigerate, covered, 1 hour.

2. Preheat the oven to 400°F.

3. Place the chicken pieces, skin side down, on a rack in a roasting pan. Bake for 25 minutes.

4. Turn the chicken pieces over, and season them with salt and pepper. Bake until the chicken is crisp and the juices run yellow when pricked with a fork, about 35 minutes. Let cool completely on a rack before chilling.

Serves 4

A GREAT PLAY

BUT AN EVEN GREATER SANDWICH

One of the most fruitless questions I am ever asked—and one that seems to come up with unerring regularity whenever I am faced with an unknown newspaper interviewer or radio show host—is: "What's your favorite comfort food, Bert?"

This query stops me cold in my tracks because *most* things I eat give me a measure of comfort. But that is not the answer they are looking for, so I rally and name a few of my food foibles that come to mind.

"Peanut butter," I will confess. "And thick malted milk shakes. Really good chocolate bars that are so rich they turn your teeth brown as they melt."

Those answers always seem to satisfy. But I will tell you a secret: all of the above are private addictions, fantasized about but rarely indulged. Comfort food is another dish altogether.

I consider the consumption of a comfort food to be in the same category as the wearing of comfortable but unsightly clothes—an act to be engaged in only in private or with a loved one who will not judge your lapse in taste. The concept summons up that warm and safe cocoon of childhood, when one was comforted with a capital C.

When I was a kid that cocoon was my grandparents' house, where I would be happily sequestered whenever my parents went off somewhere overnight.

The comfort food I ate in my grandmother's kitchen was usually cooked for the two of us alone. When I grew bored or sulky, my maternal forebear would stop and say: "I know what's the matter with you. You're hungry." Even if we had eaten breakfast not an hour before! And she was always right. In the kitchen, she would survey the wondrous array of odds and ends in her icebox, all neatly arranged like a collection of precious bibelots.

"Have you ever had a *Hamlet*?" she asked one time, knowing full well I had not. When I shook my head, she produced a bit of cheese, a tomato, bread, and some ham—which in minutes became the most delectable broiled open-face sandwich I'd ever eaten. I eat Hamlets still, whenever I feel the need of a quick restorative.

Another of my grandmother's cures for flagging spirits was a dish we always called Chicken-Fried Noodles. She prepared this from scratch in less than half an hour, while my mouth watered at the prospect of the creamy mixture of noodles, cheese, and bits of re-fried chicken. As I recall, we always ate the whole thing—sometimes at 11:00 A.M. and sometimes at 11:00 P.M.—never regretting our excesses because it was precisely the comfort we both needed!

And that's what I call real "comfort food"!

TOASTED TOMATO HAMLETS

*T*his dish bears no relation to any ham and cheese sandwich you've ever eaten. My grandmother made it with any good white cheese she had in the fridge. I prefer Brie. My friends opt for Monterey Jack. Be my guest.

½ loaf fresh French bread
Unsalted butter
1 teaspoon Dijon mustard
8 thin slices ham (Prague or
   Black Forest if available)

8 thin slices ripe tomato
5 to 6 ounces Brie cheese, cut
   into thin slices

1. Preheat the broiler.
2. Cut the bread into two 4-inch-long pieces, and cut each piece in half lengthwise. Toast them lightly under the broiler.
3. Preheat the oven to 400°F.

4. Lightly butter each piece of bread, and then spread the mustard over them. Place them in a shallow ovenproof baking dish.

5. Layer the ham slices over each piece of bread, and then the tomatoes. Cover with the cheese, and bake until the cheese is bubbly, 8 to 10 minutes.

Serves 2

CHICKEN-FRIED FETTUCCINE

ℳy grandmother would say that I'd gone ritzy if she knew I substituted fettuccine for homemade noodles, but actually they're exactly alike. I like this best when the chicken is leftover fried, with bits of crust that color the creamy sauce golden, but any cooked chicken will do in a pinch.

2 pieces leftover cooked chicken, preferably fried
1 tablespoon unsalted butter
1 shallot, minced
2 teaspoons all-purpose flour
¾ cup homemade chicken stock or canned broth
½ cup heavy or whipping cream
⅛ teaspoon freshly grated nutmeg

Salt and freshly ground black pepper
1 cup cooked fettuccine noodles
1½ tablespoons freshly grated Parmesan cheese
Chopped fresh parsley, for garnish

1. Remove the skin from the chicken pieces, and chop it fine. Set the chopped skin aside. Remove the meat from the bones, and cut it into pieces; you should have about 1 cup of meat. Set aside.

2. Melt the butter in a large heavy skillet over medium heat. Add the chopped chicken skin; cook 4 minutes. Add the shallot and cook 3 minutes longer.

3. Reduce the heat to low, and sprinkle the mixture with the flour. Cook, stirring constantly, for 2 minutes. Then whisk in the chicken stock and cream. Heat to boiling, stirring constantly. Reduce the heat to medium and cook until thickened, 4 to 5 minutes.

4. Add the nutmeg, and salt and pepper to taste. Stir in the chicken meat, and cook over medium-low heat until it is heated through, 2 minutes. Then add the pasta and toss until warmed through. Sprinkle with the cheese and parsley, and serve immediately.

Serves 2 to 4

THE ART OF BARGAINING

*T*hanks to some remarkable cooking teachers, the art of food preparation in America has improved mightily in the past fifty years. However, the talent for food shopping has gone to the dogs.

Half a century ago, no self-respecting consumer would have considered buying all the household comestibles in one store, even if such an emporium had existed. Instead, for our mothers and grandmothers shopping was a day-long excursion, starting with the butcher or poultry market (for they were rarely synonymous) and making tracks afterward to the greengrocer, fishmonger, dairy, bakery, and finally a grocery, where staples and canned goods were acquired. It was an arduous task but a rewarding one, for those old-time shoppers learned how to select superior products and, more important, how to reject inferior ones. My own mother was a fierce buyer who would pick over a carton of tomatoes or a basket of green beans until, by a series of judicious pinches and squeezes, she found the produce that finally met her standards.

My parent had many disconcerting confrontations with shopkeepers. If a skimpy head of lettuce or a fibrous cauliflower displeased her, she would hold the offending vegetable up to me for inspection, and within earshot of the proprietor, inquire in Yiddish (a language never spoken in our household and one in which I could not possibly respond) for corroboration.

Mortified, I would stare at the floor in dismay. "Mother, I don't know what you're saying," I would at last mutter. Then she would translate her remarks, the tenor of which was inevitably the same.

"He [indicating the seller] must think I'm an idiot—like the rest of his customers—or he wouldn't offer me crap like that!"

My mother's hard bargaining techniques always began in this aggrieved manner and ended with her offering less than half the stated price; and my distress notwithstanding, the greengrocer never seemed particularly offended. Most often her evaluation prevailed. Moreover, the entrepreneurs she dealt with always showed a grudging admiration for her acumen.

"Your mother's a tough lady to do business with, sonny," Mr. Molfetto, the vegetable man, once proclaimed. "But nobody can say she doesn't have a good eye!"

CARROT GNOCCHI

❧❧❧

*W*inter is a tough season for the demanding shopper, but happily root vegetables like carrots and potatoes—which meld to produce the most golden gnocchi I know—are always available.

1 cup cooked mashed
  potatoes, chilled
1 medium-size carrot,
  grated
1 medium-size shallot,
  grated
2 eggs
½ cup finely grated Jarlsberg
  cheese
¼ teaspoon freshly grated
  nutmeg
¼ teaspoon ground allspice

½ teaspoon salt
⅛ teaspoon freshly ground
  white pepper
Dash of hot pepper sauce
1 to 1½ cups all-purpose flour
3 tablespoons unsalted
  butter, melted
Freshly grated Parmesan
  cheese

1. Preheat the oven to 325°F. Generously butter an ovenproof serving dish, and set it aside.

2. Combine all the ingredients through the hot pepper sauce in a large bowl; mix thoroughly. Then work in the flour, starting with 1 cup, until a soft dough is formed (do not exceed 1½ cups).

3. Bring a large pot of salted water to boil. Roll the dough out to form long ropes; cut them into 1½-inch-long pieces. (If the dough is too sticky, place it in a large pastry bag, pipe out 1½-inch-long pieces, and cut them off with scissors, letting them fall directly into the boiling water.)

4. Cook the gnocchi, about 5 at a time, in the boiling water until they float to the top—no longer than 3 minutes. Drain them well in a colander or on paper towels, and then place them on the prepared serving dish. (It is always a good idea to taste the first batch, so you can adjust the cooking time on the others if necessary.) Repeat with the remaining gnocchi.

5. Drizzle the melted butter over the gnocchi, and bake them in the oven until they are heated through, 15 to 20 minutes. Sprinkle lightly with the Parmesan cheese, and serve with additional cheese on the side.

Serves 4 to 6

T O U S L E D
Z U C C H I N I

W hether zucchini is a vegetable of supreme tenderness or fibrous mettle, depends upon the season. My mother always scraped a zucchini's skin with her fingernail to test for freshness. If her hand turned green, we had squash for supper. Try this recent invention of mine—a luscious herbal baked omelet.

¼ cup olive oil
2 tablespoons unsalted butter
2 cloves garlic, minced
1 medium onion, chopped
8 ounces zucchini, thinly
  sliced
1 small tomato, chopped
2 tablespoons chopped fresh
  parsley
2 tablespoons chopped fresh
  basil, or 2 teaspoons dried
1 teaspoon chopped fresh
  tarragon, or ¼ teaspoon
  dried

1 tablespoon red wine
  vinegar
Salt and freshly ground black
  pepper to taste
4 eggs
¼ cup heavy or whipping
  cream
¼ cup grated Gruyère or
  Monterey Jack cheese
2 tablespoons freshly grated
  Parmesan cheese

1. Preheat the oven to 350°F. Butter a 10-inch ceramic quiche dish, and set it aside.

2. Heat the oil and butter in a large skillet. Add the garlic, and cook over medium-low heat for 2 minutes. Add the onion, raise the heat slightly, and cook for another 2 minutes. Then add the zucchini, tomato, herbs, vinegar, and salt and pepper. Reduce the heat and cook until the zucchini is slightly wilted, about 4 minutes.

3. Transfer the mixture to the prepared quiche dish.

4. Beat the eggs with the cream, and pour this over the zucchini. Sprinkle with the Gruyère and Parmesan cheeses, and bake until golden, about 25 minutes.

Serves 4 to 6

DR. GRANDMA—HOLD THE CHICKEN SOUP

Though I have written long and lovingly of my grandmother's prowess at the stove, it seems that I have never given her sufficient praise as a healer. That tiny woman (less than five feet tall) was a natural homeopath who was inspired to work miracles whenever she discovered anyone of poor health in her domain.

My grandmother's therapy was legendary. A tale often told in our family detailed, for instance, how she had nursed one of her four daughters through Spanish influenza—by means of sheer insistence and startling amounts of rye whiskey. But then liquor was a medication to which she ascribed primary restorative powers.

"Why not?" I can recall her defending the prescription righteously. "Whiskey kills the pain, which lets you sleep, right? And sleeping stimulates the appetite, so you want to eat when you wake up. And everybody knows that nourishment is the secret of good health!"

I cannot know if everybody accepted her doctrine for recuperation, but I certainly did. I remember, when I was perhaps eleven years old, feeling peaked and unable to eat when I arrived at my grandmother's house for my daily hot lunch between classes. A quick mouth on my brow (for a fever check) led to a diagnosis of grippe and the cancellation of any more school for a week.

I was put to bed in the den between the kitchen and the dining room, and dosed with rock and rye (whiskey sweetened with rock candy) over ice. I was bid to sip "very, very slowly, please!"—which was no hardship, as I hated the taste of the stuff. But it worked. The treatment put me into such a deep sleep that I did not wake until morning, and it reduced the fever as well.

After rye, my grandmother's next best home remedy was an egg. Patients had a choice of soft-boiled, poached, or frothed into a thick eggnog. I always elected mine scrambled, served up in the blue enamel pan in which they had been whisked together with a fork. My maternal forebear's scrambled eggs were like no others I have ever tasted. Neither hard-edged nor soft-centered, they were a perfect amalgam, like a custard—velvet on the tongue. As a matter of fact, the scrambled egg treatment was reason enough to become ill on my grandmother's turf, for no matter how poorly one felt before the first forkful, convalescence was always ensured by the second or third bite.

Unlike traditional Jewish matriarchs, my grandmother never served chicken soup to the sick. No, indeed; her cup of chowder was stronger stuff, most often compounded of mushrooms and beef, and always pearly with tender barley.

Two days of rye whiskey, scrambled eggs, and barley soup, and even the most debilitated human showed signs of life. And not only humans. Once my grandmother found a blue jay with a broken wing in her garden. After making a splint out of kitchen matches and creating a bed of absorbent cotton in a soap dish, she nursed it back to health—and flight too, eventually. What was her cure? Well, for starters . . . rye whiskey, eggs, and mushroom soup!

UNGRANDMOTHERLY
SCRAMBLED
EGGS

tried for years to duplicate my grandmother's remarkable scrambled eggs, but finally gave up. My version is quite therapeutic, but not for invalids alone. Consider it as a brunch or lunch dish.

6 eggs
¼ cup heavy or whipping
  cream
2 tablespoons unsalted
  butter

2 ounces goat cheese,
  crumbled or coarsely
  chopped
Salt and freshly ground black
  pepper

1. Beat the eggs with the cream in a large bowl.

2. Melt the butter in a large heavy skillet over low heat. Pour in the eggs and cook, whisking frequently, until they are velvety, about 25 minutes. Stir in the cheese just before serving, and add salt and pepper to taste.

Serves 2 or 3

MUSHROOM, BEEF, BARLEY, AND TOMATO SOUP

forgot to say that my grandmother, Minna Cohn, had yet another curative power: Her hand was always like a wondrously cool compress when placed on a sick child's forehead. She was also the only woman I ever knew who put tomatoes in her barley soup. Perhaps it began when her kitchen garden blazed scarlet one summer. Whatever the reason, her version is eminently worthy of emulation.

2 tablespoons vegetable oil
1¼ pounds stewing beef, cut into 1-inch cubes
1 clove garlic
5½ cups water
½ ounce dried sliced mushrooms
1 small onion, chopped
1 large carrot, chopped
2 large ribs celery, chopped
1 cup chopped, seeded, peeled tomatoes

½ teaspoon sugar
1 small parsnip, chopped
1 small white turnip, chopped
Pinch of dried thyme
¼ cup pearl barley
4 cups homemade beef stock or canned broth (approximately)
Salt and freshly ground black pepper
Chopped fresh parsley, for garnish

1. Heat the oil in a large heavy pot or Dutch oven over high heat. Add the meat and sauté until well browned on all sides, 12 to 15 minutes. Add the garlic and 4 cups of the water. Stir, scraping the bottom and sides of the pot, and bring to a boil. Reduce the heat and simmer, partially covered, for 1 hour. Use a spoon to remove any scum that rises to the surface.

2. Meanwhile, bring ½ cup water to a boil, and pour it over the mushrooms in a small bowl. Let stand at least 20 minutes.

3. Remove the garlic from the soup, and discard it. Add the mushrooms with their liquid. Add the onion, carrot, celery, tomatoes, sugar, parsnip, turnip, thyme, barley, beef stock, and remaining 1 cup water. Simmer, partially covered, until the meat is tender, about 1½ hours. If the soup becomes too thick, thin with more beef stock.

4. Season to taste with salt and pepper, and sprinkle with parsley before serving.

Serves 6 to 8

GREENE'S BEAN VICTORY

Raised as an Orthodox Jew by a Russian-born mother of great religious zeal but obviously little power of persuasion, my father abandoned the dietary strictures of his religion at an early age and the devotional aspects as soon as he reached manhood. He adored ham, bacon, and all manner of biblically proscribed seafood, including clams, oysters, shrimp, and lobster. Even more heretically, he always wanted lots of butter and cream in the pile of mashed potatoes that accompanied a pot roast to the table. But the one food he resolutely drew the line against was fresh pork.

Why? An emotional barrier, I can only surmise. "No, no," my father would state. "Religion has nothing to do with it. I just can't *go* the taste!" "But Daddy, you've never even tried it," my sister, Myra, would rebut. "I know." My father would shake his head stubbornly. "But even if I did, I couldn't *go* it anyway!"

To satisfy his sense of propriety, we never told him when he was eating pork. My mother once presented him with a gloriously burnished "veal roast" that he thoroughly relished until he observed a look of sneaky superiority in the faces surrounding him at the dinner table.

"If that was pork," he began, "you all should be ashamed of yourselves. Don't tell me. I don't want to know, because it would make me sick!"

Whenever we made pork and beans for Tuesday dinner, my mother, my sister, or I would skim off the offending bits of meat he was likely to encounter in the dish, so he was never the wiser. However, on the odd occasions when my father did the family shopping, there was always trouble. For he unerringly returned from the market with cans clearly labeled "Vegetarian-Style Baked Beans—No Pork Added"— tins that produced a decidedly less than tonic flavor, as he never failed to observe.

"You sure there's no pork in these beans?" He would question after tasting a mouthful gingerly. "You know how I feel about that subject." "Father!" I would begin in my most aggrieved tone. "You bought these beans yourself. Want to see the can?" "No. But they sure must be doing something funny with the product. Tastes lousy! Can't you 'gook' 'em up?"

Because I disliked the taste of any canned bean, I had hit upon a curious method for making them palatable, a prescription that never failed to please my parent.

"Now that's what I call a hill of beans," he would announce after the transformation. "For someone who can't stand to eat army food, you sure cook it good!"

The recipe for those "doctored" legumes remains evergreen to this day, though I have not put it to use in over forty years. To summon up the past, I will attempt to reconstruct it one more time:

> Sauté 3 slices of bacon until crisp. Drain and crumble, reserving 1 tablespoon drippings in the pan. In the drippings, sauté 1 minced onion until it turns golden. Add 2 tablespoons each of mustard, ketchup, chili sauce, and sweet paprika, plus ½ cup dark brown sugar. Stir well until the mixture forms a thick sludge. Add 1 can of beans. Stir well. Scatter the bacon on top, and bake this mess in a medium (350°F) oven for 1 hour, or until a respectable crust forms on top.

That was the first recipe for beans I notched on my belt as a fledgling chef, and while it presaged no brilliant culinary future, the devise plainly pleased my father. He could "go it" two or even three times a week for his supper.

GREENE'S BEANS

 n the fullness of time, I did come to appreciate a "no-fudged" hill of baked beans. The precept for Greene's beans circa 1984 follows. It is, as you can see, dependant upon bourbon, mustard, bacon, garlic, and even chili sauce for savor. But ironically, it is *sans* salt pork!

1 pound dried Great Northern or navy beans	5 tablespoons chili sauce
2 teaspoons unsalted butter	1 tablespoon dry English mustard
1 clove garlic, bruised	1 teaspoon curry powder
1 large onion, finely chopped	1½ teaspoons salt
3 strips bacon, crisply fried and crumbled	½ cup bourbon
2 tablespoons dark brown sugar	1½ cups tomato juice (approximately)
2 teaspoons Worcestershire sauce	3 strips uncooked bacon
¼ cup molasses	

1. Bring a large pot of water to a boil, and add the beans. Return to the boil; then turn off the heat, and let stand for 1 hour.

2. Meanwhile preheat the oven to 275°F. Grease a bean pot or large heavy casserole with the butter. Rub the sides of the pot well with the bruised garlic.

3. Drain the beans and transfer them to a large bowl. Add all the ingredients through the bourbon. Mix thoroughly. Then stir in 1½ cups tomato juice.

4. Transfer the bean mixture to the prepared pot and place the uncooked bacon on top. Cover and bake until soft, adding more tomato juice if the beans start to dry out, 7 hours.

Serves 6 to 8

MY MOTHER TAKES THE CAKE

Whenever I teach a class, one question always comes up at some point in the proceeding: "Was your mother *really* such a terrible cook?"

My answer is unvaryingly the same: "Yes and no."

To set the matter straight, Paula Greene, *née* Pauline Cohn, was decidedly an adept kitchen practitioner—but only when she chose to be. Which was not very often!

Trained in domestic matters at her mother's knee, she could roast a chicken or braise a pot roast blindfolded if necessary. But even with such trusted savants as Fannie Farmer and Irma Rombauer as her mentors, she could never once turn butter, flour, and milk into a relatively tranquil, or even very white, sauce. Mainly because in her heart, she considered all that stirring totally irrelevant.

"Anything that takes so damn long to prepare never turns out to be worth the effort" was her dismissal of all such refinements. When there were obvious lumps of discord in her creamed offerings, she would merely camouflage the surface with a copious dusting of parsley or paprika, sometimes both if a sauce was particularly clotted. But one thing you could be sure of: no dish ever came to her table with an apology.

My mother was born under the sign of Scorpio (with a scorpion for her rising sign as well), which may indicate a measure of her housewifely sting. For while she attacked most culinary challenges with supreme confidence and inordinate manual dexterity, she was also capable of losing interest in the task at some crucial point and ruining it entirely.

I remember her making grape jelly (a hurdle she and my grandmother vaulted together every summer), assiduously straining the cooked fruit through yards and yards of cheesecloth to achieve the perfect degree of unblemished lucidity. After waiting hours for the sticky purple juices to drip, my mother quite arbitrarily (and over the wild protests of my grandmother) squeezed the remainder of the grape pulp with her bare hands—"to get the job over and done with, for goodness' sake!"

She never admitted the error of her impetuosity, even when each Mason jar developed a formation of menacing cumulus clouds below the paraffin. "Everyone worries far too much about petty details," said my mother as she stashed the flawed jelly in the back of her jam closet in the cellar. "Who cares what something looks like, as long as it tastes okay?"

I, for one. But my parent had little or no patience with that aesthetic element in my nature. She was a do-er, as she proclaimed. I was a thinker first. We never cooked together.

Now I am sometimes sorry, for nobody I have ever met made golden cakes more effortlessly, or better for that matter. And her chocolate fudge icing was an Olympian upholstery. To her mind, what was good about it was the fact that it could be made fast. I cherished the goodness first.

My mother's cake recipes were all noted (roughly) in a loose scrawl in a blue school notebook that I hoped to inherit some day—but it went astray, so her actual formulas are lost. I can finally offer up a reasonably accurate facsimile of her fabled yellow cake, after asking everyone I ever met for their recipe—it only took about twenty years to reconstruct it. From whatever heaven my mother resides in, I can hear her comment now: "He always was a dopey kid!"

MY MOTHER'S OLD-FASHIONED YELLOW CAKE

*T*his devise is the result of many borrowed recipes and lots of failures. The fact that it is so much like my mother's original treasure is miraculous, since I make this cake with an electric mixer. Her only tools were an earthenware bowl and a long-handled wooden spoon.

1 cup solid vegetable shortening	*2 teaspoons baking powder*
1 cup sugar	*Pinch of salt*
4 eggs (1 whole, 3 separated)	*½ cup milk*
1½ cups sifted cake flour	*1 teaspoon vanilla extract*

1. Preheat the oven to 350°F. Butter and flour two 8-inch round cake pans.

2. Using an electric mixer, beat the shortening in a large bowl until light. Slowly beat in the sugar. Add the whole egg and the egg yolks, one at a time, beating thoroughly after each addition.

3. Sift the flour with the baking powder and salt. Add this to the egg mixture in three parts, alternating with thirds of the milk. Stir in the vanilla.

4. Beat the egg whites until stiff, and fold them into the batter. Pour the batter into the prepared pans, and bake until a toothpick inserted in the center comes out clean, about 25 minutes. Cool on a wire rack before icing.

Serves 8 to 10

MY MOTHER'S CHOTE ICING

his is one recipe I did manage to memorize at my mother's stove. The dense chocolate matches the lightness of the cake to a fare-thee-well. My parent always claimed that this frosting (and the cake) tasted better the day after it was made. I never can keep it on hand that long!

3 ounces (3 squares)
unsweetened baking
chocolate
1 can (14 ounces) sweetened
condensed milk
8 tablespoons (1 stick)
unsalted butter, cut into 8
pieces

1 egg yolk, beaten
1½ teaspoons vanilla
extract

1. Melt the chocolate in the top of a double boiler over simmering water. Stir in the condensed milk, and beat until smooth.

2. Add the butter, one piece at a time, stirring after each addition. Stir in the egg yolk and vanilla. Beat until smooth and thick 3 minutes. (If the icing becomes too thick, thin with a little hot water.)

Makes enough for a 2-layer cake

INHERITING THE SOUP GENE

n San Francisco recently, I was stopped at a pedestrian crossing by a reader of this column who made an extremely illegal U-turn in a red station wagon in order to be heard.

"Bert Greene?" this lady exclaimed, rolling down her car window. "What in the world are you doing in the City? And why have you short-changed your grandmother?"

It was a puzzling opener. Flattered at first (at being recognized) and flustered immediately after (for being so accused), I stammered out that I had been teaching cooking classes. The second question required some thought. Truthfully, I feared I had sung the praises of my good-cooking grandmother overmuch of late.

"That's just the point," cried my motorist friend. "You always write about your mother's mother. What about the other one?"

The other one, my father's mother, was a mail-order bride if family tales are to be believed. A very religious girl, speaking nary a word of English, she crossed the ocean on the advice of a marriage broker to wed an itinerant New York blacksmith, my grandfather. He spoke not a word of Russian, and very little Yiddish. How they communicated is sheer speculation, but they managed to produce fourteen children despite the language barrier.

Progeny aside, their union was not a happy one. My grandfather plied his trade (shoeing horses and mending pots and pans) in a covered wagon that took him across the Great Divide. According to one of his sisters, he was never home for longer than a month in all his married life. "Because," she confided, "the poor man could not bear to hear the accusations of his shrieking wife."

Grandfather Greene died before he was forty-five, leaving his widow with a houseful of young children and the nagging rumors of a dozen others born outside the state line.

My mother, who was remarkably prejudiced on the subject of her mother-in-law, declared that she got what she deserved: "Fifty years in this country and that woman never learned a word of English! And not such a hot homemaker, either!"

I could never verify this, because my father was a reticent man. I do know that toward the end of her life she became a virtual recluse, living in the ghetto of New York's Lower East Side and resisting any creature comforts pressed upon her by her children.

"All she did was pray," my mother would say, "and give money to the *shul*." She died—on her way to the synagogue for Friday night service— with over a thousand dollars in her pockets.

I have never seen a photograph of Bessie Greene, for it was against her religious principles to permit such an act of vanity, but I suspect I resemble her. She died six months before I was born and I am named to honor her memory.

My father, who was her youngest child, claimed not to remember anything special about his mother, not even her cooking. "She did as well as and no better than anyone in her circumstances," he would reply to my questioning—meaning, I knew, a life of self-denial and absolutely no joy.

One time when I asked him to recall something special, such as a dish his mother might have prepared for a high holiday meal, he simply shook his head. "Soup. She made lots of soup!"

The following recipes—a Russian soup with meat, and one without— are an uninherited legacy.

RUSSIAN
CABBAGE BORSCHT

ʘ

*T*his potful yields two courses. Green beans are my choice of vegetable with the meat.

1 onion, finely chopped

1 small head cabbage,
   shredded

1 beef brisket (3 to 4 pounds),
   trimmed of fat

1 can (13¾ ounces) beef
   broth

2 cans (17 ounces each)
   imported Italian tomatoes,
   mashed

1½ tablespoons sugar

1 green apple, cored and
   chopped

¼ cup raisins

3 tablespoons fresh lemon
   juice

1 tablespoon tarragon
   vinegar

2 teaspoons salt

1 teaspoon freshly ground
   black pepper

Pinch of ground allspice

12 to 24 boiling potatoes (2 or
   3 per serving)

1. Arrange half the onion and half the cabbage in a large Dutch oven. Place the meat on top; cover with the remaining onion and cabbage. Add the broth and enough water to barely cover the meat. Then add the tomatoes, sugar, apple, raisins, lemon juice, vinegar, salt, pepper, and allspice. Bring to a boil. Reduce the heat and simmer, covered, until the meat is tender, 3½ to 4 hours.

2. About 45 minutes before serving time, bring a large pot of salted water to a boil. Add the potatoes and simmer until tender, 20 to 30 minutes. Drain and keep warm.

3. Serve the borscht as two courses: Place 1 or 2 potatoes in each soup bowl, and ladle the soup over the potatoes. (Keep the remaining borscht warm.) When the soup course is finished, transfer the meat from the hot liquid to a platter, and slice it. Serve the meat with additional boiled potatoes; ladle some more soup over each portion to moisten.

Serves 6 to 8

CHERNICHNY SOUP

~~~

*B*lueberries are at their peak in late July and August; the perfect time to serve this fruit soup as the first course to a light summer meal.

1 pint fresh blueberries, stemmed and rinsed
1 cup sugar
1 cinnamon stick, 1½ to 2 inches long

2 cups water
1 lemon, quartered
¼ cup vodka
½ cup sour cream

1. Combine the blueberries, sugar, cinnamon stick, and water in a large saucepan. Scrape the pits from the lemon wedges, and squeeze the wedges into the pot; then add them. Bring to a boil. Reduce the heat and simmer for 15 minutes. Set it aside to cool slightly.

2. Transfer the soup (including the cinnamon stick and lemon wedges) to a blender, and blend until smooth. Chill thoroughly.

3. Just before serving, stir in the vodka. Ladle the soup into serving bowls, and garnish each with a heaping tablespoon of sour cream.

Serves 6

DUDE TOOK HIS MILK SOURED

My beloved cat, Dude, died earlier this summer. This is no tardy obituary, however. Rather, it is a testament to one cat's innate (if decidedly unfeline) taste buds.

Dude was a sleek, handsome twenty-two-pound male who came into my life as a stripling weighing less than a can of Tab. His mother, a stray calico, chose a stately townhouse on East Fifty-fifth Street for his birthplace, so he clearly was born on the posh side of town.

Technically his breed was listed as "red," but Dude's actual color fell somewhere between the melting shades of coffee mousse and vanilla ice cream. If that analogy seems pointed in the direction of the kitchen, it is, because Dude was a fellow of catholic appetite. No rote consumer of Friskies or Tender Vittles (though I never saw him refuse a bowlful), this cat's palate was challenged in the main by *haute cuisine*. To wit: shrimp jambalaya, homemade brownies, and runny Brie.

Dude ate not so much with discrimination as with fervor, at a rate of consumption that earned him a second sobriquet around the house: *Chazzah,* which means "glutton" in Yiddish. And which in short order became abbreviated to a still more stylish tag: *El Hussar.*

Whatever one called him, Dude came running—though truth to tell, he was never very far from the kitchen, particularly when serious cookery was in progress. Always ravenous, he nevertheless had exemplary manners and never attempted to lap a jot of spilled cake batter or attack a strand of pasta Genovese without a nod of approval from the chef.

Of all Dude's culinary affections, perhaps the dearest to his heart was yogurt. This cat would leap almost headlong into an open refrigerator whenever he spied a carton. His special leaning was toward exotic fruit flavorings (banana-strawberry, orange-coconut), but I have seen him slurp up the natural, unadulterated variety with the same degree of bliss. As a gastronomic pet or a pet gastronome, Dude will never have an equal.

L E M O N   Y O G U R T   C A K E

One of the most elegant cakes in my baking repertoire, a lemony ring of golden air that cats (and humans) pine for, has yogurt as a serious ingredient! As an added plus, this dessert actually improves the day after it is made.

1 cup (2 sticks) unsalted butter, at room temperature
1½ cups sugar
4 eggs
1 tablespoon grated lemon zest
1 teaspoon vanilla extract
2½ cups sifted all-purpose flour

1 teaspoon baking powder
1 teaspoon baking soda
½ teaspoon salt
1 cup plain yogurt
¾ cup finely ground blanched almonds
½ cup fresh lemon juice

1. Preheat the oven to 350°F. Butter and flour a 9-inch tube pan.

2. Beat the butter in a large bowl until light and fluffy. Slowly beat in 1 cup of the sugar. Then add the eggs, one at a time, beating thoroughly after each addition. Beat in the lemon zest and the vanilla.

3. In a medium-size bowl, sift the flour with the baking powder, baking soda, and salt. Add the flour mixture to the egg mixture in three parts, alternating with thirds of the yogurt. Then fold in the almonds.

4. Pour the batter into the prepared pan, and bake until a toothpick inserted in the center comes out clean, about 1 hour. Cool the cake, still in the pan, on a wire rack for 5 minutes.

5. Meanwhile, combine the remaining ½ cup sugar with the lemon juice in a small saucepan, and heat until the sugar dissolves. Slowly pour this over the cake, allowing the syrup to soak in. Cool the cake completely in the pan before unmolding.

Serves 8 to 10

F O O D ' S   C O F F E E   M A R B L E   C A K E

FOR THE CAKE:

½ cup firmly packed dark
   brown sugar

1 tablespoon ground
   cinnamon

2 teaspoons instant coffee
   powder

2 tablespoons unsweetened
   cocoa

½ cup raisins

½ cup chopped walnuts

¾ cup (1½ sticks) unsalted
   butter, at room
   temperature

1½ cups granulated sugar

2 teaspoons vanilla extract

3 eggs

3 cups sifted all-purpose flour

1½ teaspoons baking powder

1½ teaspoons baking soda

½ teaspoon salt

2 cups plain yogurt

FOR THE ICING:
2 teaspoons instant coffee
powder
2 tablespoons hot water
1 package (8 ounces) cream
cheese, at room
temperature
¾ cup (1½ sticks) unsalted
butter, at room
temperature

1¼ cups confectioner's
sugar
1 teaspoon vanilla extract
1 teaspoon fresh orange
juice
Chopped walnuts, for
garnish
Raisins, for garnish

1. Preheat the oven to 350°F. Butter and flour a 10-inch bundt pan.

2. *To make the cake:* Combine the brown sugar, cinnamon, instant coffee powder, cocoa, raisins, and walnuts in a medium-size bowl. Mix thoroughly, and set aside.

3. Beat the butter in a large bowl until light and fluffy. Slowly beat in the sugar, then the vanilla. Add the eggs, one at a time, beating thoroughly after each addition.

4. In a large bowl, sift the flour with the baking powder, baking soda, and salt; sift again. Add the flour mixture to the egg mixture in three parts, alternating with thirds of the yogurt. Do not overmix. The batter will be thick.

5. Spoon a fourth of the batter into the prepared pan, and sprinkle with a third of the raisin-nut mixture. Repeat the layers twice; top with the remaining batter.

6. Bake the cake until a toothpick inserted in the center comes out clean, about 1 hour. Cool in the pan on a wire rack before unmolding.

7. *To make the icing:* Mix the coffee powder and hot water; cool to room temperature.

8. In the medium-size bowl of an electric mixer, beat the cream cheese and butter until light and fluffy. Slowly beat in the confectioner's sugar. Then beat in the vanilla, orange juice, and cooled coffee mixture. Beat until almost doubled in volume, about 4 minutes. Spread the icing over the sides and top of the unmolded cake. Sprinkle walnuts and raisins over the top.

Serves 8 to 10

THE PUNCH AND DINAH SHOW

*F*or the past two weeks I have been cooking light. I am sequestered in my house near the sea in Amagansett (Long Island) with two cats, a brand-new paint roller, and at least two dozen gallons of white paint, trying to undo the winter's mildew before the summer tenants arrive.

I bring up my cats for a specific reason: They are both spoiled rotten and adept at the subtle ploys of blackmail to achieve their ends— notably uncanned cat food!

Both these felines are an American breed that is sometimes termed "marmalade," a curiously appropriate cognomen as it turns out, for they do get me into some truly inextricable jams.

Dinah, the elder, is a sleek and worldly female with a face and form that would give Twiggy a run for the money. Dinah's problems (aside from a young, aggressive, and mismatched partner named Punch) are all in the realm of culinary disquiets.

It is her pose, you see, that she is completely disinterested in food as a means of survival. And unless one has had the foresight to be able to provide her with a snack of fresh corn, asparagus tips, honeydew melon, or (and here lies the nub of this essay) bay scallops, she will adamantly refuse to eat whatever is set before her. Provide her with an expedient bowl of Friskies, for instance, and she will immediately decamp the kitchen, without so much as a sniff at the offending porringer.

Dinah won't simply reject the offering and be done with it, however. She will reproach her feeder with a series of baleful glances, then a round of unexpected acrobatics—falling over on the floor as if to demonstrate how easily a beautiful cat could expire from a case of neglect and malnutrition.

Dinah's hunger strikes have a double-edged sword, as my other cat, Punch (who will eat anything, it seems), demands her uneaten portion for himself as soon as he ascertains her disinterest. To make his appetite apparent, he will whirl about the house like a dervish, knocking over chairs, upsetting paint cans, and shredding plastic drop cloths. If all that doesn't work, he uses his loud voice to meow with a vibrato that would give Pavarotti pause. "More! More!" cries Punch, and the echo is heard for miles along the Eastern seaboard.

The only way to survive the tyranny of my cats is to pay the piper. Since neither corn nor honeydew is in season yet, and asparagus is past its prime, my dues are being paid in bay scallops.

Dinah adores this treat and purrs loudly for an hour after a meal. Punch, being somewhat more follower than leader, accepts the change of diet with good grace, and no meows. But here's the kicker: Both cats have become so accustomed to the good life that they will nibble a bay scal-lop only after it has been sautéed in butter and garlic! Of a consequence my diet has been fairly limited for a fortnight. But to look on the bright side, it's fast food to prepare, and D. and P. are quiescent in the extreme after every meal.

The house is nearly painted, too!

SCALLOPS D'AIL

❧

*F*rom the South of France, a dish I like almost as much as my cats do. What makes it memorable is the dollop of ripe tomato, the splash of vermouth—and the garlic, of course.

Serve this over rice. The recipe doubles easily for extra diners—human or feline.

1¼ pounds bay scallops

6 tablespoons (¾ stick)
   unsalted butter

3 large cloves garlic,
   minced

1 tablespoon unbleached
   all-purpose flour

1 large ripe tomato, seeded
   and chopped

6 scallions (green onions),
   trimmed and finely
   chopped

Pinch of dried thyme

⅓ cup dry vermouth

2 tablespoons fresh lemon
   juice

½ teaspoon salt

⅛ teaspoon freshly ground
   black pepper

2 tablespoons finely chopped
   fresh parsley

1. Rinse the scallops, and dry them between layers of paper towels.

2. Melt 2 tablespoons of the butter in a large skillet. Add one third of the garlic; cook over medium heat for 1 minute. Add one third of the scallops; cook over high heat, stirring constantly, until golden, 4 to 5 minutes. Transfer to a warm serving dish. Repeat twice, using up the remaining butter, garlic, and scallops. Keep the scallops warm, uncovered, in a 250°F oven.

3. Sprinkle the flour into the skillet, and stir until all the liquid is absorbed. Add the tomato, scallions, and thyme; cook over medium heat until the tomato is soft, about 5 minutes. Gradually stir in the vermouth and lemon juice; raise the heat slightly and cook until the sauce is syrupy,

5 minutes more. Season with the salt and pepper. Pour the sauce over the scallops, sprinkle with the parsley, and serve immediately.

Serves 2 to 3

GARLICKY BAY SCALLOP HASH

$\wp$

A jot more work for the chef, Bay Scallop Hash is a piece of my own culinary handiwork, produced after a steady diet of sautés. When you make it, be certain the potatoes do not overcook. The hash must have some bite if it is not to become bay scallop mush.

1 pound bay scallops

6 tablespoons (¾ stick) unsalted butter

1 tablespoon olive oil

2 cloves garlic, minced

2 large baking potatoes, cubed

3 tablespoons unbleached all-purpose flour

4 scallions (green onions), trimmed and minced

1 tablespoon fresh lemon juice

1 teaspoon grated lemon zest

½ cup chopped fresh parsley

1 teaspoon crushed dried hot red peppers

Salt and freshly ground black pepper

1. Rinse the scallops and pat them dry between layers of paper towels.

2. Heat the butter and oil in a large skillet, and sauté the garlic over medium heat until golden, 2 minutes. Stir in the potatoes. Cook, stirring constantly, until they are light golden, about 10 minutes.

3. Coat the scallops lightly with the flour, and stir them into the pota-

toes. Add the scallions, lemon juice, and lemon zest. Cook, stirring frequently, until the potatoes are tender, about 6 minutes. Toss in the parsley, dried red peppers, and salt and pepper to taste. Serve immediately.

Serves 4

HERE'S TO YOU, MYRA

M y sister, Myra, died last summer, and her passing is an incal-
culable loss.

More than a sibling, Myra was a staunch supporter and close personal
friend (made early and kept long) who monitored my welfare all her life.
When I opened The Store in Amagansett twenty years ago, she was the
original backer. None of the founding partners had either the cash or
the credit to persuade a bank to sponsor the operation, so Myra signed
The Store's first loan—and co-signed a few afterward as well. Her
reward? Functioning as its largely unsalaried manager and general fac-
totum for the next decade. But my sister was generous to a fault.
Whenever I traveled—no matter how long the trip's duration—she
always took custody of my cats. And she frequently opened her home to
my two-legged friends as well.

Myra was a counselor and guide, the person who brought culture into my young life when my parents and teachers had given up trying. A worldly type, even as an adolescent, Myra permitted me to join her in her pursuit of grace and style. Since most of her early education in sophistication was acquired from the movies we attended, her role models were inevitably screen stars, whose elegant manners and modish dress she attempted to emulate whenever our parents were out of earshot.

In order to expose my palate to *haute cuisine* (at age ten), Myra gave a luncheon party for just the two of us every Saturday afternoon—the Depression notwithstanding. An intrepid believer in *making do*, Myra reasoned that if a recipe called for alligator pears (avocados, but who knew) stuffed with Stilton cheese and black walnuts, canned Bartlett pears filled with cream cheese and run-of-the-mill walnuts would not be too diverse a substitution. It was a disaster, of course, but neither of us admitted culinary defeat as we consumed the repast on my mother's best china and damask, at the dining room table, with a bottle of bubbly (ginger ale) discreetly wrapped in a towel and placed in a bucket of ice.

A lot of water has passed under the bridge since I was that dashing *boulevardier* in short pants and knee socks, but I would like to raise a glass to my sister one more time, with your indulgence. She was, as you may have surmised, one hell of a lady!

M Y R A ' S   H A M

ひとら

*M*y sister was not a notable chef, but she had certain skills at the stove that were honored in print. She was always irritated because her ham recipe, limned by Denis Vaughan in his chapter of *The Store Cookbook,* left out the slice of toast that made it an open-face sandwich. Herewith the corrected version—better late than never.

1 slice ham, ⅛ to ¼ inch thick
1 slice crusty round bread,
   lightly toasted and
   buttered

1 or 2 slices Swiss cheese
   (enough to cover the ham)

1. Preheat the broiler.

2. Place the ham on a broiling pan and broil it for 1 minute. Turn the ham over and place it on the bread. Cover with the cheese. Return it to the broiler, and cook until the cheese is melted and bubbling.

Serves 1

MYRA'S POTATO LATKES

*T*his recipe came from my grandmother, who passed it on to my mother, who passed it on to my sister. I could never get the hang of the darn things. My sister grated her potatoes by hand, using the finest blade. Quite by accident I grated them roughly once and had to process them afterward. The trick worked, so I recommend it to all but hard-nosed latke makers. In the Greene household latkes were always served with a rich meaty gravy, plus applesauce on the side.

1½ pounds baking potatoes
1 lemon
1 small onion, finely grated
1 large egg, lightly beaten
2 tablespoons all-purpose
   flour
2 teaspoons baking powder

Salt and freshly ground black
   pepper
Solid vegetable shortening
Traditional Meat Sauce for
   Latkes (recipe follows)
   and/or applesauce

1. Preheat the oven to 250°F.

2. Squeeze the lemon juice into a large bowl of cold water. Peel the potatoes, and roughly grate them into the bowl. Let stand for 30 minutes.

3. Drain the potatoes, and squeeze them dry with your hands. Place them in a food processor and process, using the on/off switch, until fairly smooth but not wet. Transfer the purée to a large bowl, and add the onion, egg, flour, baking powder, and salt and pepper to taste. Stir until smooth.

4. Place a large cast-iron skillet over medium heat. Film the bottom of the skillet with shortening. Using about 1 large tablespoon for each, scoop 4 latkes into the skillet. Cook until golden brown and puffed, about 1 minute. Turn them over and brown the other side, about 30 seconds. Place the latkes on a rack and keep them warm in the oven while you sauté the remaining ones. Grease the skillet after each batch.

5. Serve with meat sauce and/or applesauce.

Serves 4

TRADITIONAL MEAT SAUCE FOR LATKES

1 large onion, thinly sliced
4 pounds beef brisket
1 to 3 bay leaves (optional)

1½ cups homemade beef stock
or canned broth

1. Preheat the oven to 350°F.

2. Arrange the onion over the bottom of a large Dutch oven. Add the beef, and the bay leaves if desired. Cover, and bake for 1 hour.

3. Continue to cook the meat, adding broth to the pot as needed, until it is very tender and shreds easily, about another 2½ hours.

4. Before serving, lightly shred the meat into its cooking juices.

Serves 6 to 8

BERT ON HOLIDAYS

CHAPTER TWO

FIRST COURSES
Bean Soup with Veal Balls • *page 74*
Hoppin' John Soup • *page 97*

MAIN DISHES
Fish Fillets in Green Envelopes • *page 67*
Chicken Pizzuta • *page 69*
Red-Eyed Baked Ham • *page 76*
Spicy Texas Meat Loaf • *page 80*
Crispy Cornish Hens with Jambalaya Dressing • *page 84*

SIDE DISHES
Hoppin' John • *page 58*
Roman Potato and Cheese Salad • *page 79*
Quick Cranberry-Peach Preserves • *page 89*
Hoppin' John Salad with Bacon • *page 98*

DESSERTS
Praline Cakes with Caramel Syrup • *page 59*
Zasu Pitts's Chocolate Fudge • *page 62*
Zasu Pitts's Panocha • *page 63*
Almond Sponge Cake • *page 71*
Coconut Macaroon Torte • *page 72*
Moravian Orange Bread • *page 81*
Polka-Dot Angel Cake • *page 93*
Lemon Angel Cake • *page 94*

BREAKFAST
Quick Pineapple-Apricot Marmalade • *page 90*

BEVERAGES
Irish Coffee • *page 66*
Hot Chocolate Toddy • *page 99*
Swedish Coffee Eggnog • *page 100*
Temperance Eggnog • *page 101*

A HAPPY, HEALTHY, WEALTHY, NEW YEAR

New Year's Day: When I was young, New Year's Day was notable to me for its totally alien array of comestibles. My mother always set out a dark and plummy fruitcake on the sideboard early in the day, secure in the knowledge that it would still be in prime condition whenever callers arrived because no one in my family ever ate a speck! My father, who was rarely pressed into kitchen service, would whip egg yolks, cream, and a shot or two of "hootch" with a rotary beater until the mixture was so thick that it had to be spooned, rather than ladled, into glasses. This libation, served up in my mother's best crystal, was rarely imbibed by anyone except a few maiden aunts.

But the food, not the drink, was the centerpiece of a New Year celebration. Our round dining room table, lit with branched candlesticks, was laid with all manner of curious sweets and savories: anchovies, caviar, and tiny rolled herrings in sour cream cheek by jowl with butter cookies, bowls of unshelled nuts, and coffee-flavored caramel candies.

What is even stranger than our holiday fare was our New Year's Day mien. Mother, father, sister, and I would sit around in our best clothes, waiting for unbidden guests to arrive at our "open house." Why they always appeared and ate and drank, I will never know. But they did, and those erratic dishes were inevitably consumed by the time our open house was shuttered.

In Virginia, where I went to college, a New Year's Day groaning board was more traditional. It always featured a cured ham, sliced papery thin, served with a platter of beaten biscuits and a porringer of Hoppin' John. A vinegary compound of black-eyed peas cooked with rice, this dish is supposed to bring health to the household and wealth to the pocket. And no southerner I have ever met was willing to forego the possibility, even though most Hoppin' John is served stone cold!

Rice in one form or another seems to be part of the world's New Year's bounty. In the mountainous provinces of China, rice is dyed red (with hot pepper oil) at the start of the year "to accustom the tongue to any fires a new cycle of months may bring." In Latin American countries, an extra spoonful of rice is traditionally added to every soup bowl at the first meal of the year—to encourage "seeds of prosperity" to grow and be harvested. In Provence, the women of the household bake cakes of rice and fruit that are eaten after first Mass of the new year—to "cement the bricks" that hold each family together.

My favorite New Year's Day rice alliance, aside from Hoppin' John, is a cake of a different color—a pancake studded with golden pecans. I came upon this dish in New Orleans almost thirty years ago, when it was served to me at the stroke of midnight on New Year's Eve as a surefire cure for a hangover. As a curative or not, it's a nice way to start any day.

HOPPIN' JOHN

ॐ

My very untraditional rendering of this classic southern dish is actually a warm salad. It marries happily with ham, fried chicken, or even a brisket of beef. Two variations on the theme—a Hoppin' John Soup and a cold Hoppin' John Salad with Bacon appear on pages 97 and 98.

1 package (10 ounces) frozen black-eyed peas
2 strips bacon
1 small onion, chopped
1 clove garlic, minced
1 cup cooked rice
2 tablespoons red wine vinegar

Salt and freshly ground black pepper
¼ cup finely chopped scallion (green onion) tops
2 tablespoons chopped fresh parsley

1. Drop the black-eyed peas into a medium-size saucepan filled with boiling salted water. Reduce the heat and simmer until tender, about 20 minutes. Drain, reserving ¼ cup of the cooking liquid.

2. Sauté the bacon in a large heavy skillet over medium heat until crisp. Drain on paper towels, and set aside.

3. Stir the onion into the bacon drippings in the skillet. Cook over medium-low for 3 minutes. Add the garlic; cook 2 minutes longer. Stir in the drained black-eyed peas and the rice. Cook, stirring constantly, until warmed through. Add the vinegar and enough of the reserved cooking liquid to moisten the mixture, 2 to 3 tablespoons. Cook for 5 minutes.

4. Add salt and pepper to taste. Crumble the bacon over the top, sprinkle with the scallions and parsley, and serve.

Serves 4 to 6

PRALINE CAKES WITH CARAMEL SYRUP

f these crêpe-like nut cakes are too sweet for you to face by dawn's early light, serve them for dessert after a meal of cold fare. And pass the whipped cream on the side.

FOR THE CARAMEL SYRUP
1 cup sugar
⅔ cup hot water
2 teaspoons vanilla

FOR THE PRALINE CAKES
4 egg yolks
1½ cups milk
4 tablespoons (½ stick)
    unsalted butter, melted

1 teaspoon vanilla extract
2 teaspoons brandy
1 cup all-purpose flour
2 teaspoons baking powder
2 tablespoons sugar
½ teaspoon salt
⅛ teaspoon ground cinnamon
½ cup coarsely chopped
    pecans
1 cup cooked rice, cooled

1. Prepare the caramel syrup: In a medium-size heavy skillet, heat the sugar over medium heat until it starts to melt and turn golden, about 1½ minutes. Continue to cook, stirring constantly, until the sugar bubbles and caramelizes, about 2 minutes longer. Do not allow syrup to burn. Carefully add the hot water; stir until all lumps have dissolved. Remove the skillet from the heat, and stir in the vanilla. Keep warm.

2. Make the praline cakes: In a large bowl, beat the egg yolks until light and lemon-colored. Then beat in the milk, butter, vanilla, brandy, flour, baking powder, sugar, salt, and cinnamon. Stir in the pecans and rice.

3. Heat a griddle or cast-iron skillet over medium heat. When it is hot, lightly butter it and pour about ¼ cup batter for each cake onto the griddle. Cook until bubbles form on top of the pancakes and the undersides are lightly browned, about 1 minute. Turn the cakes over and lightly brown the other side, about 30 seconds. Keep them warm in a low (250°F) oven while you cook the rest of the pancakes. Butter the griddle as necessary. Serve with syrup drizzled over the top.

Makes 16 small pancakes (serves 6)

CANDY THAT'S TRULY THE PITTS

Happy Valentine's Day: If you haven't been assiduously calendar watching, this Saturday is St. Valentine's Day. I know, because I received my first valentine well before the official date this year. And, since it was such a particularly sweet bequest, I think you all deserve to share in the spoils.

My valentine is actually a cookbook—the residual of a column written at Christmastime—about homemade candies. Aside from recipes, there was a parenthetic note to my story about a favored (lost) tome on the subject: *Candy Hits* by Zasu Pitts. This short but highly informative work was compiled by the late, beloved movie comedienne, shortly before her death in 1963 and published posthumously. A copy came into my hands as a Christmas present a long time ago and I literally used it to a faretheewell. Half the pages were caramelized and the rest so badly streaked with cocoa and vanilla stains that recipes were barely legible. But I loved every sticky paragraph.

I lost *Candy Hits* well over a decade ago—and never expected to ever see another copy again. However, almost immediately after my column ran, I received over 50 letters from readers who still had the book in their possession.

Three writers offered me their copies outright. "No strings," was one correspondent's explicit deposition. "Not even a box of homemade fudge!"

At least half the number offered to lend me books so I might transcribe favorite recipes. The other half—declaring they could not bear to part with their mint editions—proposed xeroxing the book page by page (at various copy centers) to help circumvent the flagrant breaking of any copyright laws.

In the end, I happily accepted a book—with the caveat that I be permitted to take up the slack on the cookbook shelf with one of my own books inscribed with a debt of gratitude. But a particular note from a circulation clerk in a library (on the subject of hard-to-find tomes in general) proved so enlightening, I requested permission to reprint it in part here.

"You wrote you'd looked for the book in libraries. But did you ask about borrowing it from another library? One of the few things in this country that works well and is quite cheap is the nationwide interlibrary loan system. Even a small branch may be connected with this, or can tell you where to find a participating library. For a small fee—as far as I know, usually not more than mailing charges on the book, sometimes less—you can borrow from any library in the country . . . through the OCLC computer system, centered in Ohio and known originally as The Ohio Colles Library Center. So, please do check into this if you have not found *your* candy book yet . . ."

I did find it of course. But, more importantly, I discovered there is a wonderful confederation of cookbook lovers out there who cared about my predicament—and my sweet-toothed predilection.

Here's a valentine to each and every one—and let calories fall where they may! The following recipes (both for fudge) are reprinted from *Candy Hits* by Zasu Pitts; *The Famous Star's Own Candy Recipes.*

ZASU PITTS'S
CHOCOLATE FUDGE

n her book, Ms. Pitts notes: "When I arrived in Hollywood, I could make four different kinds of candy. They were basic . . . In that day every schoolgirl had her own special fudge which she used to whip up on a Sunday afternoon with friends." Those days are obviously gone forever but if parents are listening, Pitts' fudge (pecan flecked) is still the best anodyne to MTV.

2 cups sugar
¾ cup milk
2 ounces (2 squares)
*   unsweetened baking*
*   chocolate*
Pinch of salt

1 teaspoon corn syrup
2 tablespoons unsalted
*   butter, cut into bits*
1 teaspoon vanilla extract
½ cup roughly chopped pecans

1. Generously butter an 8-inch-square baking pan.

2. Butter the sides of a medium-size saucepan. Combine the sugar, milk, chocolate, salt, and corn syrup in the saucepan. Attach a candy thermometer to the pan, and place over medium heat to melt the chocolate. Then gently boil, *without stirring,* until the thermometer reads 238°F, about 20 minutes. Test the mixture by dropping a small amount into a saucer of cold water. A soft ball should form.

3. Remove the pan from the heat. Add the butter but do not stir.

Allow the mixture to cool to 165°F, about 20 minutes. Add the vanilla and beat vigorously until the fudge has lost its gloss, 8 to 10 minutes. Stir in the nuts.

4. Spread the fudge in the prepared pan, smoothing the top. Allow to cool completely, then cut it into 1½-inch squares. Remove the squares from the pan and store them in a tightly covered container.

Makes twenty-five 1½-inch squares.

ZASU PITTS'S PANOCHA

In her book, Ms. Pitts calls this brown-sugar fudge "panocha." When I was a tyke, we knew it as "penuche." But by any name at all, this is the best molar demolishment I know! Restrict yourself to two pieces a day if you can! Incidentally a candy thermometer is a worthwhile kitchen investment if you plan to do any heavy confection-making!

2⅓ cups tightly-packed light
   brown sugar
¾ cup evaporated milk
2 tablespoons unsalted
   butter, cut into bits

1 teaspoon vanilla extract
½ cup roughly chopped
   pistachio nuts

1. Generously butter an 8-inch square baking pan.

2. Combine the brown sugar and the milk in a medium-size saucepan. Attach a candy thermometer to the pan, and place the pan over medium heat. Cook, stirring until the sugar dissolves and the syrup is gently boiling, 4 to 5 minutes. Continue boiling until the thermometer reads 238°F, about 20 minutes. Test the mixture by dropping a small amount into a saucer of cold water. A soft ball should form.

3. Remove pan from the heat and allow to cool to 165°F, about 20 minutes. Add the butter and vanilla and beat vigorously until the mixture becomes thick and starts to lose its gloss, 8 to 10 minutes. Stir in the nuts.

4. Spread the fudge into the prepared pan, smoothing the top. Allow to cool completely, then cut it into 1½-inch squares. Remove the squares from the pan and store them in a tightly covered container.

Makes twenty-five 1½-inch squares.

HELLO, THE FOOD THERAPIST IS IN

St. Patrick's Day: In my curious profession, I am often the recipient of rather strange phone calls. Not heavy breathers—these callers are almost always readers who feel they must "reach out and touch someone" (me) to claim reassurance or issue a rebuke. These phone calls come at odd hours, often after midnight, and the answers often require the well-tempered response of a therapist rather than a newspaper columnist, but there is a bonus: at least one knows someone out there is *reading*!

One of the calls I recently received came from Ireland, of all places. The caller, Eugene McSweeney, is chef-owner of a charming inn known as Lacken House, in Kilkenny. McSweeney telephoned long-distance one morning last week, with only the slightest degree of ire, to set the record straight, once and for all, about the origin of Irish coffee.

It seems that many American food writers have recently been perpetuating a rumor that Irish coffee was actually invented in the U.S., its place of origin being the bar of the august St. Francis Hotel in San Francisco. Not so, claimed McSweeney, with a sheaf of historical documentation to prove the quaff's actual source. As Saint Patrick's Day is just around the corner, it seemed high time to get the facts nailed down, so I did. And I pried a recipe for the spirited drink in passing.

According to McSweeney, Irish coffee was the invention of a barman named Joe Sheridan, who tended the pub at Shannon Airport back in 1949, when it was still known as Foyne's Flying Boat Basin. As the story goes, one morning when the clipper from America was overdue, the waiting passengers were so cold that they begged the bartender for a quick hot toddy to revive their flagging spirits. Being a creative fellow, and fast into the bargain, Sheridan whipped up a drink of what he had on hand: freshly brewed coffee, brown sugar, and Irish whisky; then he floated some heavy cream on top to "lighten the traveler's load." The rest is tippler's history, and there is even a plaque commemorating Sheridan's stirring arm at Shannon Airport. If anyone has a lingering doubt about Irish coffee's ancestry, they won't after they try the recipe below, for it is obviously pure gold in a glass.

Aside from Irish coffee, Eugene McSweeney, with his lilting brogue and fey sense of humor, is a good spokesperson for Irish food in general. Fed up to the teeth with his countrymen's image as "corned beef-and-cabbage eaters," he and his wife make a point of using only fresh local ingredients for all the dishes they prepare at Lacken House.

At my request, McSweeney gave me the recipe for a much-requested entrée he serves, a delicate fish dish of turbot (I used sole) wrapped lightly in lettuce and poached in cream. Irish ingredients probably make a difference, but even in my kitchen, this prescription would make a French chef proud. Moreover, it is relatively easy: twenty minutes from saucepan to table. When I suggested serving Eugene McSweeney's creation over rice, however, his chauvinism rose to the surface.

"Never," he insisted. "Use *potatoes,* please!"

I R I S H   C O F F E E

cSweeney's Irish coffee recipe (which is actually Joe Sheridan's original) comes with the following toast. When lifting your glass, recite:

> St. Patrick was a gentleman
> Who through strategy and stealth,
> Drove all the snakes from Ireland—
> Here's a toasting to his health.
> But not too many toastings, lest
> You lose yourself and then,
> Forget the good St. Patrick and
> See all those snakes again!

*1 cup strong brewed black
  coffee, hot
1 teaspoon dark brown sugar
1 jigger (1½ ounces) Irish
  whisky*

*¼ cup (approximately) heavy
  or whipping cream, lightly
  whipped*

Warm an 8-ounce glass with hot tap water. Discard the water and pour in the coffee until the glass is seven-eighths full. Add the brown sugar and whisky, and stir until the sugar has dissolved. Gently pour the cream over the back of a spoon and into the glass, so that it floats on top of the coffee and forms a collar on the glass. Serve immediately.

Serves 1

FISH FILLETS IN GREEN ENVELOPES

3 large fillets of fresh sole, flounder, or turbot (about 1 pound)	*⅛ teaspoon freshly ground black pepper*
6 large romaine lettuce leaves	*⅛ teaspoon chopped fresh thyme, or a pinch of dried*
1 cup heavy or whipping cream	*1 tablespoon chopped fresh parsley*
⅛ teaspoon salt	

1. Cut each fillet in half crosswise. Place each piece on the large end of a lettuce leaf, and roll up the lettuce to enclose the fish. Trim off any excess lettuce.

2. Combine the cream, salt, pepper, and thyme in a large skillet. Heat to boiling; then reduce the heat. Carefully place 3 rolled fillets in the cream mixture, and gently simmer until done, about 5 minutes per side. Using a slotted spatula, transfer the rolls to an ovenproof serving dish and keep them warm in a low (250°F) oven. Cook the remaining rolled fillets, and transfer them to the serving dish.

3. Continue to cook the cream sauce until it has thickened slightly, about 5 minutes. Spoon the sauce over the fillets, sprinkle with the parsley, and serve.

Serves 3

SWEETS FOR THE SEDER

*P*assover: My family was, by and large, a decidedly unreligious lot. Both my mother and father, having been born in this country, conspicuously denied themselves the pleasurable traditions of their Eastern European Jewish forebears—out of misguided allegiance to All-American blandness, I assume.

Even in my grandparents' home, Christmas held equal sway with Hanukkah. But Passover was the one holy day that brought out all their Jewishness—probably because it was celebrated at the dinner table. All of my relatives were hearty eaters, and my grandmother was a noteworthy cook.

There were never fewer than twenty guests for the *seder* (the ritual feast), and the preparation occupied not only my grandmother's kitchen but my mother's and aunts' as well for days in advance of the event. The courses seemed endless, and apparently were prepared in team relays. My mother, who had what she called "the lightest hand with matzo balls," always prepared these airy dumplings at home. But my father and I were elected to bring a sample to my grandmother ahead of time, so she could test one early on in a trial run of chicken soup—to be certain the hand had not lost its touch.

Grandmother was a tyrant at the stovetop every day of the year, but holidays brought out her true iron fist. If a monumental arrangement of celery, radishes, and olives (prepared by one of my aunts) displeased her eye, she would topple it with an imperious elbow and watch critically as it was reassembled to suit her exacting standard. Likewise no one was ever permitted to wash a dish in her sink or ladle a plate of soup or carve a chicken wing at her table. Though forty-odd years have passed, I can still recall watching her run to the kitchen during courses, while the others at the table happily dined, to supervise the next round of food. Entering the kitchen, she would don a voluminous apron over her lace dress, toss some meat on a platter, empty a skillet of its vegetables, and then like a proficient striptease artist, remove her protective garment with a shake of the hips as she made her way back to the dining room, the precious dish held aloft.

My grandmother was not a religious woman, and she never kept a kosher home. Her only concession to this ritual was an extra set of dishes in her china closet—which she used indiscriminately for either milk or meat when the occasion arose. But never on Passover. A scrupulous baker, she would pound almonds and matzo meal for the desserts that inevitably appeared on her dessert tray: dry macaroons and airy but decidedly unbuttery cakes. I remember her being tempted on one occasion to add a tablespoon of flour (instead of matzo meal) to a nut torte she was whipping together. But she resisted the urge, shrugging. "So what if it's dry? A tradition is a tradition, after all!"

CHICKEN PIZZUTA

This is a Roman dish that's been converted for use at Passover. Any way you look at it, it makes a highly arresting change from traditional roast chicken.

1 chicken (3½ to 4 pounds),
   cut into serving pieces
Salt and freshly ground black
   pepper to taste
1 large matzo
1 tablespoon red wine
   vinegar
3 tablespoons olive oil
   (approximately)
25 almonds, shelled

3 cloves garlic
1 cup homemade chicken
   stock or canned broth,
   heated
1 small bay leaf
3 tablespoons mayonnaise
2 teaspoons fresh lemon juice
Chopped fresh parsley, for
   garnish

1. Sprinkle the chicken pieces with salt and pepper, and set aside. Sprinkle the matzo with the vinegar, and break it into pieces.

2. Heat 1 tablespoon of the oil in a large heavy skillet over medium heat. Add the broken matzo, almonds, and garlic. Cook, stirring constantly, until golden, 4 or 5 minutes. Transfer to a food processor and process until smooth. Scrape the mixture into a medium-size bowl, and stir in the hot chicken stock.

3. Add the remaining 2 tablespoons oil to the skillet. Sauté the chicken pieces over medium heat until golden brown on all sides, 15 to 20 minutes.

4. Pour off all fat from the skillet, and add the almond mixture and the bay leaf. Cover, and cook the chicken over medium heat until tender, about 20 minutes. Then reduce the heat to low, and discard the bay leaf.

5. Combine the mayonnaise with the lemon juice, and slowly stir this into the pan juices around the chicken pieces. Heat thoroughly, but do not allow it to boil. Season with salt and pepper to taste, sprinkle with the parsley, and serve.

Serves 4

ALMOND SPONGE CAKE

ツゑ⑤

*T*his cake is remarkably like one my grandmother always made during the holidays, although perhaps a tad less dry for the shower of almond liqueur after baking. It keeps well, too!

6 egg whites
Pinch of salt
5 egg yolks
8 ounces blanched almonds, ground
1 cup granulated sugar
1 tablespoon matzo meal

2 tablespoons brandy
6 tablespoons amaretto liqueur
Confectioner's sugar, for dusting

1. Preheat the oven to 350°F. Butter a 9-inch springform pan and line the bottom with parchment paper. Then butter the paper and flour the pan.

2. Beat the egg whites in the large bowl of an electric mixer until fluffy. Sprinkle with the salt and beat until stiff. Add the egg yolks one at a time, beating thoroughly after each addition.

3. Combine the ground almonds, granulated sugar, and matzo meal in a bowl. Gradually add this to the egg mixture. Add the brandy and 2 tablespoons of the amaretto. Pour the batter into the prepared pan, and bake until firm to the touch, about 1¼ hours. Cool completely in the pan on a wire rack.

4. Remove the sides of the pan, and sprinkle the top of the cake with the remaining 4 tablespoons amaretto. Dust with confectioner's sugar just before serving.

Serves 8 to 10

COCONUT MACAROON TORTE

*A*s I have said, my grandmother favored ground almonds in most of her Passover desserts. Like my forebear, I haven't a kosher bone in my body. The following coconut macaroon torte originally called for 2 tablespoons of all-purpose flour in its devise. Ecumenically, that translates to 2 tablespoons of superfine matzo meal, with not a jot of difference to the torte. The choice is yours.

4 egg whites
Pinch of salt
¾ cup sugar
3 tablespoons light rum
1½ cups sweetened shredded
   coconut
¼ cup ground blanched
   almonds

2 tablespoons superfine
   matzo meal
½ teaspoon grated lemon
   zest
Fresh berries or sliced
   fruit

1. Preheat the oven to 350°F. Lightly grease a 9-inch round cake pan, and sprinkle it with matzo meal; shake out the excess. Set the pan aside.

2. Beat the egg whites with the salt in a large bowl until soft peaks form. Gradually add ½ cup of the sugar, 2 tablespoons at a time, and beat until the whites are stiff and shiny. Then beat in the rum.

3. Combine the coconut, almonds, matzo meal, and lemon zest in a medium-size bowl. Fold this into the egg whites.

4. Spread the coconut mixture evenly in the prepared pan, and bake until the top is lightly browned, about 20 minutes. Cool the torte in the pan on a wire rack before unmolding.

5. To serve, sprinkle the fruit with as much of the remaining ¼ cup sugar as needed. Unmold the torte onto a platter and scatter the fruit over the top.

Serves 6

THE EASTER HAM

*E*aster: I am a self-professed nontraditionalist in the kitchen, but there are a host of dishes associated with the specific holidays that I wouldn't pass up for anything in the world—even for a due-bill at Paul Bocuse!

Thanksgiving and roast turkey is one such union, and St. Patrick's Day and corned beef (boiled with cabbage, of course) is another. Fourth of July brings to mind hot dogs, preferably grilled over an open fire but paired with potato salad no matter what the landscape. Recently in these pages I noted my affection for airy-light matzo balls—but I would never think of biting into the delicate golden heart of one except at Passover time. Why? I cannot explain. But clearly particular foods have their season, early imprinted on an impressionable palate. So (as the song goes), why fight the feeling?

Another of these prandial matches is coming up on the calendar, and frankly, I can't wait for the dinner gong to sound! I am speaking of the first Sunday in April (if you haven't caught my drift) and announcing that the holiday *plat du jour* at Greene's table will be: *ham!*

Ham is one viand that I am severely addicted to, and I consume it a good deal more than once a year. Out of respect for my ham habit, however, I reserve the best recipe I know for its Easter appearance. Some years ago, doing research for a book on American foods, I came upon a method for cooking ham that I have adopted (and adapted) as the definitive formula.

Ham with red-eye gravy may be far removed from any traditional Easter rendering you have ever sampled, but it is no less intoxicating for that. The dish originated about 135 years ago in the Klondike where the miners, living in lean-to's or tents without kitchens, survived on a diet of smoked meat. A most enterprising gold digger, it is recorded, threw a spot of bourbon into his fry pan by accident one morning. When it caught fire—as such liquid is guaranteed to do—he put out the flames with a cup of coffee. Thus one of the best boozy prescriptions of American cookery was born.

Being a nontraditionalist is useful in the kitchen, and applying the same spirited basting liquor to a whole ham produces a wondrously tangy hock. My only problem with Red-Eyed Baked Ham is that I made it so often, I accrued a healthy collection of meaty ham bones in the freezer.

Out of that situation, however, arose another recipe—a thick, velvety white bean potage, dappled with veal balls, that makes a perfect after-Easter-week dinner with nothing more substantial than a loaf of bread. It's particularly good when those April showers arrive.

BEAN SOUP WITH VEAL BALLS

ꙮ

*T*he following potage is hearty fare. If April turns unexpectedly balmy, store the ham bone (not the recipe!) in your freezer till next fall.

1 pound Great Northern
    beans
3 tablespoons unsalted
    butter
1 large onion, chopped
1 small clove garlic,
    minced
2 large carrots, chopped
2 ribs celery, chopped
1 medium-size parsnip,
    chopped
1 medium-size turnip,
    chopped
1 leftover ham bone, trimmed
    of fat

1 large can (46 ounces)
    chicken broth
4 cups water
2 teaspoons red wine vinegar
8 ounces ground veal
1 small scallion (green onion),
    trimmed and minced
1 egg, lightly beaten
¼ cup water
¼ cup fresh bread crumbs
¼ teaspoon salt
¼ teaspoon freshly ground
    black pepper

1. Place the beans in a large pot of cold water, and bring to a boil. Remove from the heat and let stand for 1 hour. Drain the beans.

2. Melt 2 tablespoons of the butter in a large pot over medium-low heat. Stir in the onion; cook to soften, 2 minutes. Add the garlic, and continue to cook until lightly browned. Then add the carrots, celery, parsnip, turnip, ham bone, broth, water, vinegar, and beans. Bring to a boil; then reduce the heat, partially cover, and cook over medium-low heat until the beans are very tender, about 2 hours.

3. Meanwhile, combine the veal, scallion, egg, ¼ cup water, bread crumbs, salt, and pepper in a medium-size bowl. Mix thoroughly, and form into small meatballs. Melt the remaining 1 tablespoon butter in a large heavy skillet. Sauté the meatballs until well browned on all sides, 8 to 10 minutes. Remove them to a plate, and set aside.

4. When the beans are tender, remove the ham bone from the soup. Remove 1 to 1½ cups of the beans from the soup (depending on the thickness desired); mash them, and stir them back into the soup. Remove any ham from the bone and add it to the soup. Bring the soup back to a simmer, stir in the meatballs, and cook for 10 minutes. Serve.

Serves 6 to 8

RED - EYED
BAKED HAM

❧

*S*moked ham is sometimes on the salty side. If you have any serious doubts about your hock's saltiness, give it a fast bath in boiling water for about 15 minutes. Then drain and cool it and bring on the cloves.

1 smoked ham or smoked picnic shoulder (about 7½ pounds; I prefer Gwaltney of Smithfield)
Whole cloves
1 clove garlic, crushed
¼ cup Dijon mustard

⅔ cup (packed) dark brown sugar
1 cup strong brewed coffee
½ cup bourbon
¼ cup heavy or whipping cream

1. Remove the heavy skin from the ham. Using a sharp knife, score the top of the ham in a diamond pattern and insert a clove at each intersection. Place the ham on a rack in a roasting pan.

2. Combine the garlic, mustard, and brown sugar in a small bowl; blend well. Smear the mixture over the top and sides of the ham, and let it stand at room temperature for 30 minutes.

3. Meanwhile, preheat the oven to 350°F.

4. Combine the coffee, bourbon, and cream in a medium-size bowl. Bake the ham for 1½ hours, basting it every 10 minutes with the coffee-bourbon mixture. Serve the ham warm or at room temperature.

Serves 6 to 8

MEMOIRS OF A FINICKY PICNICKER

ndependence Day: No matter what the weather is like on this coming Fourth of July, I am planning a picnic.

Needless to say, I have made that kind of declarative statement in the past—and usually ended up cracking open the deviled eggs and uncorking a thermos of gazpacho on my living room rug when Mother Nature had other ideas on the subject.

This Independence Day, however, I am determined to dine *alfresco* even if it means dragging along an inflatable life raft instead of a blanket and supplying umbrellas for every member of the party. Because rustic foods simply do not have the desired effect on my psyche unless they are chomped in the great outdoors—with ants on the side. No, cockroaches simply will *not* do in Greene's version of a symphonie pastorale.

I suspect I came to this predilection for eating in forest glades and meadows by inheritance. My father, who was by no stretch of the imagination a naturalist, relished open-air meals. Say "cookout" or "barbecue" and his taste buds instantly flowered. Indeed, before the Depression sapped his social inclinations, I suspect he joined all the fraternal organizations he connected with (Masons, Shriners, Elks, Lions) just to get a crack at the monster picnics those various organizations gave on national holidays in the long-ago summers of my youth.

These outings usually took place in some lakeside glen or wooded camp, a good half-day's ride from our home in Queens. To a chronically car-sick kid like me, that journey was the first canker.

I usually arrived in a state of pale green biliousness, and the revels of my father's Lodge members were no palliative to the condition. Intoxicated on their own high spirits (and I suspect a few nips from pocket flasks passed around), they played hard and noisily at the various games that made up the pre-picnic activities: three-legged races, potato relays, blindman's buff, and marathon volleyball and croquet.

When it was almost time for food, the brethren and their captive families would cram together at long trestle tables. Stationed there, the men drank enormous quantities of beer and sang off-key until the food finally arrived.

What a collation it was, too! Vast platters of gilded chicken and rosy beef, cheek by jowl with lobsters, clams, oysters, and soft-shell crabs. Almost weighing the table down at either end were porringers of pickled beets, potato salad, cole slaw, and a sizzling pot of sugar-crusted baked beans.

Fare for a regiment, it was demolished with relish—by everyone but me. A finicky eater (then, not now), I would deign to eat only a peanut butter and jelly sandwich, wax-paper-wrapped, and brought from home by a prescient mother who knew her son's Achilles' heel. Or digestive system!

The picnic planned for my outing on "the glorious fourth" will be a jot more circumspect.

ROMAN POTATO AND CHEESE SALAD

*T*he secret of this dish is *barely* cooked potato strips, combined with ham and cheese. It's wonderful picnic fare, but bring it chilled in a vacuum jar, please.

8-ounce piece Swiss or Fontina cheese
6 medium-size baking or red-skinned potatoes
Juice of 1 lemon
1½ cups mayonnaise
¼ cup fresh lemon juice
1 teaspoon salt
½ teaspoon freshly ground black pepper

¼ teaspoon cayenne pepper
1 teaspoon finely chopped fresh chives
8 ounces prosciutto or Black Forest ham, cut into thin strips
2 mushroom caps, peeled and sliced
Chopped fresh parsley, for garnish

1. Place the cheese in the freezer for 20 minutes to harden slightly and ease the slicing.

2. Peel the potatoes under cold running water. Using a food processor (preferably with a shoestring French-fry attachment), cut the potatoes into fine julienne strips. As you slice them, place the potatoes in a large bowl of cold water to which you have added the juice of 1 lemon; this will keep them from turning brown.

3. Slice the hardened cheese to the same size.

4. Bring a large pot of salted water to a boil, add the potato strips, and blanch until slightly softened, 2 minutes. Rinse under cold running water. Drain and pat dry. Combine with the cheese slices in a large bowl.

5. Combine the mayonnaise, ¼ cup lemon juice, salt, black and cayenne peppers, chives, and half the prosciutto or ham with the potatoes. Mix well. Garnish with the remaining ham, the mushrooms, and the parsley.

Serves 6 to 8

S P I C Y   T E X A S
M E A T   L O A F

cool spicy meat loaf will please most picnickers more than expense pâté. Serve it with a good loaf of buttered bread, lettuce and tomatoes, and a jar of mustard.

1½ pounds ground beef
8 ounces ground veal
4 ounces ground pork
⅓ cup fine fresh bread crumbs
¼ cup minced shallots
¼ cup milk
1 egg
2 tablespoons green chile salsa

1 teaspoon minced fresh basil
1 tablespoon chopped fresh parsley
1 teaspoon seasoned salt
1 teaspoon seasoned pepper
½ teaspoon soy sauce
2 tablespoons prepared chili sauce
2 strips bacon

1. Preheat the oven to 400°F.

2. Combine all the ingredients through the soy sauce in a large bowl and mix well. Pat the mixture into a loaf shape in a baking dish.

3. Spread the chili sauce over the loaf, and arrange the bacon strips on top. Bake for 15 minutes. Then reduce the heat to 350°F and bake until cooked through, 55 minutes longer. Let stand for 10 minutes, then remove it from the dish. Serve hot or cool completely, then refrigerate to serve cold.

Serves 6 to 8

MORAVIAN
ORANGE BREAD

icnic dessert should always be fresh fruit, plus an unfrosted cake that travels and goes equally well with wine or coffee. Try this Pennsylvania Dutch sweet known as Moravian Bread.

4 cups all-purpose
flour
Grated zest of 2 oranges
1 cup sugar
2½ teaspoons cream of
tartar
1 teaspoon baking soda
Pinch of salt
8 tablespoons (1 stick)
unsalted butter, melted
and cooled
2 eggs, lightly beaten
⅓ cup milk

1 teaspoon vanilla
extract
1 egg yolk
4 teaspoons fresh orange
juice
3 tablespoons confectioner's
sugar
½ teaspoon fresh lemon
juice

1. Preheat the oven to 375°F. Grease and flour a baking sheet, and set it aside.

2. Place the flour in a large bowl. Add the orange zest, sugar, cream of tartar, baking soda, and salt. Mix well.

3. Add the butter, eggs, milk, and vanilla to the flour mixture, working it together with a fork until it is able to be kneaded. Transfer the dough to a lightly floured board, and knead it for several minutes until smooth. Roll the dough to form a long log, lift it from the floured board, and place it on the prepared baking sheet in the shape of a ring. Pinch the ends together.

4. Mix the egg yolk with 2 teaspoons of the orange juice, and brush this over the top and sides of the ring. Make several shallow diagonal cuts on the ring's surface with a sharp knife. Bake for 35 minutes.

5. Let the cake cool on a wire rack for 5 minutes. Combine the remaining 2 teaspoons orange juice with the confectioner's sugar and lemon juice in a small bowl. Mix well, and drizzle over the cake. Let it cool completely.

Serves 10 or more

A TIME OF SLOPPY STUFFING

Thanksgiving: In my family, Thanksgiving was always a very, very formidable event. The preparation of this meal, besides requiring every jot of my mother's slim culinary resources, stopped all normal activity in the household for at least two weeks prior to the actual carving of the turkey.

Indeed, our home life was so antic in the latter half of November that my sister and I would make any number of excuses to leave the house. Looking back, it is hard to believe that such monumental house purges ever existed—days and weeks during which all familial communications came to a dead standstill while my mother literally tore room after room apart, scrubbing, dusting, and waxing every inch of floor, wall, and ceiling until both hands and temper were frayed.

At the dinner table each evening, my mother would recite a litany of the next day's chores. My father made no comment. He knew better. Instead he buried his head behind the nightly newspaper while my sister and I diffidently accepted our roles in the ghastly household Olympics.

I cannot now recall just how many Oriental rugs I beat, or the quantum accumulation of tarnished silver my sister and I helped polish. Though we could see our reflections perfectly in every dessert spoon and butter knife, my mother was never satisfied.

"If something is worth doing," she would ruminate over our cleaning performances, "it is worth doing *right*! More elbow grease, please."

In the end, the airs of pungent silver polish, soap flakes, and lemon oil were never entirely compatible with the scent of sage and bacon drippings that came from the kitchen on Thanksgiving morning—but it hardly mattered in the final analysis. We were all too fatigued to care. The intensive purification had robbed the holiday of its essential joy. Early on, I made up my mind to correct that misfeasance some day. And I have.

My house is usually fairly neat but hardly aglow (in the accepted TV commercial sense) when the last Thursday in November arrives. And if my friends bring their children, with sticky fingers and unsure table manners that may occasion a spill here or a drop there—who cares? Thanksgiving is meant to be a day of gratitude, not self-pride. I propose that it be celebrated with a blessing first and a lot of carousal afterward.

CRISPY CORNISH HENS
WITH JAMBALAYA DRESSING

∧∧∧

My notion of the perfect Thanksgiving bird is never turkey, because it's always stone cold by the time I get finished carving it. This year I plan to serve the following fowl instead: Cornish hens super-stuffed with Jambalaya Dressing, and crucially crusted too!

6 fresh Cornish hens
Jambalaya Dressing (recipe
*   follows)*
8 tablespoons (1 stick)
*   unsalted butter, at room*
*   temperature*
1 large clove garlic, crushed
⅔ cup fresh bread crumbs
2 tablespoons brandy
1 quart homemade chicken
*   stock or canned broth*
1 clove garlic
1 rib celery, broken

3 sprigs fresh parsley
¼ teaspoon salt
8 peppercorns
1½ tablespoons unsalted
*   butter*
1½ tablespoons all-purpose
*   flour*
¼ cup heavy or whipping
*   cream*
Salt and freshly ground black
*   pepper*
Parsley sprigs, for garnish

1. Preheat the oven to 425°F.

2. Remove the giblets from the hens, and set them aside. Wipe the hens dry with paper towels. Stuff the cavities with the dressing, and truss.

3. Combine 8 tablespoons butter with the crushed garlic, bread crumbs, and brandy in a bowl; blend well. Smooth this mixture over the hens with a spatula. Let them stand for 30 minutes.

4. Place the hens on a rack in a roasting pan, and bake for 1 hour.

5. Meanwhile, combine the stock, garlic clove, celery, parsley, salt, and peppercorns in a medium-size saucepan. Add the giblets and heat to boiling. Reduce the heat and simmer until reduced by one third, about 20 minutes. Strain.

6. Pour 1 cup of the reduced chicken stock around the hens, and bake for another 30 minutes.

7. Transfer the hens to a platter; remove the trussing and keep warm. Degrease the pan juices.

8. Melt the 1½ tablespoons butter in a medium-size saucepan over medium-low heat. Stir in the flour and cook, stirring constantly, for 2 minutes. Whisk the pan juices and the cream into the saucepan; simmer 5 minutes. Thin with extra chicken stock if too thick. Season with salt and pepper to taste.

9. Garnish the hens with parsley sprigs, and pass the sauce on the side.

Serves 6

JAMBALAYA DRESSING

Jambalaya, which means "a jumble" in Creole dialect, is a Louisiana specialty. Consider my version—in a bird or out, for it makes a tasty treat quite on its own! Improvising chefs may even want to add a bit of sautéed chicken to the jumble.

1 teaspoon olive oil
2 sweet Italian sausages
2 tablespoons unsalted
   butter
1 medium-size onion,
   chopped
1 clove garlic, minced
¼ cup diced green bell
   pepper
¼ cup diced red bell pepper
1 cup chopped, seeded,
   peeled tomatoes
¼ teaspoon sugar
¼ cup homemade chicken
   stock or canned broth

1 tablespoon chopped fresh
   basil
½ teaspoon grated lemon
   zest
¼ teaspoon chili powder
Pinch of dried thyme
½ cup chopped cooked
   ham
5 to 6 ounces small shrimp,
   shelled and deveined
2¼ cups cooked white
   rice
Salt and freshly ground black
   pepper

1. Heat the oil in a medium-size skillet. Add the sausages, and sauté over medium heat until well browned on all sides, 6 to 8 minutes. Let them cool on paper towels. Then cut into ¼-inch-thick slices, and set aside.

2. Heat the butter in a large skillet, and sauté the onion and garlic over medium heat until golden, about 5 minutes. Add the green and red peppers; cook 3 minutes. Add the tomatoes, sugar, stock, basil, lemon zest, chili powder, and thyme; cook 3 minutes. Then stir in the ham and shrimp; cook 2 minutes.

3. Transfer the mixture to a large bowl, and add the reserved sausages and the rice. Season to taste with salt and pepper. Cool slightly before stuffing the Cornish hens.

Makes about 6 cups

HONEY, I FORGOT TO PRESERVE

Christmas Season: It probably comes as no surprise to discover that all of my favored dispensations at holiday times are homemade.

Unfortunately I must also confess that these bottled and beribboned goodies are usually a last-minute enterprise. When normal folk are occupied unraveling their Christmas tree lights or recycling last year's tinsel, I am always to be found bent over a hot stove, stirring up great piles of scarlet berries (most often from California) into jam or sterilizing jars to hold some conserve I have just cooked up out of a mess of dried fruits.

Definitely "out of sync" with the calendar, I am as unlike my maternal grandmother, Minna Cohn, as can be—though I sometimes suspect that that good lady, if she were alive today, would make some allowance for my wayward style because of the peripatetic life I lead. Hers, devoted to only house and garden, afforded the luxury of "putting up" in a proper season.

My earliest memories of my grandmother's house are of those occasions when I would be allowed to stay over while my parents traveled to visit my sister in summer camp. The time was probably late summer, because that remembrance is enveloped in a commingled scent of steaming fruit and paraffin wax.

My grandmother's life seemed to revolve around her coal stove. Mornings, after she had walked through her large garden, snipping a rusty rose leaf here and pinching an errant chafer there, she would always shake out the ashes, never allowing me to assist as she laid in a new supply of kindling and coal for the day.

How I would wait, impatient for the time of cookery to begin while she made her morning "feeding" rounds, first throwing seeds to the blue jays, then to Lucky, a fat gray pigeon that lived in a cage above the carless garage.

"Grandma," I would admonish, "isn't it time to light the stove if we're making jam?"

She would nod yes, but first the yard squirrel would be permitted to approach, poking his cool nose into her apron for peanuts. Then Snoozy, the fine, sleek, fat Scottish terrier who followed her everywhere, had to be given her snack too.

"It's really getting late, Grandma. If we don't hurry, there will never be time to get all those peaches [or pears, plums, even chokecherries] into the jars!"

It was never too late, of course. And no matter what the temperature, my grandmother would get the enormous pans of fruit boiling away on her shiny black coal stove before I had time to repeat my concern. That woman was indubitably the best jam maker who ever lived. Without resorting to commercial pectin or unlimited sugar (as she was a diabetic), her creations would be boiled to a state of thick and oozy perfection, with only her eye as a jelly thermometer! When a pan was ready, she knew it, and removed it from the fire without even dipping a spoon into its silken surface—never sloshing a bit on a cold saucer to make sure it jells, as I inevitably do. Obviously to my grandmother preserving was an instinctive form of expression—one I never quite inherited. I "put up" with the same degree of enthusiasm, but my tongue gets burned with regularity nonetheless—probably as punishment for doing the job in the wrong season!

If you too must make your Christmas confections on the fly, try the following duet. Both may be prepared from the December largesse readily available on greengrocer, freezer, and supermarket shelves. So, in the words of a most appropriate carol, "let nothing you dismay."

QUICK
CRANBERRY-PEACH
PRESERVES

*T*he following sweet (slightly on the spicy side, if truth be told) can be made and jarred in less than 45 minutes. It makes a fine accompaniment to cold meats, curries—and toast in a pinch!

1 package (12 ounces) fresh
    cranberries (about 2 cups)
3 cups sliced peeled peaches,
    fresh or frozen
1 teaspoon slivered orange
    zest

½ cup fresh orange juice
2 cups sugar
Pulp of 1 orange, chopped
1 teaspoon freshly grated
    ginger

Combine all the ingredients except the ginger in a large saucepan, and heat to boiling. Reduce the heat and simmer for 20 minutes. Stir in the grated ginger, pour into sterilized jars, and seal.
Makes 3 pints

QUICK PINEAPPLE-APRICOT MARMALADE

*T*his traditional British upholstery for muffins and scones will liven the breakfast break of any lucky recipient—or so I am assured by my friends.

1 large pineapple, peeled, cored, and cubed (about 3 cups)
Pulp of 1 orange, chopped
½ cup fresh orange juice
¼ cup fresh lemon juice
1 tablespoon grated orange zest
1 teaspoon grated lemon zest
3 cups sugar
1 package (11 ounces) dried apricots, cut into strips
Pinch of ground cloves
Pinch of ground cinnamon
¼ cup orange liqueur
1½ cups coarsely chopped walnuts

1. Place 2 cups of the pineapple in a blender or food processor, and process until smooth.

2. Combine the puréed pineapple with the remaining cubed pineapple in a large saucepan. Add the orange pulp, orange juice, lemon juice, grated zests, and sugar; heat to boiling. Reduce the heat, and stir in the apricots. Simmer until the mixture is fairly thick, about 30 minutes.

3. Add the cloves and cinnamon to the mixture, and stir in the orange liqueur and the walnuts. Cook 6 minutes longer. Pour into sterilized jars, and seal.

Makes 3 pints

MAY YOUR CAKES BE ANGELIC

*C*hristmas: To me, the most important aspect of Christmas is the tree itself. Long before the calendar dips downward in December, I find myself speculatively eyeing the bundled spruce and pine on the sidewalks of my neighborhood, mentally equating the height and girth of one tree after another to the proportions of my low ceilings and narrow staircase. Though, well as I know that tidings of comfort always precede joy, I am dead certain the tree that will be finally chosen will be a ceiling-scraper!

The ritual has never changed since I was a child. For years my father, mother, sister, and I would troop down to the hub of the town where I grew up—inevitably on the coldest night of the year, it seemed—to argue publicly about the size of our Christmas tree while the tree sellers refereed. My mother always contended that a tabletop model would be a sensible choice (though what she really wanted was an artificial pine), a tree that could be dispatched to the garbage the day after Christmas without spilling needles on her Oriental rugs, while my father and I always held out for the tallest, broadest conifer we could find. My sister, as I recall, never took sides in this size war. What she wanted was to get out of the cold and shop for the tinsel and silvery trimmings that were replaced yearly. The other ornaments on our tree never changed.

Most were old; some had even belonged to my mother when she was a girl. And while a few of these delicate glass treasures broke each year (usually at my hands), the gilt angel that topped the highest branch remained intact for half a century—until my Scotch terrier, who could digest anything, impulsively crunched it between his teeth one Christmas Eve. The angel was irreplaceable, so he went unpunished for the crime—possessed, as it were, with Yuletide zeal.

I will never know why Christmas (and Christmas trees) meant so much to my mother and father. For while they were both admittedly unobservant (second-generation) Jews, this holiday often caused them grave difficulties and uneasy dialogues with some of their more rigid peers.

"I don't know why some people make such a darn fuss about Christmas," my mother said on more than one occasion, usually when placing the glass angel in its accustomed place. "It's the *idea,* not the religious aspect, that's important to your father and me. And besides"—flicking a strand of spun glass on the angel's wing—"who in the world would want to be against the idea of peace on earth, good will to men?"

Nobody in our house, certainly!

The angel on our family Christmas tree has certainly influenced my cooking on more than one Yuletide occasion. The following beatific (easy-to-whip-up) angel cakes make a perfectly happy ending for a filling holiday meal.

P O L K A - D O T
A N G E L
C A K E

♈♓♋

This is a fairly recent kitchen invention at my house. We got the idea for this white-and-black dessert just when the world deemed that the chocolate chip craze had peaked. Now it may start over again, with this fresh ammunition. A scoop of chocolate chip ice cream on the side might be considered overkill by some, but not by me!

1 cup sifted cake flour
1½ cups granulated sugar
1¼ cups egg whites (10 to 12),
  at room temperature
1¼ teaspoons cream of
  tartar
¼ teaspoon salt

1 teaspoon vanilla extract
¼ teaspoon almond extract
¾ cup semisweet chocolate
  chips
Confectioner's sugar, for
  dusting

1. Preheat the oven to 325°F.

2. Sift the flour and ½ cup of the sugar together four times.

3. Beat the egg whites until foamy; add the cream of tartar and salt. Beat until moist peaks form. Add the remaining 1 cup sugar, 2 tablespoons at a time, beating thoroughly after each addition. Add the vanilla and almond extracts. Sift about ¼ cup of the flour-sugar mixture over the meringue; fold in until no flour shows. Repeat, using up all the flour. Fold in the chocolate chips.

4. Transfer the batter into an ungreased tube pan, and bake until firm to the touch, about 1 hour. Invert the pan on a wire rack and allow the cake to cool completely in the pan. Then unmold and dust it with confectioner's sugar.

Serves 8 to 10

LEMON ANGEL CAKE

≈

*T*he is is a gilded version of the classic lily-white confection. Fresh-squeezed lemon juice, in place of vanilla, gives angel cake a halo of another color. And more pertinently, a bright new flavor!

1 cup sifted cake flour	*2 teaspoons fresh lemon juice*
1½ cups sugar	*½ teaspoon finely grated*
1¼ cups egg whites (10 to 12),	*lemon zest*
at room temperature	*Fresh strawberries*
1¼ teaspoons cream of tartar	*Sweetened whipped cream*
¼ teaspoon salt	*(optional; see Note)*

1. Preheat the oven to 325°F.

2. Sift the flour and ½ cup of the sugar together four times.

3. Beat the egg whites until foamy; add the cream of tartar and salt. Beat until moist peaks form. Add the remaining 1 cup sugar, 2 tablespoons at a time, beating thoroughly after each addition. Add the lemon juice and zest. Sift about ¼ cup of the flour-sugar mixture over the meringue; fold in until no flour shows. Repeat until all the flour is used up.

4. Transfer the batter into an ungreased tube pan, and bake until firm to the touch, about 1 hour. Invert the pan on a wire rack and allow the cake to cool completely in the pan before unmolding. Then unmold and surround with fresh strawberries. Serve with whipped cream if desired.

Serves 8 to 10

Note: To make sweetened whipped cream, add 1 teaspoon sugar (or to taste) to every 1 cup heavy (whipping) cream before whipping.

WELCOMING IN THE NEW YEAR GREENE'S WAY

New Year's Eve: The first time I was aware of New Year's Eve celebrations, I was seven years old. My parents had gone partying, and my twelve-year-old sister, Myra, woke me sharply at 11:45.

"Get dressed. Quickly!" she commanded. "Come downstairs, get a pot and a spoon from the kitchen, and button up your overcoat!"
"Why?" I asked sleepily.
"Because we're going to celebrate the New Year. It's 1930!"

What I remember best of this escapade is Myra and I, joined by the Johnson kids next door, walking around the dark suburban streets of Queens like a band of raggle-taggle midgets, banging our pots and striking pan covers together like cymbals, screaming: "Happy New Year!" And succeeding only in waking the chickens in our neighbor's yard across the street.

They crowed nice and loud!

When I grew older, my taste in New Year's Eve festivities changed. For years I would go to the theater, eat a midnight supper at some expensive hostelry, and allow myself to be crushed into a state of indigestion by the surging mobs in Times Square afterward. After a dozen of these masochistically enchanted evenings, I decided to pass on that ritual as well.

House parties to celebrate the dying of the old year and the birth of the new were my next attempt at annual conviviality. Another bust!

I found I was unutterably dispirited by so much desperate merriment—not to mention the sight of old friends, drunk as the dickens, making the same darn fools of themselves year after year with only some half-warm midnight casserole to take up the slack!

If it sounds to you as though Greene is growing crotchety with each passing year, I deny it to the death. Merely more selective in my need for revelry! If anything, New Year's Eve becomes a precious gift with each twelve-month passage of time. How I choose to spend its commemoration, I find, becomes a more and more personal option.

My happiest way to inaugurate the beginning of another auspicious year is with a very small dinner party—never more than six at the table, and in the best of all possible worlds, two. There are only two ingredients necessary for this assemblage: true amicability among the dinner partners and enough good Champagne to cherish it.

I wish the same joyous gift to each and every one of you dear friends. Happy, healthy, fruitful, new year!

HOPPIN' JOHN SOUP

$\mathcal{A}$ traditionalist host, whenever I prepare New Year's Eve dinner for friends, I try to include some version of beans and rice—what southerners dub "Hoppin' John"—as one of the adjuncts of the meal. Why? Because it's meant to bring good luck to the householder for the whole next year, and I for one will take that on hearsay alone!

1 tablespoon unsalted butter
2 tablespoons olive oil
1 large onion,
 minced
1 large clove garlic,
 minced
1 pound dried black-eyed
 peas, picked over
1 ham bone (or 8 ounces
 smoked ham)
½ teaspoon chopped fresh
 thyme, or ¼ teaspoon
 dried

1 bay leaf
1 quart homemade chicken
 stock or canned broth
 (approximately)
1 quart water
½ cup brown rice
Juice of 1 lemon
1 teaspoon grated lemon
 zest
Salt and freshly ground black
 pepper
1 teaspoon chopped fresh
 chives

1. Heat the butter and oil in a large pot over medium-low heat. Add the onion; cook 1 minute. Add the garlic; cook 5 minutes. Stir in the black-eyed peas. Add the ham bone, thyme, bay leaf, chicken stock, and water; bring to a boil. Reduce the heat, cover partially, and simmer for 1 hour.

2. Stir the rice into the soup and continue to cook, partially covered, until the peas and rice are tender, about another 30 minutes. If the soup is too thick, add more stock.

3. Remove the ham bone from the soup. Cut off any meat from the bone, chop it fine, and add it to the soup (or chop the smoked ham and return it to the pot). Cook for 2 minutes. Then stir in the lemon juice and zest. Season with salt and pepper to taste, sprinkle with the chives, and serve.

Serves 6 to 8

H O P P I N ' J O H N S A L A D W I T H B A C O N

∾

A second variation on the theme, this one served at room temperature.

1 package (10 ounces) frozen
*   black-eyed peas*
2 strips bacon
1 small onion, chopped
1 clove garlic, minced
1 cup cooked white rice
2 tablespoons red wine
*   vinegar*

Salt and freshly ground black
*   pepper*
¼ cup finely chopped fresh
*   chives or scallion (green*
*   onion) tops*
2 tablespoons chopped fresh
*   parsley*

1. Drop the frozen peas into boiling salted water in a medium-size saucepan. Simmer until tender, about 20 minutes. Drain, reserving ¼ cup of the cooking liquid.

2. Sauté the bacon strips in a large heavy skillet over medium heat until crisp, 4 to 5 minutes. Drain on paper towels and set aside.

3. Stir the onion into the bacon drippings in the skillet. Cook for 3 minutes. Add the garlic and cook 2 minutes longer. Stir in the drained peas and the rice. Cook, stirring constantly, until warmed through, about

5 minutes. Add the vinegar and enough reserved cooking liquid from the peas to moisten the mixture, 2 to 3 tablespoons. Cook for 5 minutes.

4. Season the mixture with salt and pepper to taste, and crumble the reserved bacon over the top. Allow the salad to cool to room temperature. Then sprinkle with the chives and parsley, and serve.

Serves 4 to 6

HOT CHOCOLATE TODDY

ot drinks, like the chocolate number here, should be served warm—temperate enough so the spirited flavors fuse, but not so hot that the liquid burns your lips. Heat the toddy in a heavy non-corrosive saucepan to just below the boiling point. Remove it from the heat and allow it to cool slightly before transferring it to preheated glass or ceramic mugs for serving.

3 ounces (3 squares) unsweetened baking chocolate
1 can (14 ounces) sweetened condensed milk

1 quart milk, heated
½ cup hazelnut liqueur
Unsweetened whipped cream (optional)

Combine the chocolate and the condensed milk in the top of a double boiler over simmering water, and stir until the chocolate has melted. Slowly whisk in the hot milk. Then add the liqueur, and whisk until heated through and frothy. Serve in mugs, topped with whipped cream if desired.

Serves 6 to 8

SWEDISH COFFEE EGGNOG

*E*ggnog is a drink that is usually stowed away with the Christmas lights and tinsely baubles from one December to another. However, this version is a drink for all seasons. Rich and redolent with coffee as well as other intoxicating adjuncts, it makes a great dessert or brunch offering year-round.

1 cup light cream or half-and-half
3 eggs, separated
½ cup granulated sugar
2½ cups heavy or whipping cream
1 cup light rum
1 cup strong brewed coffee, chilled

½ cup bourbon
¼ cup coffee-flavored liqueur
Dash of salt
1 tablespoon confectioner's sugar
Grated orange zest, for garnish

1. Heat the light cream in a medium-size saucepan over medium heat just until scalded, about 3 minutes.

2. Beat the egg yolks in a large bowl until they are light and fluffy. Gradually beat in the scalded cream and granulated sugar until the mixture is thick and lemon-colored. Stir in 1½ cups of the heavy cream, rum, coffee, bourbon, liqueur, and salt. Refrigerate, covered, until cold, about 2 hours.

3. Beat the remaining 1 cup heavy cream with the confectioner's sugar until stiff. Fold into the eggnog mixture.

4. Beat the egg whites until stiff peaks form. Fold them into the eggnog mixture. Cover, and refrigerate for 1 hour. Stir lightly and sprinkle with the orange zest before serving.

Makes about twenty ½ cup servings

Note: This recipe contains raw eggs. Recently, some uncooked eggs have been a source of salmonella, a serious infection. If you are unsure of the quality of the eggs you buy, avoid recipes that use them raw.

T E M P E R A N C E
E G G N O G

*T*raditional holiday drinks are usually strong-tempered stuff, but for the non-imbiber, this eggless nog makes an excellent stand-in. For the peak of hostly perfection, make sure all of the ingredients are very, very cold before they are combined.

2 cups fresh orange juice	*1 teaspoon finely grated*
2 cups pineapple juice	*orange zest*
1 pint vanilla ice cream	

Combine the orange juice, pineapple juice, and ice cream in a food processor (or in two batches in a blender), and process until frothy. Pour into goblets, garnish with the orange zest, and serve immediately.

Makes 8 to 10 servings (6 cups)

BERT ON PEOPLE

CHAPTER THREE

A CASTLE OF COCONUT

Do you dream of lost loves? Or the golden chances that have passed you by, perhaps? Not me. My recurrent dreamland images are all confectionery. I dream of the coconut cakes of yesteryear.

When I was a late adolescent and our family resources had recovered somewhat from the debacle of the Depression, my mother decided to hire a cleaning woman to tidy our living quarters once a week. The practitioner she chose for this detail (recommended by my charitable grandmother) was a needy widow with four small children and a sad family history. Her husband had been murdered during a robbery attempt on his grocery shop some years before.

One would never have suspected such a note of genuine tragedy from Mrs. Pendleberry's mien, for she was a doggedly cheerful soul. Large, red-faced, of considerable girth and unfortunately endowed with ill-fitting dentures, she loved to talk as she worked. Or to be more accurate, she loved to talk *rather* than work!

Most of her tales centered around herself and "the years before the bad times," as she put it. But all of her anecdotes seemed to require a response. If a story was told and pointedly ignored, Mrs. Pendleberry would repeat it again (and again) until the listener gave some form of acknowledgment and the conversation finally could be bridged.

"You never know what life has in store for you, Sonny," she would announce apropos of nothing at all as I did my homework at the kitchen table. When I did not react, she reiterated it, louder.
"I say, *you* never know what life has in store!"
"Yes, ma'am. I heard you the first time."

A response in kind never satisfied Mrs. Pendleberry. "Because that's how life is!" she continued. *"Un-predict-able."*

By nature she was unpredictable herself. Ill-equipped to be a house-worker, she was too fat to bend or stretch and had water on the knee and a bad left arm into the bargain. My mother declared, after her first sortie, that her household abilities left much to be desired. But she loved to cook and bake, and of a consequence took any excuse at all to quit the dust mop and soap suds for a stint at our stove.

On one occasion that I recall, when she was washing down venetian blinds according to my mother's injunction, Mrs. Pendleberry became so enraptured over coconut cake (the fresh-grated kind she had learned to make as a girl) that she stopped working altogether. Abandoning a sponge in midsentence and producing a quarter from her shoe, she sent me to the market to buy a coconut. Together we spent the whole sweet-scented afternoon paring, grating, stirring, separating eggs, measuring flour and sugar, and ultimately whipping up the most extravagant cake that I had ever seen.

Fully four inches high, this confection was crusted with snowy frosting and blanketed like an igloo with drifts of tender coconut snow. My family was absolutely awestruck at the sight of this dazzling creation when they returned home from work that night.

Truthfully, if I live to be a hundred I will never forget the consummate delight when I first tasted it. Nor my mother's acrimony when Mrs. Pendleberry (the venetian blinds still unwashed) reminded her that she had laid out twenty-five cents for the coconut.

Mrs. Pendleberry's tenure was of a brief duration, but her cake will live forever! At least in my dreams.

MRS. PENDLEBERRY'S UNFORGETTABLE COCONUT CAKE

The cake that troubles my sleep has never been precisely duplicated, in my kitchen or out. Maybe I am mixing memory with desire, but this delicate compound of butter, cream, flour, and eggs seems a very notable facsimile. However, the coconut *must* be fresh!

FOR THE CAKE
1 small coconut
⅓ cup unsalted butter, at
    room temperature
⅓ cup solid vegetable
    shortening
1⅔ cups sugar
3 eggs
2½ cups sifted cake flour
3½ teaspoons baking powder
¼ teaspoon salt
¾ cup heavy or whipping
    cream (approximately)
1 teaspoon vanilla extract

FOR THE ICING
½ cup water
⅓ cup light corn syrup
2½ cups sugar
⅛ teaspoon salt
3 egg whites
1 teaspoon fresh orange
    juice
1¼ teaspoons vanilla
    extract
2½ cups grated fresh coconut
    (see step 2 and 3)

1. Preheat the oven to 350°F. Butter and flour two 9-inch round cake pans.

2. Make the cake: Poke an ice pick through the eye of the coconut, and drain the coconut milk into a glass. Strain the milk through a doubled layer of cheesecloth into another container, and set it aside.

3. Break the coconut shell with a hammer into small pieces. Carefully peel the shell from the meat with a sharp knife. Shred the coconut meat in a food processor, and set it aside.

4. Beat the butter with the shortening in a large bowl until light and fluffy. Slowly beat in the sugar. Then add the eggs, one at a time, beating thoroughly after each addition.

5. In another bowl, sift the flour with the baking powder and salt. Combine the reserved coconut milk with enough heavy cream to make 1¼ cups. Stir both mixtures, in alternating thirds, into the batter. Then stir in the vanilla.

6. Spoon the batter into the prepared cake pans, and bake until a toothpick inserted in the center comes out clean, about 30 minutes. Cool on wire racks. When completely cool, loosen the edges with a knife, and remove the layers from the pans.

7. Make the icing: Combine the water, corn syrup, sugar, and salt in a medium-size saucepan; bring to a boil. Reduce the heat and simmer until a small spoonful of the mixture forms a firm ball when dropped into cold water, or until the mixture registers 242°F on a candy thermometer.

8. Beat the egg whites in the large bowl of an electric mixer until soft peaks form. With the mixer on high speed, slowly add the syrup in a thin trickle. Continue beating until of spreading consistency. Then beat in the orange juice and vanilla.

9. Place the bottom layer on a rack, topside up. Spread one fourth of the icing over the layer. Sprinkle with some of the reserved shredded coconut. Add the second layer, and spread the remaining icing over the top and sides of the cake. Press the remaining coconut into the icing.

Serves 8 to 10

C O C O N U T   W A F E R S

ᘐᘐᘐ

*H*aving cracked a coconut for the fabled cake above, it seems like the pettiest bit of larceny to swipe 3½ ounces of the stuff for the crunchiest cookies in the world.

8 tablespoons (1 stick)	*⅓ cup evaporated milk*
* unsalted butter, melted*	*3½ ounces shredded fresh*
1 cup sugar	* coconut*
1 egg	*½ teaspoon finely grated*
1 cup sifted all-purpose flour	* lemon zest*
1 teaspoon baking powder	*¾ teaspoon fresh lemon juice*

1. Preheat the oven to 350°F. Lightly butter a baking sheet.

2. Beat the melted butter with the sugar in a large bowl until well mixed. Beat in the egg.

3. Sift the flour with the baking powder in another bowl. Add this to the batter in three parts, alternating with thirds of the evaporated milk. Stir in the coconut, lemon zest, and lemon juice.

4. Drop the batter by small teaspoonfuls on the prepared baking sheet, and bake until the edges are lightly browned, about 7 minutes. Cool completely before removing from the pan.

Makes about 72 cookies

DR. BERT FORESEES

GREENE FOLLOWS THROUGH

I am a logical man, not given to flights of fancy—in or out of the kitchen. But sometimes the supernatural throws me a curve I cannot quite ignore.

Trying to find a radio station in downtown Los Angeles recently, I became hopelessly lost. Driving along the Harbor Freeway, I finally pulled off at an exit ramp to ask directions. The neighborhood in which I found myself was almost totally vacant, great yawning warehouses and no street life whatsoever. The few pedestrians I stopped spoke no English, and all the public phones were either smashed or inoperable. Growing desperate—for I was scheduled to be interviewed in less than half an hour—I noticed a very old black woman several blocks away. She was standing on a street corner, arranging piles of tattered magazines on the sidewalk, presumably for sale.

When I drove alongside the display and showed her the address I was looking for, she shook her head.

"Yo is miles out of yo way, baby," she said gravely. "But yo is also in luck. For I knows this city like a open book."

The truth is, she did. After scratching her chin several times, she dictated the route precisely. When I thanked her, she grinned toothlessly.

"If you so grateful, be a sport, baby. Buy a book!"

I stared at the dismal array spread out on the pavement without much real enthusiasm. Before I could choose, however, she seemed to read my mind. Reaching into a cardboard box, she handed me a tan pamphlet, not unlike some volume of privately printed poems.

"This one has yo name on it," she said knowingly. "Only five bucks, too."

The cover had a design of cabalistic symbols, with a legend printed over it: "Dr. Bert's Book of Magic, Dreams and Occultism," it said. That might have given me real pause if I had not been so late. Instead I handed over the money, stashed the book in my raincoat pocket, and took off for the interview. In the rearview mirror, I could see the old woman on the curb, laughing and laughing.

Actually I didn't think about the book again until several weeks later, when I returned home to New York. My cleaner discovered it when the raincoat had to be pressed.

"Did you write this?" he asked.
"No. Just a coincidence."

But was it? When I opened the book for the first time, the pages flipped apart, revealing in the dead center a section entitled "Dreams of Cooks." Scanning that, I came upon a long list, some of which appeared to be underlined: "To dream of prawns . . . means great ambition. To dream of onions . . . means tears without a serious cause. To dream of hot pepper or fiery seasoning . . . means you must be on guard against the devil's wiles."

Now you must understand that up until this point, I had had absolutely no visions of those ingredients in any form. But I certainly did that night. I dreamed I was in a well-appointed kitchen, preparing a wonderfully spicy dish of shrimp, bacon, scallions, and chili powder. While I cooked, the old woman stood at my side, nodding. After I tasted the mixture, she held open a checkbook.

"Write yo own ticket, baby," she announced. "This dish gonna make you rich."
"And famous, too," I added confidently.
"No! Only rich. Yo can't have yo cake and eat it too!"
"Go to the devil!" I cried. And promptly woke up because the phone was ringing. The caller was an account executive for a public relations firm. She wished to inquire whether I would consider developing some spicy regional recipes for a client who made a hot pepper sauce.

I am afraid I stopped her in midsentence. "Would I receive credit for developing these recipes?"

"Actually, no. The client is thinking of attributing them to fiery media personalities. But they will *pay* well . . ."
"Thanks. Thank you for calling." I replied. "But no thanks." And I hung up the phone.

Later I wrote down all the ingredients I had put together in my dream, and I made the dish shortly afterward. So far it has made me neither rich nor famous—but it tastes supernaturally delicious all the same!

DEVILISH CHILIED SHRIMP WITH BACON

8 ounces bacon strips

2 bunches scallions (green onions), bulbs and green tops chopped separately

1 large clove garlic, minced

¼ cup finely chopped red bell pepper (about ½ pepper)

1 hot green pepper, seeded, deveined, and minced

1 large tomato, seeded and chopped

1 tablespoon chopped fresh basil

1 pound shrimp, shelled and deveined

1½ tablespoons chili powder

½ tablespoon mild ground chiles or paprika

¼ cup homemade chicken stock or canned broth

¼ cup vodka

½ teaspoon hot pepper sauce

Salt and freshly ground black pepper

Cooked white rice, heated

1. Sauté the bacon strips in a large heavy skillet until crisp. Drain the bacon on paper towels, crumble, and set aside.

2. Discard all but 2 tablespoons of the bacon drippings from the skillet. Add the chopped scallion bulbs and cook, stirring frequently, over medium heat for 2 minutes. Add the garlic and both peppers; cook 1 minute. Add the tomato and basil; cook 1 minute longer. Toss in the shrimp, and sprinkle with the chili powder and mild ground chiles. Continue to toss until the shrimp turn pink, about 3 minutes. Then add the chicken stock, vodka, chopped scallion tops, and the reserved crumbled bacon. Continue to toss until slightly thickened but not dry, about 2 minutes. Add the hot pepper sauce, and salt and pepper to taste. Serve immediately over hot cooked rice.

Serves 4

A MISSED OPPORTUNITY— A LIFE LONG REGRET

Having lived a rather full life, it is surprising how few regrets I've accumulated along the way.

One disappointment I do harbor, however, is the fact that I never learned to bake cake from one of the unacknowledged masters of the art. The person I am speaking of (whose name is lost to the ages) was a huge man of unbelievable culinary ability who never gave a cooking lesson in his life. He had been a cook and one-man *batterie de cuisine* for Zoe Chase, a tearoom-type restaurant in New York City, for almost half a century when I discovered him. And he remained there, whipping up incredible concoctions until the landmark establishment closed a decade ago. But I missed my chance to learn his prodigious skills—out of sheer inanition and, to be frank, fear of incurring his legendary wrath. But I am getting beyond the story.

I used to eat at Zoe Chase (it was on Sixtieth Street on Manhattan's East Side, near Bloomingdale's) at least once a week when I was young and footloose. Then in the mid-1960s, when I began to cook professionally and opened The Store in Amagansett, my visits to the restaurant became an almost daily occurrence. Without calling attention to the fact, I was trying to determine the secret ingredient in the fabulous layer cakes that were a magnet for most diners.

Feeling brave one day, I cornered Miss Chase after lunch. She was an elderly southern woman, on the frail side and with a tendency to be distracted. Not on this occasion, however.

"I admire your cakes," I began.
"So I notice. You eat two kinds daily."
"I want to learn how to make that cake. Teach me. I'm willing to pay!"
"Oh, my dear." She laughed until she blushed. "Dear young man, I don't make the cakes. Our chef does that. He comes in here at dawn to bake. And when the cake is gone . . . it's gone."
"Would he teach me?"
"Heavens, I don't know! Go in the kitchen. Ask him yourself."

I started toward the kitchen. Like all restaurant galleys, it was utter chaos. But a dozen perfect layer cakes, rising like swans, blinded my eyes to the squalor. The chef—a giant of a man, twice my size and a head taller—was upbraiding a pale assistant with carefully chosen epithets. He stopped in mid-curse as I entered.

"What do you want?"
"Cake. That is, I want you to teach me to bake cake."
"Why?"
"For money. I'll pay a hundred dollars a week if you'll let me watch while you work."
"I don't like people in my way." He glowered. "Besides, I start at four in the morning. Can you get up that early?"
"I can try."
"Trying don't cut any ice with me. You be here at that hour or no deal. 'Cause I don't need the money."
"Yes, sir."

The first lesson was scheduled for the following Tuesday. The day before, I withdrew a hundred dollars from the bank. When I went to bed, early, I set the clock for 3:00 A.M. to be certain I would be early.

What can I tell you? The heart was willing but the flesh was weak. I turned off the alarm at the first clarion—and did not rise till noon, out of guilt and remorse. I'd forever blown my chances to learn cake-making with this man—that much was self-evident.

I didn't show my face at Zoe Chase's restaurant for a month. When I did, the genteel Miss Chase inquired discreetly, "What happened to you?"

"Appendicitis," I lied without blinking.

She clucked ever so slightly but offered no condolences or get-well wishes. "He was *very, very* angry!"

"I'm sorry."
"So am I. But please don't go near the kitchen while meals are being served."
"I won't!"

The truth of the matter is, I never came back to the restaurant again—to my sincere regret then, and to this day still.

What follows is a cake, roughly adapted by yours truly, from Zoe Chase's repertoire. It would have been better with those lessons, but it's still a darn good dessert.

VANILLA-CARAMEL LAYER CAKE

FOR THE CAKE
8 tablespoons (1 stick)
   unsalted butter, at room
   temperature
1 cup granulated sugar
3 eggs
1 tablespoon vanilla extract
1 teaspoon fresh lemon
   juice
2 cups sifted all-purpose
   flour
¼ teaspoon salt

4 teaspoons baking powder
⅔ cup milk

FOR THE ICING
1 cup heavy or whipping
   cream
2¼ cups (packed) light brown
   sugar
2 tablespoons unsalted
   butter
2 teaspoons vanilla extract

1. Make the cake: Preheat the oven to 375°F. Butter and flour two 9-inch round cake pans.

2. In a large bowl, beat the butter with the sugar until light and fluffy. Add the eggs, one at a time, beating well after each addition. Stir in the vanilla and lemon juice.

3. Sift the flour with the salt and baking powder in another bowl. Stir the flour mixture into the butter mixture in three parts, alternating with thirds of the milk. Pour the batter into the prepared cake pans, and bake until a toothpick inserted in the center comes out clean, about 25 minutes. Cool on wire racks. When completely cool, loosen the edges with a knife, and remove the layers from the pans.

4. Make the icing: Combine the cream and brown sugar in a medium-size saucepan, and bring to a boil. Reduce the heat, and simmer over medium heat until the mixture forms a ball when a small spoonful is dropped into cold water, about 20 minutes. Place the pan in a bowl of cold water, and stir in the butter and vanilla. Continue to stir until the icing is thick enough to spread. Place the bottom layer on a rack, topside up. Spread one fourth of the icing over the layer. Add the second layer, and spread the remaining icing over the top and sides of the cake. (Add a few drops of boiling water if the icing thickens while you are working.)

Serves 8

FAME MAY WITHER

BUT SUNDAY DINNERS—NEVER

For my birthday last year, a fan in Michigan—who is also a good friend after a near decade of steady correspondence—sent me a cookbook that had been in her family for years. Written by Mrs. Elizabeth O. Hiller and titled *Fifty-Two Sunday Dinners,* this wonderful volume was published in 1913 and came with the following inscription on its yellowed flyleaf:

> *For Bert,*
> *Because I know you will love this old treasure as much as I did.*
> *—Clara Less, October 1986*

Since its arrival, I have dipped into the recipes of *Sunday Dinners* with a great deal of pleasure, and, I must admit, a tinge of trepidation. Aside from its status as a culinary document, this book has a way of putting a contemporary cookbook author like myself in his proper perspective.

In 1913, for instance, it was not unusual for a commercial food manufacturer to underwrite the publication of a cookbook. Point of fact, it is still not an outmoded practice—though it certainly should be. Elizabeth O. Hiller's sponsor (for want of a better term) was a kitchen ingredient named Cottolene, a shortening that the author recommends as a substitute for butter or lard when (and I quote) "today the visible supply of these two products is in insufficient quantity to supply the demand, taking into consideration the amount of butter required for table use."

Setting Mrs. Hiller's commercial ties aside (Cottolene has long joined the ranks of other forgotten American commodities), her book of "company dinners" is a true delight—crammed to the nines with all manner of wonderful recipes that I have managed to get on the table from Monday to Saturday as well.

However, there is one aspect of this old volume that frankly gives me pause. On page eight, prior to the actual recipe section and the discreet endorsements of Cottolene's efficacy by eminent physicians of the time, there is a full page of printed quotes about the book, all highly laudatory of course, from "Noted Cooking Experts." The list is long and the names are set in impressive bold type. But I am pained to report that not a single one of these food authorities can be recalled, even in dim memory, by this long-in-the-tooth cookbook collector!

So, let Julia, Craig, Jacques, Giuliano, Marcella, Paula—and Bert, too—take a clear-cut message from that augury. Cooking fame does not last forever. With luck, recipes do!

COLD JELLIED MEAT LOAF
WITH WHIPPED-CREAM HORSERADISH DRESSING

☙❧☙

*T*wo excellent notions for a summer Sunday dinner (or buffet), freely adapted from recipes in Elizabeth O. Hiller's 1913 book: a seasoned meat loaf in aspic with a creamy-but-tangy sauce to pass alongside. (Note that this is a day-before preparation.)

*1½ pounds veal shoulder
(with bones)
1½ pounds lamb shoulder
(with bones)
1 bay leaf
1 teaspoon salt
5 peppercorns
2 onions, sliced
½ teaspoon grated lemon zest
1 teaspoon freshly ground
black pepper*

*½ teaspoon minced fresh
ginger
½ teaspoon ground allspice
1 envelope unflavored gelatin
½ cup strong homemade
chicken stock or canned
broth
Watercress leaves, for garnish
Whipped-Cream Horseradish
Dressing (recipe follows)*

1. Butter or oil a 9 x 5-inch loaf pan, and set it aside.

2. Place the meats, bay leaf, salt, peppercorns, and half the onions in a large pot with water to cover. Bring to a boil. Then reduce the heat, cover, and simmer until the meat is tender, 1½ to 2 hours.

3. Remove the meat and discard the bones. Strain the cooking liquid into a saucepan; discard the seasonings. Bring the strained liquid to a boil, and cook over high heat until reduced to about 1 quart, about 20 minutes.

4. Grind the meat with the remaining onion in a meat grinder or finely chop together in a food processor. Transfer to a large bowl, and stir in the lemon zest, pepper, ginger, and allspice. Add the meat mixture to the cooking liquid, and cook over low heat for 10 minutes. Remove from the heat.

5. Combine the gelatin and the chicken broth in the top of a double boiler. Place it over hot water, and stir until the gelatin has dissolved. Stir this into the meat mixture, and mix thoroughly. Pour the meat mixture into the prepared loaf pan, and allow it to cool. Cover with plastic wrap and refrigerate overnight.

6. Unmold the meat loaf and garnish it with watercress. Pass the Horseradish Dressing on the side.

Serves 6 to 8

WHIPPED-CREAM HORSERADISH DRESSING

¼ cup fresh grated
 horseradish
¼ teaspoon fresh onion juice
⅛ teaspoon cayenne pepper
1½ tablespoons white wine
 vinegar

½ cup heavy or whipping
 cream
Salt and freshly ground black
 pepper

1. Combine the horseradish, onion juice, cayenne pepper, and wine vinegar in a medium-size bowl. Mix thoroughly.

2. Whip the cream until soft peaks form, and fold it into the horseradish mixture. Add salt and pepper to taste. Chill before serving.

Makes about 1 cup

WINGING ACROSS HEAVEN WITH THE STARS

One of the dividends of my recurring TV appearances with Gary Collins on *Hour Magazine* this year has been the conspicuous cross-country consumption I have enjoyed aboard American Airlines to and from California every other month.

I say "dividend" with tongue placed securely in cheek, you understand, because I always debark these excursions sick as the proverbial dog. Not so much out of atmospheric turbulence as sheer inability to refuse any food or drink that the overly solicitous flight attendants press on their captive voyagers.

Now I have flown far and wide enough in my time to know the so-called Captain's First-Class Service (consisting of a half dozen effulgently described courses plus appropriately matched California vintages) is merely a ploy to keep passengers drugged into submission during the time span of a dreadful in-flight movie. But somehow or other, despite my awareness of the dark design, I am compulsively unable to refuse a single caloric option. From the first sluice of Champagne and orange juice before takeoff to the last alignment of weak coffee and strong brandy before landing, I swallow it all! And usually exist on a diet of Maalox for the rest of my sojourn in the Golden West.

This week's flight, however, was a model of dietary self-control, occasioned by the example of two notable traveling companions. Joanne Woodward and Paul Newman were fellow wayfarers in the very same row of the silvery DC-10 that took me to Los Angeles. And their eating habits (on board, at least) were downright infectious.

For the record, I must report that this talented pair not only looked startlingly attractive but seemed to be models of good humor into the bargain. The fact that our departing plane left Kennedy Airport an hour behind schedule rattled them not a jot—as far as I could observe behind their enormous (and co-equally tinted) sunglasses. Miss Woodward either assiduously knitted or read her morning newspaper (aloud) while her handsome spouse yawned or nodded, refusing all manner of spirited libations pressed upon him by overattentive stewardesses.

Being a movie star obviously has advantages. The captain of the airplane left his post for a moment or two (after we were finally aloft) to assure the startled Newmans that their flight would be most comfortable, since the tailwinds were completely on *their* side. To the credit of most first-class passengers, no one stared—except me. But I at least had a perfectly valid excuse. They were both in my peripheral line of vision, you see.

Which brings me to their observed eating habits. Movie stars are obviously not mortal. Paul Newman and Joanne Woodward drank only club soda on this long and boring journey, and while their fellow travelers elected such diverse menu aberrations as double-broiled lamb chops coupled with lobster tails or sirloin roast carved at the armrest, they dined on nothing weightier than a double portion of tossed green salad. They eschewed the shrimp appetizer, hot rolls, fudge sundae, and choice of red and white wines.

Do movie stars have any kinks in their gastronomic armor? Well, yes. Pretzels. Mr. Newman made several trips to the fore-section buffet for a very healthy collection of assorted cocktail nibbles, and both he and his wife quietly chewed pretzels while all around them lesser men gorged without restraint.

The green salad served these superstars was certainly no bowl of originality. In Newman and Woodward's honor, therefore, chef Greene has concocted some arrestingly verdant variations. American Airlines, feel free to copy!

CHEF GREENE'S
CHEF SALAD

n this variation on the classic chef's salad, artichokes, a dash of sour cream, and mustard make a tonic difference.

1 package (9 ounces)
   frozen artichoke
   hearts
4 ounces mushrooms, sliced
   (about 1 cup)
4 ounces Monterey Jack cheese,
   cut into thin 1½-inch-long
   strips (about ½ cup)
6 to 7 ounces leftover roast
   beef, ham, chicken, turkey,
   or tongue, cut into strips
   (about 1 cup)

1 large scallion (green onion),
   trimmed and minced
1 small clove garlic, crushed
¼ teaspoon salt
1 teaspoon Dijon mustard
Juice of ½ lime
⅓ cup olive oil
1 tablespoon sour cream
1 teaspoon red wine vinegar
Salt and freshly ground black
   pepper

1. Cook the artichoke hearts in boiling salted water until tender, 5 to 8 minutes. Drain and allow to cool.

2. In a large bowl, combine the artichoke hearts with the mushrooms, cheese, meat, and scallion. Toss lightly.

3. Mash the garlic with the salt in a small bowl. Stir in the remaining ingredients through the vinegar, and pour over the salad. Toss well, and season with salt and pepper to taste. Serve at room temperature or slightly chilled.

Serves 4

MELON MELEE

mêlée is a fray. It is also a Key West salad (by way of Cuba) composed of bits of melon and assorted smoked meats along with greens. The dressing is my own notion, substituting melon liqueur for vinegar. This dish makes a nifty first course as well.

4 ounces sliced prosciutto or Black Forest ham, cut into strips

4 ounces sliced smoked turkey or chicken, cut into strips

½ large melon (such as Cranshaw or honeydew), scooped into balls

1 cup cherry tomatoes, halved

¼ to ⅓ cup Melon Vinaigrette (recipe follows)

Assorted torn lettuce leaves and watercress

1 tablespoon chopped fresh basil leaves, or ½ teaspoon dried basil chopped with 2 teaspoons fresh parsley

Combine the meats, melon balls, and cherry tomato halves in a mixing bowl. Toss well. Add the Melon Vinaigrette and toss again. Serve over a bed of lettuce and watercress, and garnish with the basil.

Serves 2 to 4

MELON VINAIGRETTE

1 small clove garlic, crushed
½ teaspoon coarse salt
½ teaspoon Dijon mustard
Juice of 1 lime

2½ tablespoons melon liqueur
(I prefer De Kuyper)
1 cup olive oil

Mash the garlic with the salt in a small bowl until smooth. Slowly stir in the remaining ingredients.

Makes about 1¼ cups

NOTES FROM NEW ORLEANS

*T*errific cooks abide everywhere in New Orleans, you don't even have to scratch the surface to find them. Denizens of the Crescent City (so named, I am told, because its geography resembles a puffy croissant) are all conversant on two subjects. Those are: how to cook and how *not* to cook!

I learned about New Orleans' tasty sobriquet from an airline attendant. A portly man, he had recently observed a recipe for croissants made with yogurt in a national magazine, and the very idea rankled enormously.

"My Cajun-French granddaddy, who was a maître boulanger, would turn over in his grave at the thought," he declared with disdain. "Real croissants [croy-sants, he pronounced them] are made of only butter, flour, and willpower!" End of lecture, as my suitcase hit the trunk of a waiting cab.

The driver was an equally ample gray-haired woman, whose slightly outmoded Lincoln Continental was chilled sufficiently to cool a case of Champagne.

"I like weather outside my car," she announced righteously. "Since God provided us with air-conditionin', I think we got to use it or lose it. Besides, hot weather takes my appetite away! And that's too high a price to pay!"

This lady, whose name is Sister Cora Harper ("I'm a Christian at the wheel"), told me her life story in the twenty minutes it took to reach the French Quarter.

"Came here from Laurel, Mississippi, in '38 with one dress on my back, four children in my arms, and a no-good man who don't like work, nohow!" she reported. "Should have all starved. But didn't. Cause I had a secret weapon kept the wolf away from our door: a talent for making things taste good." She laughed, remembering it. "Worked as a cook. Startin' at three dollars a week—mornin' till night—for good people and bad. Learnin' all kinds of tricks in the kitchen that no amount of money could buy." She winked in the rearview mirror. "After I get rid of the no-account man, I find me a better one and open up a restaurant. My my . . ." She sighed, making a detour from the traffic-clogged expressway to a rural dirt road. "That was a lovely time, I can tell you. For twenty years."

How did she get from a hot stove to a cool cab? I asked her somewhat inquisitively.

"God. God did it. The good man, my husband, got sick, so we sold the restaurant. I used to take him to a hospital every day but he was a big man [another nod in the mirror] like you. Cab drivers don't like to bother with big people who're sick. Too much trouble liftin' and settin' down. So I said to myself, 'Cora, buy a cab and do it yourself!' Which I did—till he died. And just kept riding ever after."

"Do you miss cooking?"

"Does a shrimp miss the Gulf Stream?" She laughed loud and clear. "Naw. I still cook. And when I drive, I just keep saying my cookin' secrets to myself so's I don't forget 'em."

Sister Cora Harper's secrets could fill a book. Here are a few:

- *Spoon apple juice instead of water into a pie crust to make it short.*
- *Use prepared mustard instead of flour for thickening a sauce.*
- *For a tender Cornish hen, boil the bird first in broth for about 30 minutes. Then roast it.*
- *Whenever it says vanilla in a recipe, substitute rum.*

In return for her dispensations, I gave Sister Cora the recipes that follow.

COUNTRY CAPTAIN

〰

Sister Cora Harper knew this old Louisiana dish , but with a different name. She recalled the spicy chicken stew as "Country-man's Hot Dog!" Figure that one out! Serve over hot steamed rice.

½ cup all-purpose flour
½ teaspoon seasoned salt
¼ teaspoon freshly ground
    black pepper
1 chicken (3½ to 4 pounds),
    cut into serving pieces
7 tablespoons unsalted butter
    (approximately)
1 onion, chopped
1 red bell pepper, cored,
    seeded, and chopped
1 large clove garlic, mashed
2 ripe tomatoes, peeled,
    seeded, and chopped
1 can (8 ounces) Italian tomatoes

1 teaspoon sugar
1½ teaspoons curry powder
1 teaspoon fresh thyme
    leaves, or ½ teaspoon dried,
    crumbled
8 ounces green beans, halved
    lengthwise
½ cup slivered almonds
1 large shallot, finely chopped
⅓ cup dried currants
Fresh thyme, for garnish
Mango chutney

1. Season the flour with the seasoned salt and pepper, and coat the chicken with the mixture.

2. Melt 4 tablespoons of the butter in a large heavy skillet or Dutch oven. Add the chicken; sauté until crisp and golden brown, about 10 minutes on each side, adding more butter if necessary.

3. Remove the chicken and all but 2 tablespoons of the butter from the skillet. Add the onion; cook 1 minute. Add the bell pepper and garlic; cook, stirring frequently, 5 minutes. Stir in the fresh tomatoes, canned tomatoes, sugar, curry powder, and thyme. Return the chicken to the skillet, pressing the pieces into the sauce. Spoon some of the sauce over the chicken pieces. Cover, and cook over medium heat until tender, 30 to 40 minutes.

4. Meanwhile, preheat the oven to 400°F.

5. Bring a medium-size pot of salted water to a boil, and add the beans. Bring back to a boil, and immediately drain. Rinse the beans under cold running water, and drain again.

6. Spread the almonds on a baking sheet, and toast them in the oven until light brown, about 10 minutes.

7. Melt the remaining 3 tablespoons butter in a skillet over medium-high heat. Add the shallot and beans; cook, stirring, just until warmed through, about 5 minutes. Stir the currants into the chicken; then stir in the bean mixture and the almonds. Garnish with fresh thyme. Serve with chutney on the side.

Serves 4

AVOCADOS VINAIGRETTE, NEW ORLEANS STYLE

This dish came to me in the 1950s—just about the time Sister Cora Harper was cooking for her living—from another wonderful woman named Sadie Lovenjoy, who cleaned my first bachelor apartment fitfully but cooked like an angel of mercy whenever either of us grew bored.

1 hard-cooked egg, chopped	*1 tablespoon red wine*
1 teaspoon chopped fresh	*vinegar*
chives or scallion (green	*¼ cup olive oil*
onion) tops	*2 slices Milano or Genoa*
1 teaspoon chopped fresh	*salami, cut into thin*
basil, or ¼ teaspoon	*1-inch-long strips*
dried	*2 avocados*
1 teaspoon chopped fresh	*Juice of 1 lemon*
parsley	*Freshly ground black pepper*

1. Combine the egg, chives, basil, parsley, vinegar, oil, and salami in a small bowl. Toss well.

2. Cut the avocados in half lengthwise, and remove the pits. Sprinkle with lemon juice.

3. Fill each avocado half with the salami-egg mixture, and sprinkle with pepper to taste. Cover, and chill well before serving.

Serves 4

THANK YOU, AGAIN, DIONE

ulinary debts are rarely paid in full. I, for instance, have never properly acknowledged the overwhelming influence of the late Dione Lucas (my first and only cooking teacher) on my kitchen sensibilities.

Dione was a handsome Englishwoman who had been apprenticed to a French chef at an early age. Her lineage, like her domestic status, was a well-guarded secret. But early on, I adjudged Dione to be of royal blood (a duchess at the very least) by the degree of hauteur she exhibited while performing the most demeaning scullery tasks.

Dione (it was pronounced Dee-OH-nee) was at the helm of a small storefront cooking school named Le Cordon Bleu when I first came into her orbit. This was barely after the close of World War II, and the culinary academy doubled as an omelet shop at midday in order to support its chic East Side address. Like a few other curious wage-earners in the territory, I appeared at the lunch counter one day. And knowing little of French cookery, I blindly ordered an *omelette brouille*.

Until the first bite, I had considered omelets to be a purely American kitchen exercise. But never again, for there was nothing to compare with the like of Mrs. Lucas's airy fabrication. Color? Pale gold. Texture? A compound of ozone and fire encircling a heart of runny velvet. Definitely kin to no other egg I had ever tasted.

I consumed two portions at that first visit—to Mrs. Lucas's deep pleasure, for she herself was the short-order cook. Garbed in an apron over a long flowing gown, her arms clattering with gold baubles and her hair (the color of cinnamon bark) coiled down her neck in a resplendent wreath, she appeared to be an empress playing at chef. But this woman's culinary skill was mesmerizing.

I ate at her counter every day for a month, exhausting an entire repertoire of omelet fillings, before she finally spoke to me. Leaning over a bowl of eggs, she lowered her voice discreetly so I alone would hear.

"Have you managed the secret yet, young man?" she inquired.
"I am not sure."

"Oh. I suspected utter proficiency. Very well, I shall instruct you today! Observe the steps carefully. The pan must be very hot. The eggs beaten to a fare-thee-well. Never with milk or cream, mind, but water alone! Butter? The size of a thumbnail and melted quickly before the eggs are poured on." She performed the glittering exercise even as she held forth. "Now the mixture must be scrambled madly—*madly*—until the omelet refuses to budge!" Her eyebrows raised a bit more imperiously. "But, see here, come 'round and do it yourself!"

The hour was late. Only a few straggling lunchers dawdled over coffee. My instinct was to flee, but I did as I was bidden.

Dione Lucas watched my tentative stove debut with a critical frown.

"Not bad," she allowed, as my omelet was folded onto a waiting plate. "Not good, either. You hesitated a moment before scrambling; that leathers the eggs' surface. But . . . definitely not bad! You must come to my classes."

"What classes?" I queried timidly.

"My school. Here. Tonight. But"—pointing to a fresh spot on my necktie—"you are obviously a slipshod boy. Purchase an apron first!"

I never had time to demur.

Dione's tenure in my life far exceeded the several months' tutelage I undertook at her elbow. And though I still bear a small pinkish scar on my wrist where she cracked me with a wooden spoon for "punishing" a delicate sauce, I truly learned to think in the kitchen from this astute and totally irresistible mentor.

I loved her as one adores an autocratic (and sometimes outrageous) parent. But never, I must confess, did I praise her sufficiently for the legacy of good cooking she bestowed—not just on me, but on many chefs of my generation who profited by her awe-inspiring expertise. The best tribute I can offer at this late date is one of her own dazzling recipes. It is the most exquisite dessert I have ever tasted. Consume it with a glass of Champagne as an overdue toast to the creator.

ROULAGE LEONTINE

ᘒᘒᘒ

8 ounces (8 squares) dark
    sweet baking chocolate,
    broken into bits
⅓ cup cold water
8 eggs, separated (see Note)
1 cup superfine sugar
1 tablespoon unsweetened
    cocoa powder

1½ cups heavy or whipping
    cream
3 tablespoons confectioner's
    sugar
1 teaspoon vanilla extract
Unsweetened cocoa powder,
    for dusting
Toasted slivered almonds

1. Preheat the oven to 350°F. Oil a jelly-roll pan, and line it with waxed paper extending 1 inch beyond the ends of the pan.

2. Combine the chocolate bits and the water in the top of a double boiler, and stir over hot water until smooth. Set aside to cool.

3. Beat the egg yolks until they are light and lemon-colored. Slowly beat in the superfine sugar. Stir in the cooled chocolate mixture.

4. Beat the egg whites until stiff but not dry, and fold them into the chocolate mixture.

5. Spread the batter in the prepared pan, and bake until it has puffed up, about 17 to 18 minutes. Remove the pan from the oven, and cover the cake with a layer of damp paper towels. Let stand for 20 minutes.

6. Remove the paper towels and dust the cake with the 1 tablespoon unsweetened cocoa. Dampen a tea towel and place it over the cake. Working quickly, invert the pan. Lift the pan from the cake and gently peel off the waxed paper.

7. Beat the cream with the confectioner's sugar and vanilla until very stiff. Spread it evenly over the cake. Working with the tea towel, quickly roll the cake toward you and onto a jelly-roll board or serving platter. Chill it thoroughly.

8. Just before serving, dust the top of the roll with unsweetened cocoa and sprinkle with toasted almonds.

Serves 10 to 12

Note: This recipe uses raw eggs. Recently some uncooked eggs have been a source of salmonella, a serious infection. If you are unsure of the quality of the eggs you buy, avoid recipes that use them raw.

LA MAESTRA

*F*or months I had heard that the liveliest cooking seminars in town take place in a small kitchen on West Twelfth Street, where Anna Teresa Callen expounds on the joys of seasonal Italian cookery to six rapt students per session. So I finally went crosstown to have a look (and a taste) for myself.

Reports of Signora Callen's culinary expertise and her utter unflappability in the kitchen were not exaggerated. The dishes she teaches are exquisite rustic creations from her homeland, honed to fit the specifications of apartment-dweller cooks. Most ingredients, she advises, come from a local supermarket. Moreover, when something goes wrong in the Callen galley (like a nonfunctioning processor) the direttrice di scuola is totally undismayed.

"Machines are not important to a good cook," she says. "Let them fall apart if they want. I still have a good muscle in my arm to chop with. And so do you!"

To prove the point, she sets her class to making pasta by hand, coaxing mere flour and eggs into a golden ball of fleecy dough. But when the students are eager to feed this dough into the waiting rollers of a pasta-making device, Callen restrains them.

"Not ready yet," she states with authority. "Knead it longer! You can tell the dough is ready to become good pasta when it is e-lastic! If you punch it, it punches back."

When Anna Teresa Callen is teaching Italian cuisine, she is the utter pragmatist. If she decides to slosh a bit of cream into a *sugo di carne* (meat sauce) that she is stirring, she does so without apology, even though that ingredient is missing in her students' printed recipe sheets.

"This sauce needs cream," she pronounces flatly, "so I am adding it. My tongue *told* me to!"

Anna Teresa Callen's prodigious skill as a teacher is evidenced by the sumptuous fare shared by her sextet of students after every class. For further proof, try her extraordinary lasagne.

L A S A G N E
S T R A O R D I N A R I E

*L*ike no other lasagne you will ever consume in your life (even if you travel to Bologna), this dish represents at least two hours' work. But to my opinionated tongue, it's more than worth the effort!

Bolognese Sauce (recipe
    follows)
¼ cup chopped cooked
    spinach
2 eggs
Pinch of salt
2 cups all-purpose flour
    (approximately)
8 ounces mozzarella cheese,
    coarsely grated

1 cup plus 3 tablespoons
    freshly grated Parmesan
    cheese
Besciamella Sauce (recipe
    follows)
2 tablespoons unsalted
    butter

1. Prepare the Bolognese Sauce. Preheat the oven to 375°F.

2. Prepare the pasta: In a food processor, process the spinach for 5 seconds. Add the eggs and salt. With the machine running, slowly add 1½ cups of the flour through the feed tube. Add more flour, 1 tablespoon at a time, until a smooth ball is formed. Transfer the dough to a lightly floured board, and knead for 5 minutes. Cover with a bowl; let stand at room temperature for 30 minutes.

3. Roll out the pasta dough as thin as possible, either by hand or using a pasta machine; add more flour if the dough seems sticky. Cut the dough into strips 9 inches long and 2½ inches wide. (The size can be adjusted to fit the dish you are using.)

4. Bring 4 quarts of water to a boil. Add the lasagne noodles, a few at a time, and boil for 3 minutes. Place the cooked pasta between damp towels while you cook the remaining pasta.

5. Spread 2 tablespoons of the Bolognese Sauce over the bottom of a lasagne pan or a 2½-quart ovenproof baking dish. Add a layer of noodles. Spread a thin layer of Bolognese Sauce over the noodles, and sprinkle with some of the mozzarella and Parmesan. Continue layering until all the sauce, mozzarella, and 1 cup Parmesan have been used, ending up with sauce and cheese. If you have rolled the pasta thin enough, there should be excess for the freezer. (*Note:* The dish can be prepared in advance to this point and refrigerated. Let it stand at room temperature for 30 minutes before continuing.)

6. Make the Besciamella Sauce.

7. Spoon the Besciamella Sauce over the top of the lasagne, gently pushing in the sides to allow some sauce to run down. Dot with the butter, and sprinkle with the remaining 3 tablespoons Parmesan cheese. Bake for 45 minutes. Let stand for 10 minutes before cutting and serving.

Serves 8 to 10

BOLOGNESE SAUCE

3 tablespoons olive oil
1 tablespoon unsalted butter
4 ounces prosciutto (the end
    piece is fine), finely
    chopped
1 medium-size onion, finely
    chopped
1 medium-size carrot, finely
    chopped
1 rib celery, finely chopped
1 sprig fresh parsley, finely
    chopped
⅓ pound ground beef

⅓ pound ground veal
⅓ pound ground pork
3 fresh sage leaves, chopped,
    or a pinch of dried
⅓ cup dry white wine
3 tablespoons tomato paste
2 cups homemade chicken or
    beef stock or canned broth
¼ cup heavy or whipping
    cream
Salt and freshly ground black
    pepper

1. Heat the oil and butter in a medium-size saucepan over medium heat. Add the prosciutto, onion, carrot, and celery, and sauté until lightly browned, about 5 minutes. Add the parsley and ground meats. Cook over high heat, breaking up any lumps, until the meat is well browned, about 10 minutes.

2. Reduce the heat, and add the sage, wine, tomato paste, and stock. Cover, and simmer over medium-low heat for 1 hour.

3. Stir in the cream, and add salt and pepper to taste.

Makes about 4 cups

BESCIAMELLA SAUCE

2½ tablespoons unsalted
    butter
2½ tablespoons all-purpose
    flour

2½ cups milk
Salt
Freshly grated nutmeg

Melt the butter in a small saucepan over low heat. Stir in the flour and cook, stirring constantly, for 2 minutes. Beat in the milk, and bring to a boil over medium-low heat. Allow the sauce to puff two or three times; then remove from the heat. Stir in salt and nutmeg to taste.

Makes about 2½ cups

GOOFS, BIG NAME STYLE

Do great chefs ever goof up in the kitchen? That is a question I am often asked at the cooking classes I teach around the country. My answer is usually speculative, for my friendship with most culinary greats is marginal at best.

Once, however, I was invited to dine with Julia Child and her husband in Cambridge, Massachusetts. Since the meal was to be taken in their big, homey kitchen, the Childs and I indulged in a few drinks and a lot of talk while Mrs. C. busied herself at the range. Perhaps we talked a bit overanimatedly, for at one point the lady of the house broke off what she was saying in mid-sentence and tossed a pot in the sink.

"What are you doing, Julia?" I queried after a discreet lapse of time. "Trying to determine what to do with scorched carrots," the dauntless French Chef replied. "What do you suggest?"

My advice was freshly grated nutmeg over the offending members— with lots of butter, parsley, and no apologies whatsoever. Happily Mrs. Child concurred.

Paula Wolfert, the doyenne of Moroccan cuisine, invited me to a small dinner last fall, with the express understanding that all dishes to be served would be "tests." In our business, you see, one is usually sweating out another cookbook, so the food we prepare for guests is often offered with that caveat. If the "test" succeeds, the dish is included in the repertoire. If it fails, the diners merely pass the wine.

Paula's first four entrées were sublime—such unqualified successes that perhaps we overtoasted the "tests." But no matter—the dessert (fragile pink, individual raspberry soufflés), destined to rise majestically in the oven, unpredictably collapsed instead. Needless to say, the dinner ended with postmortems and brandy.

Recently I planned a gala Christmas dinner in true Dickens tradition: a huge rosy roast to be escorted to the table with an equally upright Yorkshire pudding. The menu seemed a breeze, the fruitcake was made in advance, and even Christmas day turned white for the occasion. But somehow or other the cook miscalculated his oven time. Instead of allowing a mere ten minutes per pound for a pinkish slice of meat, I allotted twenty-five. Ever see a genuine tattletale-gray roast beef?

Guests are noble creatures. Mine ate what they were served with grace, and even faintly praised the "pot roast"!

Do yourself a favor—buy an oven thermometer. I have. And try the following, if on true pot roast you would dine.

POT ROAST WITH GREEN SAUCE

❧

*T*his is one of Greene's better efforts in the traditional pot roast division—a Sunday dinner prescription, laced with a subtle horseradish-tinged parsley sauce for much distinction.

2 tablespoons plus 1 teaspoon unsalted butter

1 small clove garlic, minced

2 medium-size onions, chopped

2 shallots, chopped

1 boneless chuck roast (3½ to 4 pounds)

1 small clove garlic, bruised

1 tablespoon black peppercorns, crushed

1 teaspoon olive or vegetable oil

1 cup homemade beef stock or canned broth

1 sprig fresh thyme, or a pinch of dried

2-inch curl of lemon zest

4 to 6 medium-size potatoes

6 medium-size carrots

1 small shallot, minced

1½ tablespoons freshly grated horseradish, or 1 tablespoon commercially prepared

¾ cup chopped fresh parsley

1. Melt a tablespoon of the butter in a Dutch oven over medium heat. Add the minced garlic, onions, and chopped shallots, and sauté until golden, about 5 minutes. Set aside.

2. Rub the meat well with the bruised garlic. Press the crushed peppercorns into the flesh. Heat 1 tablespoon of the butter with the oil in a heavy skillet over medium-high heat. Add the meat, and brown it well on all sides, about 8 minutes. Transfer the meat to the Dutch oven.

3. Add the stock, thyme, and lemon zest to the skillet, and cook briefly, scraping the bottom and sides of the skillet. Pour the sauce over the meat, cover, and cook over medium-low heat for 1½ hours.

4. While the meat is cooking, cut the potatoes into eighths, and cook in boiling salted water for 15 minutes; drain and set aside. Halve the carrots lengthwise, then cut them into 1-inch chunks, and cook in boiling salted water for 5 minutes; drain and set aside. Preheat the oven to 375°F.

5. Remove the meat from the Dutch oven. Strain and reserve the cooking liquid. Degrease the liquid, reserving the fat. Return the meat and the degreased juices to the Dutch oven, cover, and continue to cook until the meat is tender, another 45 to 60 minutes.

6. Meanwhile, pour the reserved fat into a shallow baking dish. Add the potatoes, turning to coat them well. Bake, turning once, for 40 minutes. Add the carrots, toss to coat, and cook another 15 to 20 minutes.

7. Remove the meat from the Dutch oven, place it on a serving platter, and keep warm. Melt the remaining 1 teaspoon butter in a medium-size saucepan, and sauté the minced shallot until soft, about 5 minutes. Add the meat juices, horseradish, and parsley. Boil for 2 minutes. Pour the sauce over the meat, surround with the potatoes and carrots, and serve.

Serves 4 to 6

B A R B E C U E D
P O T   R O A S T

S ame pot, but a different roast entirely—a tangy red Colorado variation, devised to perk up jaded winter appetites.

1 small onion, chopped

1 boneless chuck roast (3½ to
    4 pounds)

1 small clove garlic,
    bruised

½ cup homemade beef
    stock or canned broth
    (approximately)

1 can (8 ounces) tomato
    sauce

2 tablespoons dark brown
    sugar

¼ teaspoon paprika

½ teaspoon dry English
    mustard

¼ cup fresh lemon juice

¼ cup ketchup

¼ cup cider vinegar

1 tablespoon Worcestershire
    sauce

Chopped fresh parsley, for
    garnish

1. Preheat the oven to 325°F.

2. Spread the onion over the bottom of a Dutch oven. Rub the meat well with the bruised garlic, and place it on the onions. Cover, and bake for 2 hours. Add some beef stock if the juices in the bottom of the pot begin to dry up.

3. Combine the tomato sauce, brown sugar, paprika, mustard, lemon juice, ketchup, vinegar, and Worcestershire sauce in a medium-size bowl. Pour the mixture over the meat. Continue to cook, covered, until the meat is tender, about 2 hours more. Baste the meat with the sauce, adding beef stock as needed, every 20 minutes.

4. Remove the meat from the Dutch oven, and place it on a serving platter. Spoon 2 tablespoons of the sauce over the top, and sprinkle with the parsley. Pass the remaining sauce.

Serves 4 to 6

RELISH THE RADISH

One's natural inclination for a certain food, I have discovered, is often heightened by some completely irrelevant set of circumstances. Recently, on an airplane trip to the West Coast, I met a woman who was a radish lover in the extreme. The reason behind her unnatural affection for that rosy root illustrates my point exactly.

Seatmates on a Boeing 747, we became acquainted when the meal of the day was served. Since I travel quite a bit, I have finally learned my lesson and eat only what lies lightest on the midriff in transit, and consequently opt for a seafood platter when my ticket is purchased. The woman at my side, however, was the recipient of the day's special: a chicken pancake that appeared slightly on the soggy side.

After some while, I noted that rather than attacking her food, this woman was staring at my plate. Not, as one might surmise, at the shrimp or crab, but rather at a large and imposing radish that I had pushed to one side before sluicing the salad greens with dressing.

"You don't eat radishes?" is the way my fellow traveler began our conversation.
"Only on the ground," I explained, "when I am certain they will be well digested. Would you care for mine?"

"Oh, yes," she replied, accepting the radish without any embarrassment whatsoever and chewing it at once. "I adore radishes and have for twenty—no, twenty-one—years!"

Obviously the specific date puzzled me. She smiled knowingly, sat back in her seat, and told the following story:

"I once had a bad case of hiccups, the kind that went on for almost a week, night and day. And nothing, no home remedy or patent-medicine cure, seemed to have any effect on them. I drank water upside down. I held my breath, sucked sugar through a straw, and blew into paper bags until I was red in the face, but nothing affected those darned hiccups! Finally, in utter distraction, I went to the emergency ward of the nearest hospital. Sitting there, bouncing on my seat every ten or twelve seconds, I noticed this rather cute guy holding a brown paper sack. He couldn't help but observe what was the matter with me, I guess. Because out of the blue, he came over to where I was sitting. From the sack he handed me . . . you guessed it, didn't you? A *radish*!

" 'Eat this with your eyes closed,' he commanded.
"I did. And he kissed me."

My fellow passenger (she was really very pretty) smiled in retrospect and pushed away the tray of uneaten food.

"I left the infirmary with him. He'd sprained his wrist, you see, reaching for those radishes at a vegetable stand . . . so I taped it for him. And in no time at all, we got married."

It seemed unnecessary to inquire whether the union had been a happy choice. Twenty—no, twenty-one—years later, radishes were still her favorite vegetable.

Since the end of all my tales invariably includes a recipe, here is hers. It's a formula for a terrific chicken salad (with radishes) that I wrote down on my napkin.

RADISH AND CHICKEN SALAD

❧❧❧

The secret of this salad is freshly poached chicken breasts cooked in a strong broth that will season the mayonnaise. I always slice up all the ingredients and toss them together at the last minute, because radishes not only cure hiccups, they wilt too!

1 rib celery, with leaves,
*   coarsely chopped*
1 carrot, sliced
3 parsley stems
1 onion, unpeeled, stuck with
*   1 clove*
Pinch of dried thyme
1½ cups strong homemade
*   chicken stock or canned*
*   broth*
1 large whole chicken breast,
*   halved*
½ cup finely minced celery

8 to 10 large radishes,
*   trimmed and thinly sliced*
*   (about 1½ cups)*
1 shallot, minced
1 tablespoon finely chopped
*   radish tops*
¾ cup mayonnaise
Salt and freshly ground black
*   pepper*
1 tablespoon chopped fresh
*   parsley*

1. Combine the celery, carrot, parsley stems, onion with clove, thyme, and stock in a medium-size saucepan; bring to a boil. Reduce the heat and simmer for 10 minutes. Then add the chicken breasts, skin side down. Cook, covered, until done, 12 to 15 minutes. Remove the chicken breasts from the broth, and let them cool. Strain the broth and let it cool.

2. Remove the meat in chunks from the chicken breasts, and place it in a serving bowl. Add the radishes, celery, shallot, and radish tops. Toss lightly.

3. Combine the mayonnaise with 2 to 3 tablespoons of the reserved broth in a small bowl (the mixture should be slightly thin but not runny). Pour the mayonnaise over the salad, and toss well. Season with salt and pepper to taste, sprinkle with the parsley, and serve.

Serves 4

R A D I S H ,   R I C E ,   A N D   S H R I M P   S A L A D

*T*his recipe is inspired by one I used to make at The Store in Amagansett. The original had many more ingredients, but as I grow older, the will to refrain culinarily has increased considerably.

2 cups cooked white rice, chilled

1 shallot, minced

8 to 10 large radishes, trimmed and thinly sliced (about 1½ cups)

¼ cup thinly sliced black olives

8 ounces cooked shrimp, shelled, deveined, and halved

1 small cucumber, peeled, seeded, and minced

1 tablespoon chopped fresh basil

1 teaspoon chopped fresh parsley

1 teaspoon finely slivered lemon zest

½ cup Vinaigrette Dressing (recipe follows)

Salt and freshly ground black pepper

Combine all the ingredients through the lemon zest in a large bowl, and toss lightly. Pour the vinaigrette over the salad, and toss well. Season with salt and pepper to taste. Chill slightly before serving.

Serves 4 to 6

VINAIGRETTE DRESSING

1 small clove garlic, crushed
½ teaspoon coarse salt
1 teaspoon Dijon mustard
Juice of ½ lemon

⅓ to ½ cup olive oil
2 teaspoons red wine vinegar
½ teaspoon freshly ground
   black pepper

Combine the garlic and salt in a small bowl, and mash together with the back of a spoon until the mixture forms a paste. Stir in the mustard and lemon juice. Then whisk in the oil, vinegar, and pepper.

Makes about ½ cup

TALENTED, AND GENEROUS TO BOOT

Anyone who has cracked open a cookbook in the past decade, or turned on the TV to watch a cooking show recently, will recognize

Jacques Pépin's handsome face at a glance. And more to the point, will probably be an enthusiastic admirer of his straightforward manner and unpretentious cooking style.

I recently spent a weekend with Pépin and a clutch of other notable kitchen practitioners, teaching cooking classes at the Culinary Festival '84 in the Scottsdale Center for the Arts in Arizona. After two days in his company, my esteem for this man's humor, tact, and absolutely unflappable French levelheadedness rivaled my admiration for his culinary expertise. Jacques Pépin teaches a class of two hundred spectators how to whip up a perfect French crêpe as though he were giving the advice to his daughter's teenage friends—dropping culinary footnotes along with provincial wisdom, family gossip, and tidbits of historical information. As I waited in the wings to begin my own class, I learned (after a lifetime of producing fairly decent pancakes) the precise spot in the pan where one should pour the crêpe batter so the pancake will always form a perfect circle: near the handle, so that gravity will do all the work!

Of course Pépin is a trained chef (and was personal chef to three French presidents before he came to America), but it is not his skill alone that makes him so engaging; it is his utter humanity.

When classes ended, a dinner was held in Jacques' honor at a posh restaurant. The chef-owner, Vincent Guerithault, is young, French, and a brilliant culinary innovator. However, on this occasion the menu could best be described as Drop-Dead Haute Cuisine. There were eight or nine extravagant courses. I watched Pépin (who is a spare type) manfully plow his way through each with praise and no demurral until coffee was served. "In France," he said *sotto voce,* "no one in his right mind eats like this. They would expire if they did. But . . ." He shrugged. "Here it is expected."

After the long day and longer meal, all I wanted was bed and Bromo Seltzer. But Pépin had other plans. "Berrt!" he hissed. "You cannot leave without visiting the kitchen."

"Of course, Jacques," I replied obediently, following him to the interior of this grand hostelry, where (despite the hubbub) the entire staff rose to greet him. Jacques had taught a class in this place a day before, and the air was heavy with esteem. Clearly every kitchen worker adored him as a member of their profession who had "made good." Lest I think of escape during the colloquy of praise, Pépin kept a strong arm around my shoulder. "Listen, Bert," he said, handing me a pen. "We must write a message on the menu to convey our gratitude to the staff." Who can argue with such good grace? I sat down to sign one, and Pépin handed me forty more. A menu, in fact, for everyone in the kitchen—and their wives.

"Are you sure they want a message from me?" I said. "After all, this dinner was in your honor, not mine."

Pépin's thick eyebrows knitted with dismay. "No, no. Of course they want you. I know it! Write something nice," he commanded. And I did, for an hour, while everyone from the sous-chef to the scullery girl beamed with pleasure. And Jacques Pépin's smile was the broadest of all. Now that is *humanity* in my book!

LEMON
AND CARAMEL
SOUFFLE

❧

One of my favorite Jacques Pépin recipes is the following dessert soufflé, which may be consumed straight from the oven and puffy, or in Pépin's way, fallen after a stint in the fridge. It's from his book *La Méthode*.

1⅓ cups sugar

¼ cup water

1½ cups milk

4 egg yolks

1 teaspoon vanilla extract

2 teaspoons finely grated
   lemon zest

2 tablespoons cornstarch

7 egg whites

Whipped cream (optional)

1. Preheat the oven to 350°F.

2. Combine 1 cup of the sugar with the water in a medium-size saucepan. Cook over medium heat until the sugar melts, 3 to 4 minutes. Then raise the heat slightly and cook, stirring constantly, until the mixture turns a light caramel color, 4 to 5 minutes longer. Pour into a 1½- to 2-quart soufflé dish, carefully turning the dish to coat the bottom and sides.

3. In a small saucepan, slowly heat the milk to boiling; remove from the heat.

4. Combine the egg yolks and the remaining ⅓ cup sugar in a saucepan, and beat until light. Beat in the vanilla, lemon zest, and cornstarch. Then whisk in the hot milk. Place the mixture over medium heat and bring to a boil, whisking constantly. Pour into a large bowl.

5. Beat the egg whites in a large bowl until stiff. Fold them into the soufflé mixture, and pour into the prepared soufflé dish. Place the dish in a roasting pan, and add hot water to the pan to reach halfway up the sides of the dish. Bake for 1 hour.

6. Allow the soufflé to deflate and cool to room temperature. Cover and refrigerate overnight.

7. About 1 hour before serving, invert the soufflé dish over a platter, and return the dish and platter to the refrigerator. The soufflé will fall from the dish by itself. Serve with whipped cream if desired.

Serves 6 to 8

TARTE A L'ORANGE

hough it has changed over the years that it has been in my repertoire, this dish is based on one of Jacques Pépin's recipes. I
always bless the creator when I make it.

Pastry for a 10-inch pie	½ cup heavy or whipping
⅓ cup sugar	cream
3 tablespoons water	
	FOR THE TOPPING
FOR THE FILLING	4 large navel oranges
3 egg yolks	½ cup apricot preserves
¼ cup sugar	1½ tablespoons sugar
¼ teaspoon vanilla extract	1½ tablespoons Grand
1½ tablespoons cornstarch	Marnier liqueur
¾ cup milk, scalded	

1. Preheat the oven to 400°F.

2. Roll out the pastry on a lightly floured board, and ease it into a 10-
inch loose-bottom tart pan. Trim and flute the edges. Line the shell with
aluminum foil, and weight it with rice or beans. Bake for 15 minutes.
Remove the weights and foil, and bake 10 minutes longer. Cool on a wire
rack.

3. Combine the ⅓ cup sugar and the water in a small saucepan, and
bring to a boil, stirring constantly. Cook until the sugar melts and turns
caramel color, 8 to 10 minutes. Drizzle the caramel over the bottom of the
cooled tart shell.

4. Make the filling: Combine the egg yolks, sugar, and vanilla in a
large bowl, and whisk until light. Whisk in the cornstarch, and slowly add
the milk. Transfer the mixture to the top of a double boiler. Cook, stirring
constantly, over simmering water until thick, about 12 minutes. Transfer
the custard to a bowl, and allow it to cool. Cover and refrigerate until
cold.

5. Beat the heavy cream until stiff. Fold it into the chilled custard,
and spoon the mixture into the tart shell. Refrigerate.

6. Prepare the topping: Peel and section the oranges, and set them aside. Combine the preserves, sugar, and Grand Marnier in a small saucepan, and bring to a boil. Reduce the heat and simmer for 5 minutes. Strain through a fine-mesh sieve.

7. Arrange the orange segments in an attractive pattern over the custard and drizzle the apricot glaze over the top. Refrigerate until ready to serve.

Serves 8

IN LOVE WITH A COLD FISH

Do you ever think about the changing fashion of appetite? Time was, not so long ago, when the only fish dish adjudged safe for consumption in summer months (particularly when the temperature soared) was canned tuna or salmon salad.

Nowadays, terrines of pike or sole, scallop mousse, and cold poached bass are as standard to a restaurant's survival in June as is its air-conditioning repairman!

When I was growing up in the late 1930s, the term "cold fish" was purely a pejorative statement, in the kitchen and out. And no one but invalids ate a deep-sea comestible any way other than fried to a golden mean. Usually with ketchup on the side. It took a long, long while to break that dietary pattern, I can tell you.

For me, the change of palate occurred when I was about eighteen, and hotly wooing a young lady who had emigrated with her parents from war-torn (and glamorous) Paris shortly before.

My appearance at this alien dinner table became a weekly occurrence. And though the fair daughter of the house never actively encouraged or discouraged my attentions, it became apparent to both wooer and wooed that it was her mother's remarkable ability to cook that truly kept my suit at the sticking point.

The Woolfs were the first family I ever encountered who drank wine at the table nightly. They also, more pertinently, often ate fish instead of meat in the summer—served chilled with any manner of elegantly temperate sauces.

My own mother, who took some vicarious interest in this romance under the guise of latent gastronomy, would usually quiz me about the dishes we ate.

"So, what kind of cold fish was it?"
"White."
"That's a big help."
"With a yellow sauce."
"Baked, broiled, or poached?"
"I don't know, Mother. I never ask for recipes. I am merely invited to dinner . . . not to play 'Information, Please.' "

Such conversations often ended with a hard look from my parent. "Well, I think you will discover that recipes last a whole lot longer than kisses" was her last word on the subject.

Are mothers always right?

I never married the girl. But I did manage to rack up some interesting ways to serve flounder (cold) from her generous mother during the long interval of courting.

And the kisses? Still sweet as a summer memory!

C O L D   F I L L E T
R O M A N O F F

*E*legant party fare all year round—easy as the dickens to prepare too! But caviar, of course, makes the dish special.

COURT BOUILLON
4 cups water
1 cup dry white wine
1 small onion, stuck with 1
  clove
½ rib celery, with leaves
1 small bay leaf
½ lemon
6 peppercorns
1 teaspoon salt

12 small sole or flounder
  fillets (or 6 medium, cut in
  half)

¾ cup sour cream
¾ cup mayonnaise
4 teaspoons Dijon mustard
1½ teaspoons fresh lemon
  juice
1 clove garlic, crushed
1 shallot, minced
¼ teaspoon salt
¼ teaspoon freshly ground
  white pepper
¼ cup good-quality vodka
1 small jar (2 ounces) red
  caviar

1. Combine the court bouillon ingredients in a heavy saucepan (not aluminum), and bring to a boil. Reduce the heat and simmer the bouillon for 5 minutes.

2. Meanwhile, roll up the fillets and secure them with toothpicks.

3. Add the fish to the bouillon, and poach gently until it flakes when pierced with a fork, 4 to 5 minutes. Drain the fish well; remove the toothpicks. Cover and refrigerate for at least 6 hours.

4. At the same time, whisk together the sour cream, mayonnaise, mustard, lemon juice, garlic, shallot, salt, white pepper, and vodka. Refrigerate, covered, for at least 6 hours.

5. When you are ready to serve them, arrange the rolled fillets on a platter, and spoon some sauce over each. Top each fillet with a small spoonful of caviar, and serve.

Serves 6

PAIN DE POISSON
PROVENCALE

*L*iterally "a fish bread" from the fishermen-chefs of the South of France. This ring of flounder and crunchy vegetables is also satisfying when served hot from the oven, but with a different sauce—say, a pale tomato sauce thinned with cream or yogurt.

1¼ pounds whitefish fillets
    (such as flounder, fluke, or
    sole)
2 egg yolks
3½ tablespoons Pernod
Salt and freshly ground black
    pepper to taste
2 pinches freshly grated
    nutmeg
⅛ teaspoon hot pepper sauce
1½ cups heavy or whipping
    cream
3 medium-size shallots

2 small green bell peppers,
    cored, seeded and cut into
    1-inch pieces
4 medium-size carrots, cut
    into 1-inch pieces
1 cup mayonnaise
1 tablespoon finely grated
    lemon zest
1 tablespoon fresh lemon
    juice
Watercress sprigs and cherry
    tomatoes, for garnish

1. Preheat the oven to 400°F. Grease a 9-inch ring mold. Cut a ring of waxed paper to fit the top of the mold. Set the mold and the paper aside.

2. Cut the fish into cubes, removing any bones. Place half the fish in a food processor, and add 1 egg yolk, 1 tablespoon of the Pernod, and half of the salt, pepper, nutmeg, and hot pepper sauce. With the machine running, gradually add half the cream. Process until smooth; scrape into a large mixing bowl. Repeat with the remaining fish, egg yolk, 1 tablespoon Pernod, and seasonings.

3. Wash the processor bowl, and process the shallots until finely chopped. Add the peppers and carrots; process just until chopped. Add the vegetables to the fish, and mix thoroughly. Add more salt and hot pepper sauce if necessary.

4. Spoon the fish mixture into the prepared ring mold. Press the waxed paper over the fish mixture. Place the mold in a roasting pan, and pour boiling water into the pan to half the depth of the ring mold. Bake until set, about 35 minutes.

5. Remove the ring mold from the oven, and let it stand for 5 minutes. Then place a wire rack over the pan and invert it over the sink (some hot liquid will spill out). Drain the mold thoroughly. Turn the mold right side up, remove the wire rack, and discard the waxed paper. Unmold the fish onto a serving plate. (Use paper towels to sop up any remaining juice that may spill onto the plate.) Allow the fish to cool; then chill well.

6. Beat the mayonnaise in a large mixing bowl until light. Add the lemon zest, lemon juice, and remaining 1½ tablespoons Pernod. Stir well, and season with salt and pepper to taste. Chill well.

7. Before serving, decorate the fish mold with watercress and cherry tomatoes. Pass the sauce.

Serves 8 to 10

PICNICKING ON MORE THAN COLD CHICKEN

*B*eing a friend of the family has its rewards. For one thing, you usually get served first at the table!

I traveled to the tiny hamlet of Rib Falls, Wisconsin (between the Big and Little Rib rivers), in the role of adopted sibling rather than professional recipe seeker. I came to celebrate a large family reunion of friends (the Schulz clan) at a picnic celebration held on the lush and rolling 340-acre farm that their forebears settled, tilled, and stocked with cattle, a hundred years ago.

Today Rib Falls is little changed. No condos, no tract housing, in sight so far. The Schulzes, however, are a large family who have spread like weeds and put down roots all over the U.S. To round up even a portion of the tribe for a homecoming picnic at the farm requires as much tactical planning as getting a man on the Moon. However, the rewards (if we are speaking of vittles) are 100 percent more compelling in corn-tall Wisconsin than in outer space.

The comestibles—brought in relays of covered dishes, coolers, cartons, and baskets—were all homemade, for one thing. And for another, of such forgotten goodness that even a jaded appetite like my own burst into second bloom at first bite!

Before the dinner bell rang, however, the feast itself was in imminent danger of demolition. Not from ravenous Schulzes, mind you, but from the Wisconsin elements. Like a scene from an outdoor spectacle in Cinerama, storm clouds suddenly gathered in the sky, and within seconds, rain and then hail completely obliterated the landscape.

Luckily the Wisconsin-born know how to deal with such exigencies of nature. Every family member, age eight to eighty, grabbed a bowl, platter, crock, pitcher—even the smoking grill laid out with bratwurst—and rushed the food to shelter till the storm passed.

Aside from the city slicker (me), everyone at the farm seemed to know that it was "merely passing weather." When the sun came out again and clean cool air had dried the trestle tables and chairs, they laughed at my concern—and I did too!

Food on the "Schulzland" farm, even in the middle of summer, is hearty fare, healthily apportioned. No diet food. Lots of cured ham, grilled "brats," chicken, and bolognas of every stripe and size. Not to mention pots of baked beans, chili, four kinds of cole slaw, and twice that amount of rainbow jellied salads. However, for me the star of the groaning board was a special Wisconsin treat: traditional German hot potato salad spiked with vinegar and crispy bits of bacon and sausage.

The menu roll call could go on forever: fresh snap beans and lettuce from the garden, homemade buns and bread and cheese, and, oh yes, lots of wonderful Wisconsin Cheddar and Cojack—the latter best paired with Point beer and glasses of the best non-ultra-pasteurized milk I've drunk in years. Followed by brownies, chocolate cake, cookies, and hand-dipped ice cream cones for everyone.

Are you thinking I flew to Milwaukee and drove 300 miles to Rib Falls for an unbridled food orgy? Not a bit of it—just a normal Wisconsin midday meal.

HOT GERMAN POTATO SALAD

*F*or the best ever potato salad, ponder this golden Wisconsin bequest: a hot spud slaw flavored with fringes of crisp bacon and spicy pink chunks of knockwurst or kielbasa.

4 strips thick bacon, cut into 1-inch-long pieces
1 tablespoon unsalted butter
1 clove garlic, minced
4 scallions (green onions), trimmed and chopped
3 medium-large potatoes, sliced ¼ inch thick
Pinch of dried thyme
⅛ teaspoon crushed dried red pepper flakes

8 ounces knockwurst or kielbasa, cut into ½-inch cubes
2 tablespoons olive oil
2 tablespoons red wine vinegar
Salt and freshly ground black pepper
Chopped fresh parsley, for garnish

1. Cook the bacon in a large heavy skillet over medium-low heat to render the fat. Do not brown. Add the butter and garlic; cook for about 4 minutes.

2. Stir in the scallions, potatoes, thyme, and dried red peppers; mix well. Then add the knockwurst or kielbasa and cook, stirring occasionally, until the potatoes are tender, about 20 minutes. Sprinkle with the oil and vinegar; cook 5 minutes longer. Season to taste with salt and pepper, garnish with parsley, and serve.

Serves 4

DIRTY RED COLE SLAW

≈

My favorite summer cabbage slaw is inevitably red-purple, though I no longer can remember why. I didn't find the following at the Schulzes, but I plan to send it along. It is my bread-and-butter note of appreciation for the next Schulz outing.

6 slices bacon
1 small red cabbage (3 pounds), shredded
2 large carrots, shredded
1 green bell pepper, cored, seeded, and finely chopped
1 onion, finely chopped
2 small shallots, minced
2 cups mayonnaise
½ cup sour cream
¼ cup heavy or whipping cream

1½ tablespoons Dijon mustard
1 teaspoon beef bouillon powder
½ teaspoon ground allspice
½ teaspoon chili powder
½ teaspoon salt
½ teaspoon freshly ground black pepper
2 tablespoons chopped fresh dill
1 tablespoon chopped fresh parsley

1. Sauté the bacon in a heavy skillet until crisp. Drain on paper towels; then crumble and set aside. Reserve the bacon drippings.

2. Combine the cabbage, carrots, green pepper, onion, and shallots in a large mixing bowl.

3. Beat the mayonnaise with the reserved bacon drippings in a large bowl until smooth. Add the sour cream, heavy cream, mustard, bouillon powder, allspice, chili powder, salt, pepper, and dill. Blend thoroughly. Pour the dressing over the vegetables, and mix well. Sprinkle with the crumbled bacon and the parsley, and serve at room temperature.

Serves 8

LADIES LINGERIE FOR THE BIG CHILL

dearly love intrepid women in the kitchen. You know the kind I mean? Not those strong-armed damsels who can butcher steers or hoist ten-gallon stockpots over their shoulders. No, what I have in mind is a different breed of cook entirely: the kind of woman who thinks nothing of shelling peas or whipping cream in a basic black dress and a string of pearls. A female who can't decide what becomes a legend most—her mink or her mixer!

In my time I have known several glamorous creatures who were equally at home at the range and in the Royal Box. Dione Lucas (my first formal cooking teacher) was such a culinary iron butterfly. To the manner born, she could still scrub a pot or peel a pound of potatoes faster and better than an army mess sergeant. Years later, I met another of these distaff daredevils of the skillet: Marilyn Harris, director of L. S. Ayre's Cooking School in Cincinnati, Ohio. A lady who could have given the late great Dione a run for her money in hauteur and hard work too, Marilyn still looks like a million bucks, even stirring up a stew.

The undisputed doyenne of cuisine in the Midwest, Marilyn is also one hell of a pragmatist, as the following tale will, I hope, demonstrate.

Succumbing to Marilyn's blandishments, I agreed to teach classes last fall. L. S. Ayre's is one of America's top emporiums, but its cooking school, in the dead center of a thriving main floor, has two obvious drawbacks: small space and low voltage—cavils that Mrs. Harris's dogged optimism dismissed forthwith. She informed me that a photographer was coming to take my picture, in color, for the local paper. "So you'd just better look damn good," she announced.

"I'll only look good if he gives me a lot of light," I countered, "to wash out the wrinkles."

To say the shooting went well would be an understatement. Those pics prove photography can and does lie, for I look twenty years younger. After the photo session, however, I aged perceptibly, for the arc lights the photographer supplied also managed to trip the department's circuit breakers.

We didn't realize it at the time, though, and nothing went awry until, with three convection ovens filled to capacity with spicy corncake and tangy broiled chicken, I flipped the switch on the electric ice cream maker. Then everything went black.

Or gray, to be precise. Auxiliary overhead lighting allowed the class to continue, so I kept teaching the thirty-odd students, whose stomachs rumbled audibly at the thought of no sampling period afterward. "You'll all simply have to shop and come back later, when the power returns," I joked lamely.

But Marilyn the glamorous was having none of that. Instead of waiting for the engineering staff to make repairs, like a five-star general she deployed ovens and ice cream maker all over the store. Corncake baked in Men's Clothing. Tangy broiled chicken in Stationery, and the fateful strawberry ice? Frozen to perfection in Ladies' Lingerie!

When the lights returned, so did the appliances and my own good humor. Not Marilyn's—but then, she'd never lost hers in the first place. That's why I love intrepid women in the kitchen.

BLACK FOREST ONION TART

∽

*M*arilyn Harris is one of those dedicated cooks who scouts the globe for good recipes. Cincinnatians are lucky to have her on their home turf—particularly when she demonstrates the gorgeously gilded onion tart she recently brought back from the Black Forest.

Pâte Brisée (recipe follows)
6 strips thick bacon, diced
4 tablespoons (½ stick)
unsalted butter
1 pound (about 3 medium)
onions
½ teaspoon salt

1½ teaspoons caraway
seeds
2 tablespoons all-purpose
flour
5 large eggs, beaten
1½ cups half-and-half or
light cream

1. Preheat the oven to 400°F.

2. Roll out the pastry to ⅛-inch thickness, and line an 11-inch loose-bottom tart pan with it. Line the pastry with aluminum foil or parchment paper, and weight it with rice or beans. Bake in the lower third of the oven for 10 minutes. Remove the weights and foil, and bake 2 to 3 minutes longer. Allow the pastry to cool. Reduce the oven heat to 375°F.

3. Sauté the bacon in a heavy skillet over medium heat until crisp. Drain it on paper towels and set aside. Pour off the excess grease from the skillet.

4. Melt the butter in the same skillet over medium heat. Add the onions and sauté until tender, about 12 minutes. Then add the salt, caraway seeds, and the flour. Cook, stirring constantly, 2 minutes longer. Allow to cool slightly.

5. Beat the eggs with the half-and-half in a large bowl. Add the bacon and the onion mixture; mix well. Pour this into the prepared pie shell, and bake until puffed and golden, about 30 minutes. Serve immediately.

Serves 8 to 10

PATE BRISEE

1½ cups all-purpose
   flour
½ teaspoon salt
1 large egg yolk

8 tablespoons (1 stick)
   unsalted butter, chilled,
   cut into bits
5 tablespoons cold water

Place all the ingredients except the water in the container of a food processor, and process until the texture resembles coarse crumbs. Add the water, and continue to process until the mixture forms a ball. Wrap in plastic wrap, and refrigerate for 2 hours before using.

Makes enough for one 9- to 10-inch tart

NEW POTATOES IN WHITE WINE

*T*he Harris cooking style is very personal. Mississippi miscellany liberally mixed with European modishness is how I'd describe it. For better evidence, try out the next dazzling Harris side dish—a bequest from the lady to yours truly that was published in *Greene on Greens*.

1¼ pounds small new
potatoes, red or white
4 tablespoons (½ stick)
unsalted butter
⅔ cup dry white wine
Salt and freshly ground black
pepper

3 tablespoons chopped fresh
parsley
1 tablespoon chopped fresh
dill

1. Using a vegetable peeler, cut away a small strip of peel around each potato. (The potatoes should look candy-striped.) Cook the potatoes in boiling salted water until barely tender, 8 to 10 minutes. Drain.

2. Melt 2 tablespoons of the butter in a large skillet over medium heat. Add the potatoes and roll them in the skillet until a light crust forms, 4 to 5 minutes. Do not let them brown. Add the wine and the remaining 2 tablespoons butter. Raise the heat and cook, stirring constantly, until the wine is reduced and the sauce is fairly thick, about 5 minutes. Sprinkle with salt and pepper to taste, and the parsley and dill. Stir gently to coat the potatoes with the herbs. Serve immediately.

Serves 4

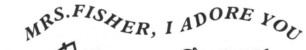

*B*y and large our lives are not often brushed with true greatness. I consider myself a jot luckier than most in that department, because I have been permitted a warm, long (although very often long-distance)

friendship with a lady whom I regard as one of the great writers of the twentieth century.

Her name is M.F.K. Fisher, and her bailiwick is much too readily acknowledged to be the world of food. To my mind it is a far deeper appetite she chronicles: the taste for life's circuitous mysteries and the relish in its manifest foibles. I suppose one might say she writes about "the human condition," but she manages it with such perceptive skill and disarming candor that her genius insight appears as almost offhand reflection.

As you may have observed, I am a fan of this lady's work. I have been ever since I first cracked open a book titled *Consider the Oyster* back in 1941. From that moment on, I have waited for more Fisher volumes with the kind of breathless anticipation not expended on any literary output since I outgrew the Bobbsey Twins.

The good tidings are that Mrs. Fisher has a new book on the shelves at the moment, a reason for much public and private rejoicing. Called *As They Were,* it is a collection of what she dubs "lodestars," those points of reference that have been guiding forces in her life. Her memory, for instance, of a kitchen in France summons up not only the scent and sight of an effulgent Provence summer but a philosophic musing on the very order of Nature itself: "first freshness, then flavor and ripeness, and then (finally) decay."

I first met Mary Frances Kennedy Fisher in the mid-1960s, when she was brought to my house in Amagansett as a guest of a dinner guest. Actually, from the moment I learned she was coming to dinner, the meal became a celebration of her influence on my sensibilities (cooking and otherwise), and rarely have I tried harder to please. To my utter delight she consumed every morsel with relish—and I loved her from that moment on.

Parenthetically, I was also bewitched by her appearance. She was (and is) a very sensuous lady with a deceptively soft voice and an ever-so-slightly feline manner that suggests she is capable of purring when pleased—and of unsheathing a sudden sharp nail when she is not! Although I have never observed any demeanor other than indulgent good humor, I sense it by some dark and divine instinct.

We became friends at first sight. Better than that, for me she became a lodestar. We have spent scant times together, but whether here or in Sonoma, California, where she lives, it is always a meeting that leaves me both exhilarated and revived. What can I say, other than that I adore this woman?

Reader, do yourself a favor and start with *As They Were*. Then work back through her long and equally satisfying collection of other writings. I promise, you will not be sorry!

To many, M.F.K. Fisher is the ultimate gastronome. Yet no food writer before or since has ever managed to elicit more real hunger for absolutely raggle-taggle foods (like fried egg sandwiches or brown-sugared rice pudding) than this *agent provocateur* of the palate. The following recipes entered my kitchen repertoire long ago.

S L O W - C O O K E D
S P I N A C H   T A R T

᰾

*T*his so-called tart is really a heavenly cracker-wafer-toast fabrication. A very unusual canape or accompaniment to cold or hot dishes, it is a devise well worth notching on your kitchen belt. But make sure you bake it for the required four hours. It may look done before, Mrs. Fisher cautions, but it is not!

1 package (10 ounces) frozen
   spinach, thawed (½ cup
   juice reserved)
1 medium-size onion,
   coarsely chopped
1 clove garlic
2 large ribs celery,
   chopped
⅓ cup coarsely chopped
   fresh parsley
8 to 10 fresh basil
   leaves

2 sprigs fresh thyme
¾ cup olive oil
2 eggs
1 cup grated Jarlsberg
   cheese
Salt and freshly ground black
   pepper
⅛ teaspoon freshly grated
   nutmeg
1 cup dried bread crumbs
¼ cup freshly grated
   Parmesan cheese

1. Preheat the oven to 275°F. Lightly oil a 10 x 15-inch rimmed baking sheet.

2. Combine the spinach and its juice with the onion, garlic, celery, parsley, basil, thyme, and ½ cup of the oil in a blender. Blend until smooth. Add the eggs, and blend 30 seconds longer.

3. In a mixing bowl, combine the spinach mixture with the Jarlsberg cheese, salt and pepper to taste, and nutmeg. Spread the mixture evenly over the prepared baking sheet. Sprinkle with the bread crumbs and Parmesan cheese, and drizzle with the remaining ¼ cup oil. Bake until dry and crisp, about 4 hours. Serve hot or cold, sliced into squares.

Makes 30 to 36 squares

Note: Store in a dry container. These wafers last a week or longer. Frozen, they can be stored for 3 months.

COOL AND COLLECTED CELERY

☙

*M*y favored cold first course (or salad in a pinch) is this wondrous M.F.K. amalgam of poached celery, anchovies, and
chopped eggs, swooshed in a good vinaigrette dressing.

*1 large, thick head Pascal
    celery
3½ cups homemade chicken
    stock or canned broth
    (approximately)
Simple Vinaigrette Sauce
    (recipe follows)
1 hard-cooked egg, yolk and
    white chopped separately*

*4 anchovy fillets
4 canned pimiento strips
Chopped fresh parsley, to
    taste
Freshly ground black pepper,
    to taste*

1. Trim off the tough outer ribs of the celery, and trim off the leaves,
leaving a head of celery about 8 inches long. Pare the bottom of the head
with a vegetable peeler, but do not cut it off. Slice the trimmed head into
four lengthwise pieces, and place them in a large shallow saucepan. Add
enough chicken stock to cover, and heat to boiling. Reduce the heat and
simmer until tender, 20 to 25 minutes. Remove the pan from the heat,
and let the celery cool in the stock.

2. Drain the cooled celery (reserve the stock for another use).
Arrange the celery in a shallow serving dish. Chill.

3. Pour the vinaigrette over the celery, and continue to chill it, turning the celery several times. A couple of hours total chilling time is best.

4. When it is well chilled, garnish the celery with alternating bands of
chopped egg white, chopped egg yolk, anchovy fillets, and pimiento
strips. Sprinkle with parsley and freshly ground pepper, and serve.
Serves 4

SIMPLE VINAIGRETTE SAUCE

1 small clove garlic, crushed
½ teaspoon coarse salt
1 teaspoon Dijon mustard
Juice of ½ lemon

½ cup olive oil
2 teaspoons red wine vinegar
½ teaspoon freshly ground
black pepper

Mash the garlic with the salt in a small bowl until smooth. Whisk in the remaining ingredients.

Makes about ½ cup

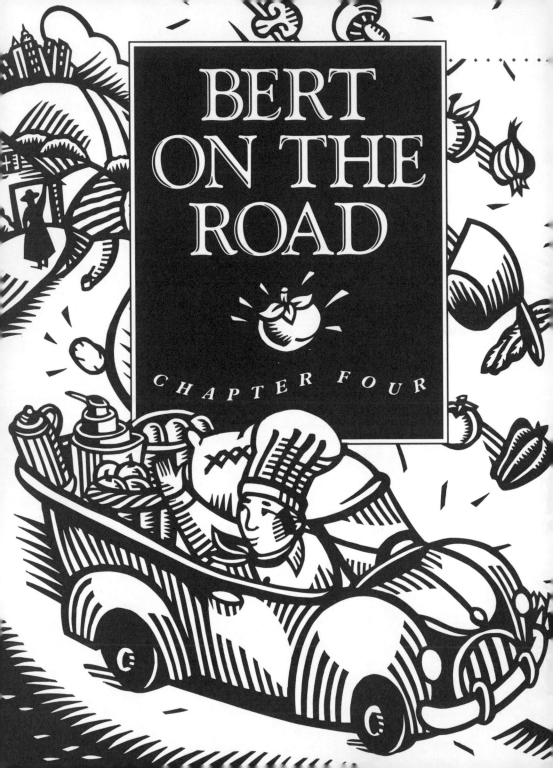

BERT ON THE ROAD

CHAPTER FOUR

TEXAS GOES ASIAN

H **ouston:** If you assume, as I did, that the language spoken in Houston is exclusively "Panhandle Provincial," take another look at those urban cowboys, please! For this sprawling Lone Star city is not only one of the fastest-growing metropolises in Texas, it was adjudged to be the fourth-largest city in the U.S. by the most recent census count—and more important, is an area of true cosmopolitan stripe.

Walking west on Westheimer (one of Houston's major downtown thoroughfares) yesterday morning, I counted three burnooses to every Stetson. And the colorful accents I overheard would certainly have seemed more at home in Saudi Arabia, Libya, or Kuwait, despite the Neiman Marcus and Sakowitz shopping bags in every speaker's hand.

Houston is an oil town that has pushed its skyline and its freeways to remarkable limits to accommodate the new Texans who have arrived during the past decade, and lifelong denizens of the city have assimilated the foreign population with what can only be described as super southwestern hospitality.

One of the more surprising facets of Houston's foreign invasion has little or nothing to do with the city's petro-economics. Fully one quarter of the most recent emigrés came to this semitropical geography from Southeast Asia, as refugees of the Vietnamese war. Block after block of Houston's downtown inner city, once exclusively Mexican, is now totally Asian in character. Indeed, a ride through the sector dubbed "Hou-nam" is so ringed with Oriental signs and banners and so pungently perfumed that a newcomer might easily mistake it for Saigon at first glance.

Being an assiduous shopper (and taster), I wandered through the local supermarkets for hours; but I gave up trying to identify the foodstuffs after a scant perusal, for most of the viands were wholly unknown to my eye, nose, and tongue. However, I observed that shoppers of all description were piling these Oriental goodies in shopping carts as though they were grits and chiles and refried beans. So the times are indeed changing, at least as far as diets go!

I sampled the two Vietnamese dishes that follow at a fabulous restaurant named Dong Ting, and later reconstructed them at home with the assistance of *The Classic Cuisine of Vietnam* by Bach Ngo and Gloria Zimmerman. Both of these excellent dishes make fine seasonal fare and are devised of fairly garden-variety ingredients, except for a sluice or two of *nuoc mam*. *Nuoc mam* is a delicately piquant sauce that may be purchased at Vietnamese groceries, or you can make a reasonably accurate facsimile at your own stovetop.

T O M A T O E S
S T U F F E D   W I T H
P O R K

(*Ca Chua Don Thit*)

ஒ

Dishes from Vietnam are catching on with Americans because they are "fast foods"—easy to prepare and on the light side too. Serve these tomatoes with rice on the side.

4 medium-size tomatoes (not
   overripe)
Salt
2 cloves garlic, finely
   minced
1 small white onion,
   chopped
2 shallots, finely minced
6 ounces ground pork
   (shoulder or hock)
½ teaspoon sugar
Pinch of ground ginger
2 teaspoons commercial or
   homemade nuoc mam
   (see page 178)

Freshly ground black pepper
¼ cup vegetable oil

FOR THE SAUCE
¼ cup water
1 tablespoon nuoc mam
1 tablespoon sugar
1 tablespoon soy sauce
1 teaspoon vegetable
   oil
1 clove garlic, finely
   minced
1½ teaspoons tomato
   paste

1. Slice the tops off the tomatoes, and scoop out the pulp. Sprinkle the inside of the tomato shells with salt and turn them upside down on paper towels to drain.

2. In a medium-size bowl, combine the garlic, onion, shallots, and pork. Mix well, and add the sugar, ginger, *nuoc mam*, and pepper. Mix again.

3. Blot the tomatoes dry, and stuff them with the pork mixture.

4. Heat the oil in a wok or heavy skillet over medium-high heat. Add the tomatoes, meat side down, cover, and cook for 6 minutes. Turn the tomatoes over and cook 6 minutes longer.

5. Meanwhile, make the sauce: Combine the water, *nuoc mam*, sugar, and soy sauce in a small bowl. Heat the oil in a saucepan over high heat, and cook the garlic until lightly browned, about 1 minute. Stir in the tomato paste and *nuoc mam* mixture and cook for 3 minutes. Pour the sauce over the tomatoes, and serve.

Serves 4

CHICKEN STEAMED WITH HAM AND VEGETABLES

(GA CHUNG JAMBON)

✺✺✺

*A*nother reason Vietnamese dishes are popular is that most are light on oil. The following dish is steamed *in toto*. The sauce gives it remarkable savor and Oriental dash!

5 chicken thighs, skinned, boned, and cut into 1-inch-wide strips
1 small onion, finely chopped
1 clove garlic, minced
2 shallots, finely chopped
3 teaspoons commercial or homemade nuoc mam (recipe follows)
¾ teaspoon salt
¼ teaspoon freshly ground black pepper

1½ teaspoons sugar
5 slices boiled ham
2 stalks bok choy (Chinese cabbage), or 8 ounces regular cabbage, or 1 pound green beans
2 teaspoons cornstarch
½ teaspoon soy sauce
1 cup homemade chicken stock or canned broth

1. Combine the chicken strips, onion, garlic, shallots, 1 teaspoon of the *nuoc mam*, ½ teaspoon of the salt, the pepper, and ½ teaspoon of the sugar. Mix well.

2. Cut each slice of ham into 4 pieces. Arrange them, overlapping, over the bottom and sides of a lightly buttered 3-cup bowl. Place the chicken mixture in the center, patting to press it down.

3. Set the bowl in a wok or pan, and fill the pan with boiling water to reach halfway up the sides of the bowl. Cover the pan, and steam the chicken for 40 minutes total. While the chicken is cooking, add the vegetable: If you are using bok choy, cut it into 2-inch pieces, and slice each piece in half; place them over the chicken after it has cooked for 35 minutes, and steam it with the chicken for the remaining 5 minutes. For regular cabbage, cut the head into 8 wedges; place them over the chicken after it has cooked for 28 minutes, and steam with the chicken for the remaining 12 minutes. If you are using green beans, slice them lengthwise, and place them over the chicken after it has cooked for 30 minutes; steam with the chicken for the remaining 10 minutes.

4. Meanwhile, prepare the sauce: Combine the cornstarch, soy sauce, stock, and the remaining 2 teaspoons *nuoc mam*, ½ teaspoon salt, and 1 teaspoon sugar in a saucepan. Heat to boiling and simmer until thick, about 20 minutes.

5. When the chicken and vegetables are done, uncover and arrange the vegetables on a platter. Turn the chicken and ham out onto the vegetables. Spoon the sauce over the top, and serve.

Serves 4

N U O C   M A M

2 fresh red chiles, seeded and chopped

1 clove garlic

1 teaspoon sugar

Juice of 1 lemon

1 tablespoon distilled white vinegar

1 tablespoon water

¼ cup soy sauce

¼ cup clam juice

Combine all the ingredients in a processor or blender, and process until smooth. Strain into a saucepan and boil for 5 minutes. Allow the mixture to cool, then cover and store in the refrigerator. It will keep for several months.

Makes about ½ cup

EVERYTHING'S STILL UP TO DATE

Kansas City: Inveterate food shoppers never die—they move to the Midwest instead!

I am speaking of Kansas City, Missouri (a buyer's paradise), where the rampant consumerism observed at the downtown City Market during the predawn hours on a recent rainy Saturday rivaled the fervor of football fans in Arrow Stadium the following afternoon.

Kansas City has long enjoyed a reputation for being a stronghold of down-home cuisine. For years, two fabled raffish hostelries—Arthur Bryant's Barbecue and "Chicken Betty" Lucas's Diner—made the turf an imperative stopover for every American food buff of hearty appetite. Unfortunately both those stovetop craftsmen are dead, and their kitchen descendants' yield these days is (to put it kindly) a pale shade of culinary gold.

As a stranger in town, I fully anticipated the K.C. fare to be pedestrian—or even worse, compulsively "continental." What a pleasure to be wrong on both counts!

For everyone (restaurateurs and homemakers alike) in this place seems to be dedicated to preparing and serving only what is fresh, prime, and seasonal. For evidence of the local good taste, hie yourself, as I did, to the bespoke City Market. There, in a scant three-block radius, you will discover almost all of the urban cooking population. On the day of my visit, they were not only wide awake but on the prowl amid the truck beds and trestle tables, assiduously scouting green bargains well before the hour of 6 A.M.

I cannot speak for the others, but to me the Market was a banquet for the senses. Just comparing the Mennonite farm folk, who arrange their winter produce (burly red cabbage, jade kohlrabi, and butternut squash) in pyramids like hex signs, with the local Italian tradesmen, who spray their bunches of fennel and celery with atomizers to keep them glistening, is a crash course in cultural relations. But then, the market is truly diverse.

Gypsies sell bangles, playing cards, and hair restoratives at one end of the street while bearded woodsmen chop hickory logs into kindling at the other. If the space is limited (and it is), the produce is always ripe perfection. Last week, enormous baskets of lightly frosted vegetables and cold-stored pears and apples shared the narrow sidewalks with giant sacks of unshelled pecans and black walnuts straight off the tree. Farm cheeses, jams, syrups, relishes, and pickles of every persuasion were displayed like bright jewels below ropes ornamented with pale loops of sausage, back bacon, and home-cured hams.

Among my purchases were a brace of Wolferman's Original English Muffins (made and sold in Kansas City since 1888) and a hard round object known as a *buckeye*. The seller of the latter promised it would bring good luck. The muffins are a mere memory, but the buckeye is still in my pocket. Hopeful.

ENGLISH MUFFINS

ۿ

Wolferman's muffins can often be found in fancy food stores nowadays. Or, they can also be ordered by direct mail (call 800-999-0169). But for a truly memorable breakfast, make your own. The following do it yourself version is made with potato dough.

1 small boiling potato
1 package active dry yeast
Pinch of sugar
1¼ cups warm water

1 teaspoon salt
2½ cups all-purpose flour
Cornmeal

1. Cook the potato in boiling salted water until tender, 15 to 20 minutes. Drain, peel, and mash it by putting it through a food mill or potato ricer. Set it aside.

2. In a large bowl, dissolve the yeast and the sugar in ¼ cup of the warm water; let stand 10 minutes. Stir in the remaining 1 cup warm water and the salt. Add 5 tablespoons of the reserved potato to the yeast mixture, and stir until blended. Then stir in 2 cups of the flour.

3. Scrape the dough onto a floured board. Knead in the remaining ½ cup flour to make a smooth dough, but do not overwork. Shape the dough into a ball, place it in a lightly floured bowl, and cover it tightly. Let it rise until doubled in volume, about 1 hour.

4. Turn the dough out onto a floured board, and flatten it with your hands. Divide it into 10 pieces, and roll each piece into a ball. Press the balls out to form 4-inch rounds. Arrange the rounds on the floured board if you will be baking them on baking tiles; if you will be using a metal baking sheet, sprinkle the sheet with cornmeal and arrange the rounds on the cornmeal. Cover, and let them rise for 1 hour.

5. Preheat the oven to 425° F.

6. If you are using a tile baking surface, sprinkle it with cornmeal, and arrange the muffins on the surface. Bake until the muffins sound hollow when tapped, 12 to 15 minutes. Remove them from the baking sheet or tiles, and cool on wire racks. Before serving, split the muffins with a fork and toast them under the broiler.

Makes 10 muffins

DOUBLE CHEESE MUFFIN BREAD

◖◗◖

first tasted Cheddar cheese muffins at the City Market, and became inspired to duplicate them on home territory. The recipe below (adapted from breadmaker James Beard) is zapped with two varieties of cheese for extra bite. Serve it toasted, please.

1 package dry yeast
1 tablespoon sugar
½ cup warm water
2½ cups all-purpose flour
2 teaspoons salt
7 ounces milk, warmed

¼ teaspoon baking soda
  dissolved in 1 tablespoon
  warm water
1 cup grated Cheddar cheese
¼ cup freshly grated
  Parmesan cheese

1. In a large bowl, dissolve the yeast and the sugar in the warm water. Let stand for 10 minutes.

2. Combine the flour and salt, and stir vigorously into the yeast mixture with a wooden spoon, in alternating portions with the milk. Hold the bowl tightly, and beat the dough hard until it shows some elasticity and looks almost ready to leave the sides of the bowl. (Unlike a kneaded dough, it will remain loose and sticky.) When it is almost gummy, cover the dough and let it rise in a warm place until doubled in volume, about 1½ hours.

3. Stir the dough down with a wooden spoon. Add the dissolved baking soda and the cheeses, and beat vigorously for about 1 minute, being careful to distribute the soda thoroughly.

4. Butter a 10 x 5 x 3-inch baking pan, and fill it with the dough, using a rubber spatula to scrape it from the bowl. Cover with plastic wrap, and let it rise again in a warm place until it rises over the top of the pan, 1 to 1¼ hours.

5. Preheat the oven to 375° F.

6. Bake the bread in the baking pan until it is golden and shrinks slightly from the sides of the pan, about 1 hour. Let it cool in the pan for 5 minutes; then turn it out on a rack to cool completely. (Loosen the edges with a knife, if necessary.) Cut the bread into ⅜-inch-thick slices for toasting.

Makes 1 large loaf

WHY THINGS HAD TO GET BETTER

St. Louis: The Newspaper Food Editors and Writers held their annual Food News Forum practically in the shadow of the Gateway Arch this year. Symbolic geography? Perhaps. For Eero Saarinen's soaring parabola on the Mississippi is a heck of a lot like the national appetite at the moment: on a decided downward curve!

Chief topics on the food editors' agenda in 1981: an overview of soy-beans (including some fairly dreadful samplings of current soy prod-ucts and analogs on the market); a discussion of how the disabled cope in the kitchen; and, oh yes, a heated debate on cholesterol. This latter contest, between two highly qualified and voluble M.D.'s, ended in what I would term a standoff, as neither doctor would predict a measure of increased life expectancy for cholesterol sufferers by any diet changes made after middle age.

I was invited to fly to St. Louis to conduct a seminar on regional foods of America. My panel of experts was a cross-section of editors, the most knowledgeable local food authorities in the nation. But their reports were all surprisingly dismal. The hearty, substantial fare that America once consumed three times a day lies amoldering, having largely been replaced by bland, stereotyped dishes in the 1980s—food concocted, moreover, of packaged instant mixes and convenience items straight off supermarket freezers and shelves, with nary a thought to the insidious ingredients listed in fine print on every package.

A notable example of the downright bad food we seem to be devouring with such gusto came in a report of a dessert that is reputedly sweeping the west coast of Florida at the moment. Tabbed "Better Than Sex," this confection is composed of a single layer of packaged yellow cake mix, topped with an upholstery of canned crushed pineapple (boiled down with sugar until it becomes thick and sludgy), plus a heavy layer-ing of Cool Whip (or whipped cream if you have the time or energy), a dusting of canned flaked coconut, and last but not least, grated sweet chocolate!

After the recipe was given, the question unanswered in my mind was: "Better than sex with whom?"

In an honest environment, one wants honest cookery. But for the life of this slightly petulant food writer, I cannot tell where or why the art of preparing simple food has gone! Good American cuisine, be it from

West, East, North, or South, is so varied and tonic that to blunt it with sauce or sorcery is to overkill the golden goose.

The state of the national appetite today stems from a lack of pride in our culinary heritage. But perhaps it is not a permanent disaffection. A common maverick sensibility seems to swing us back from fad to fundamental in everything we do, art or politics. And I think it may very well be time for a "plain cooking" upswing.

The following are a few samplings of honest-to-gosh American cuisine that returned with me from St. Louis. Each is local, and good as gold!

CRAB CAKES MARYLAND

A mid-Atlantic bequest from the Chesapeake Bay, this handed-down recipe makes the lightest fish cakes I have ever set fork to. The mayonnaise is the secret ingredient.

1 pound lump crabmeat
1 cup fresh bread crumbs
⅓ cup milk (approximately)
1 egg, lightly beaten
¼ cup mayonnaise
½ teaspoon baking powder
2 tablespoons finely chopped fresh parsley
2 tablespoons minced scallion (green onion)

½ teaspoon salt
¼ teaspoon freshly ground white pepper
All-purpose flour, for dusting
Unsalted butter or vegetable oil
Tartar sauce

1. Place the crabmeat in a large bowl. Add the bread crumbs and enough milk to moisten.

2. Combine the beaten egg with the mayonnaise in a medium-size bowl. Beat in the baking powder, parsley, scallion, salt, and white pepper. Pour the mayonnaise mixture over the crabmeat, and toss lightly until well mixed. Form into 10 large crab cakes, wrap in plastic wrap, and refrigerate for 1 hour.

3. Dust the crab cakes lightly with flour and sauté them in hot butter or oil until golden, 3 to 4 minutes per side. Serve with tartar sauce.

Serves 4 or 5

BUFFALO
WINGS

uffalo, New York, gave birth to this golden treat—tangy deep-fried chicken wings dished up with celery sticks and a mess of blue cheese dressing. The precept is said to have originated at the Anchor Bar on Main Street.

20 to 24 small chicken wings
Vegetable oil for deep-frying
¼ cup (½ stick) unsalted
*   butter*
6 ounces Frank's Louisiana
*   Red Hot Sauce (see Note)*

Creamy Blue Cheese Dressing
*   (recipe follows)*
4 ribs celery, cut into strips
*   3 inches long and ¼ inch*
*   thick*

1. Cut the tips off the chicken wings (reserve them for use in making stock). Cut the wings in half at the joint. Pat dry.

2. Heat enough oil in a heavy pot to deep-fry the wings. The oil should be very hot but not smoking. Add the wings and fry until golden brown and cooked through, about 12 minutes.

3. Meanwhile, combine the butter and Red Hot Sauce in a pot large enough to hold the wings, and place over medium heat.

4. Drain the wings on paper towels, and stir them into the sauce. Toss until well coated with sauce.

5. Serve the wings with the dressing and celery strips on the side.
Serves 4

Note: If you can't find Frank's (made by Durkee), any spicy hot barbecue-type sauce will do.

CREAMY BLUE CHEESE DRESSING

2 tablespoons minced onion
1 clove garlic, mashed
¼ cup chopped fresh parsley
1 cup mayonnaise
½ cup sour cream
1 tablespoon fresh lemon
  juice

1 tablespoon white wine
  vinegar
¼ cup crumbled blue cheese
Salt and freshly ground black
  pepper to taste
Cayenne pepper to taste

Combine all the ingredients in a large bowl, and whisk until smooth. Chill well before serving.
Makes about 2½ cups

COWPUNCHER BEANS

*F*rom Arizona comes the devise for Cowpuncher Beans. Neither chili nor carne, it might be termed an exhilarating amalgam of both—with a difference. Sou-West-Mex cookery!

12 ounces dried pinto beans
4 quarts water
2 strips bacon
4 ounces salt pork, diced
1 pound lean pork, cut into strips 2 inches long and ½ inch thick
1 pound round steak, cut into strips 2 inches long and ½ inch thick
2 onions, chopped
3 cloves garlic, minced
½ teaspoon dried oregano

⅛ teaspoon ground cumin
3 tablespoons chili powder
1 teaspoon salt
¼ teaspoon freshly ground black pepper
3 cups chopped canned plum tomatoes with their liquid
1 medium-size jalapeño or other hot green pepper, seeded and minced
1 teaspoon Worcestershire sauce
¼ teaspoon hot pepper sauce

1. Place the beans in a large heavy saucepan, and add 2 quarts of the water. Heat to boiling, and boil for 2 minutes. Remove the pan from the heat, and let it stand for 1 hour.

2. Drain the beans, wipe out the pot, and return the beans to it. Cover with the remaining 2 quarts water and bring to a boil over medium heat. Reduce the heat and simmer until barely tender, about 30 minutes. Drain, and set aside.

3. Sauté the bacon strips in a large Dutch oven over medium heat until crisp. Transfer the bacon to paper towels to drain, and set aside.

4. Add the salt pork to the Dutch oven, and sauté until golden brown, 3 minutes. Remove with a slotted spoon, and set aside.

5. Add half the pork strips to the Dutch oven, and brown well on both sides, 1 minute per side. Remove the pork with a slotted spoon. Sauté the remaining pork, and remove it. Repeat the process, in two batches, with the beef strips. Set the meats aside.

6. Add the onions and garlic to the Dutch oven, and sauté over medium heat until golden, about 5 minutes. Return the pork and beef strips to the Dutch oven; stir in the oregano, cumin, chili powder, salt, and pepper. Mix well. Add the tomatoes, jalapeño, and reserved salt pork. Cook, covered, over low heat until the meat is almost tender, about 1 hour.

7. Stir in the Worcestershire, hot pepper sauce, and reserved beans. Cook, covered, for 30 minutes. Taste and adjust the seasonings. Crumble the bacon over the top before serving.

Serves 6

MY FIRST FRITTATA

taly: Breaking bread can sometimes be a crash course in geopolitics. Who, for instance, but the eternally resourceful Italians would have the *audacia* (read *chutzpah*) to compose a dish entirely of leftovers and eggs and fry it to a state of culinary immortality?

I am thinking specifically of that homely provincial luncheon phenomenon known as *la frittata,* which translates into basic English as a rather wayward omelet. However, even noncooks in Italy know that "to make a frittata" in your life means making a real mess of it, whether the shambles occurs in the kitchen or the bedroom!

I first tasted a frittata on the *autostrada,* that silvery super-highway system that crisscrosses the nation from heel to bootstrap. My journey was midcalf, between Bologna and Milano. The dining place was Motta, a chain of very large, hi-tech fast-food eateries that dot the glorious roadsides but where the viands are no more inviting (or tasty) than the kind we chomp at the U.S. equivalents.

Starving, as always when I travel, I inquired in my very best Berlitz-Italian what was the *capriocciosa* (cook's specialty) at the steam table.

The young girl behind the counter was so taken aback by this question that she began to laugh and cough violently, and had to be replaced at her station. Her successor, a middle-aged matron amicably scornful of gastronomic wayfarers, merely placed a slice of leathery-looking pie on my plate.

"Torta?" I inquired hopefully.
"Non. Frittata. Americano-style. You'll like."

American-style indicated the filling: cubes of ham and processed cheese.

That initial disappointment only whetted my appetite for more solid satisfactions. Returning home and dipping into the works of Signora Hazan and Signor Bugialli, I discovered that most of these pie-like creations are of a vegetarian stripe (composed of green tomato slices, leeks, asparagus, artichokes, and even green beans on occasion), but the filling possibilities seemed infinite to a chef with a refrigerator full of arresting culinary trivia.

So, herewith a few of Greene's freeform variations on the Italian theme.

Unlike the tried-and-true Italian authorities on the subject, I think frittatas are best served warm or at room temperature rather than stone cold. Also, I prefer them for brunch or lunch rather than as appetizers. A frittata makes for admirable fall tailgate picnic fare as well. For such alfresco dining, I would advise wrapping the pan (straight from the oven) in several layers of aluminum foil, then two or three sheets of newspaper and an extra covering of foil. That insulation will keep your frittata tastefully tepid until halftime at the very least!

ALL-AMERICAN FRITTATA

๛

*M*y nationalist version of a frittata also has ham, and two kinds of cheese, in its devise as well as spaghetti. I consider it a salute to the land of its origin.

3 tablespoons unsalted butter
2 teaspoons olive oil
1 medium-size onion, finely chopped
1 small clove garlic, minced
1 medium-size tomato, seeded and chopped
1 small green or red bell pepper, cored, seeded, and chopped
Pinch of sugar
1 teaspoon red wine vinegar
½ cup diced cooked ham
2 tablespoons chopped fresh basil, or ½ teaspoon dried
1 tablespoon chopped fresh parsley
20 strands spaghetti, broken into 4 pieces
5 eggs
¼ cup freshly grated Parmesan cheese
½ cup shredded mozzarella cheese
¼ teaspoon freshly ground black pepper

1. Heat 1 tablespoon of the butter with the oil in a large heavy skillet over medium-low heat. Add the onion and garlic; cook 2 minutes. Add the tomato, bell pepper, sugar, vinegar, and ham. Cook, stirring occasionally, for 15 minutes. Then stir in the basil and parsley, and set aside to cool.

2. Drop the spaghetti into a large pot of boiling salted water. Stir once, and cook until tender, about 12 minutes. Drain thoroughly.

3. Meanwhile, preheat the broiler.

4. Beat the eggs in a large bowl. Stir in the cooled ham-vegetable mixture, the spaghetti, 2 tablespoons of the Parmesan, all the mozzarella, and the pepper. Mix well.

5. Heat the remaining 2 tablespoons butter in a heavy 10-inch skillet over medium heat. When the foam subsides, pour in the egg mixture and reduce the heat to low. Cook without stirring until the bottom of the mixture has set, 12 minutes. Sprinkle with the remaining 2 tablespoons Parmesan, and cook under the broiler until the top is set and lightly browned, about 1 minute.

Serves 4 to 6

SAUSAGE AND PEPPER FRITTATA

nother favorite rendering. Frittatas seem to be best when the ingredients are on the piquant side. The following can also be made any time you have leftover peppers and sausages.

3 sweet Italian sausages
2 tablespoons unsalted butter
1 large onion, thinly sliced
1 small red bell pepper,
    cored, seeded, and cut into
    strips
1 small green bell pepper,
    cored, seeded, and cut into
    strips

¼ teaspoon crushed dried hot
    peppers
Salt and freshly ground black
    pepper
5 eggs
1 tablespoon freshly grated
    Parmesan cheese

1. Sauté the sausages in a large heavy skillet over medium heat until well browned on all sides, 4 to 5 minutes. Cover, and cook over medium-low heat, stirring occasionally, for 8 minutes.

2. Transfer the sausages to paper towels to drain, and remove the excess grease from the skillet. Add 1 tablespoon of the butter, the onion, and the fresh and dried peppers. Cook, stirring constantly, over medium heat until the onions are lightly golden, about 4 minutes. Cover, and cook over low heat until the peppers are tender, about 5 minutes. Remove from the heat. Cut the sausages into slices and return them to the pepper mixture. Season to taste with salt and pepper.

3. Preheat the broiler.

4. Beat the eggs in a large bowl. Stir in the sausage-pepper mixture, and mix well.

5. Heat the remaining 1 tablespoon butter in the skillet over medium heat. When the foam subsides, pour in the egg mixture and reduce the heat to low. Cook without stirring until the bottom of the mixture has set, 12 minutes. Sprinkle with the Parmesan, and cook under the broiler until the top is set and lightly browned, about 1 minute.

Serves 4 to 6

P I P E R A D E

iperade is the frittata's Spanish cousin, dissimilar only in the choice of filling ingredients. For some elusive reason, most piperades contain shellfish, and they are stirred from time to time. The sea change (Mediterranean) makes for an arresting culinary adjunct to your brunch collection, no matter what the nationality.

3 tablespoons unsalted butter
1 onion, thinly sliced
2 small green bell peppers,
   cored, seeded, and cut
   into strips
3 tomatoes, peeled, seeded,
   and chopped
1 clove garlic, minced
1 teaspoon finely grated
   orange zest

Salt and freshly ground black
   pepper
1 pound shrimp, shelled and
   deveined
8 eggs
¼ cup heavy or whipping
   cream
Buttered toast

1. Melt the butter in a large heavy skillet over low heat. Add the onion and peppers; cook until tender but not brown, 6 to 8 minutes. Add the tomatoes, garlic, orange zest, and salt and pepper to taste. Cook, stirring occasionally, for 20 minutes. Then stir in the shrimp and toss for 1 minute.

2. Beat the eggs with the cream until light. Stir them into the skillet, and cook, stirring constantly, over low heat until the eggs are velvety in texture, 15 to 20 minutes. Serve immediately, with buttered toast.

Serves 6

A FLING WITH GOOD FOOD

Scotland: After publicly hankering after the taste of authentic Scottish food earlier this year, I was presented the opportunity to sample scones and shortbread on native soil recently—along with a slight, though not altogether unpleasing, handicap. *Ladies' Home Journal* invited me to pack a bag and junket through Scotland, to report on the current state of the Scots' ancient art: whisky making. Since I was permitted to eat as well as drink on this assignment, I accepted the chore with, if you will forgive the pun, decidedly high spirits.

Visiting distilleries in the Low- and Highlands of that remarkably green (if relatively unpopulated and untilled) countryside provided me with an insight into the Scottish national character as well as into the hundreds of years of tradition it takes to produce "a cup o' kindness." Whether it is served up neat, on the rocks, or sluiced with fresh lake water, excellent Scotch single-malt whisky is available everywhere, from the smallest thatched-roof pub to the poshest urban hostelry. Honest Scottish fare, on the other hand, is as hard to find as the Loch Ness monster.

It is there, just as the famed serpent may be, but it requires a pilgrim's diligence to scout it out. But one can hardly blame the Scots for that. After whisky, the country's second major industry is tourism; and since the palate of most travelers is so notoriously parochial, local foods have practically disappeared—except in small and relatively untraversed hamlets.

One such purlieu is the Highland town of Oban (OH-ben), where seagoing ferries shuttle back and forth to the Inner and Outer Hebrides and the scent of salt is so strong one can taste it on one's toothbrush in the morning. Oban is a holiday resort for the Scottish, but a visitor with an appetite for traditional local dishes—plus an eye for *ceilidhs* (KAY-leh, entertainment with bagpipers and folk-dancers)—would do well to pencil it into a travel itinerary.

The place to eat (and roister a wee bit if y'hae a mind to) is McTavish's Kitchen. A spare upstairs room overlooking the harbor, it is short on decor but long on clamorous good fellowship as well as plainly prepared good food. (Parenthetically, it is moderately priced, so one puts up with the din and simply dines with good grace.) The kitchen serves the best (brown) salmon trout and Loch Fyne kippers I uncovered anywhere. The latter are small herrings smoked over oak chip fires and then grilled to perfection. McTavish's is also notable for its haggis. This is a dish I had been warned about—a meat, innard, and oat pudding (the national specialty), usually steamed in a sheep's stomach. I found it surprisingly tasty and worthy of a return engagement any time I get back to Scottish shores. But the very best offering at McTavish's is the show: a constant parade of kilt-clad pipers, folksingers, Highland flingers, and even jigging children who perform as the clientele wash down the "bashed neeps" and "tatties" (turnips and potatoes) with cold Scotch and warm beer.

The audience at McTavish's is a raucous and photo-snapping lot, which I (the traveling masochist) assumed to be all fellow Americans. At the show's close, however, just before the crowd held hands and sang "Auld Lang Syne," we were asked to identify our nationalities. The noisiest and brashest turned out to be Scandinavians and Germans. Denizens of the U.S. (a scant ten or twelve aside from me) kept the lowest profile imaginable. Know why? They were all busy eating!

GIRDLE SCONES

~~~

Scones are a biscuit-muffin-roll much admired by the Scots. They come in as many varieties as the yellow gorse that covers the moors. The following recipe is for a scone made on a "girdle" (griddle).

2 cups sifted all-purpose flour	4 tablespoons (½ stick) unsalted butter, chilled, cut into small pieces
½ teaspoon salt	
2 teaspoons cream of tartar	⅔ cup heavy or whipping
1 teaspoon baking soda	cream

1. Sift the flour with the salt, cream of tartar, and baking soda into a large bowl. Gradually cut in the butter, blending it with a pastry blender until the dough resembles coarse meal. Then add the cream, and stir until the mixture has the texture of a soft dough. Do not overwork it.

2. Place the dough on a lightly floured board, and knead it briefly into a ball. Roll or press it out to form a circle ½ inch thick. Cut into 6 wedges.

3. Rub a cast-iron griddle or skillet with flour, and place it over medium-low heat for 5 minutes. Add 3 of the scones, and cook for 8 minutes per side. Reduce the heat if the scones cook too fast; they should be dark brown but not burned. Repeat with the remaining scones. Serve warm.

Makes 6 large scones

SCOTCH WHISKY CHICKEN

My favorite chicken dish is a union of crunchy meat and velvety mushrooms enveloped in a creamy and spirituous sauce. Scotch, of course.

1 chicken (about 3 pounds),
    cut into serving pieces
Juice of 1 lemon
3 strips thick bacon, diced
8 tablespoons (1 stick)
    unsalted butter
3 large shallots, finely
    chopped
½ cup all-purpose flour
1 teaspoon salt
½ teaspoon freshly ground
    black pepper
½ cup Scotch whisky

½ teaspoon sugar
½ cup dry white wine or
    vermouth
1 cup sliced mushrooms
½ cup homemade chicken
    stock or canned broth
½ cup heavy or whipping
    cream
2 tablespoons fresh lemon
    juice
2 egg yolks
Chopped fresh parsley, for
    garnish

1. Marinate the chicken pieces in the juice of 1 lemon for at least 1 hour.

2. Cook the bacon in boiling water for 1 minute; drain and pat dry on paper towels. Melt 7 tablespoons of the butter in a heavy skillet, and sauté the bacon and shallots until golden. Remove with a slotted spoon and set aside.

3. Combine the flour, salt, and pepper in a bowl. Remove the chicken from the marinade (reserve the marinade), and pat the pieces dry. Dust with the flour mixture, and sauté in the butter until golden on all sides, 3 to 4 minutes per side.

4. Warm the whisky in a small saucepan, and pour it over the chicken. Using a long match, carefully ignite the whisky. When the flame subsides, add the cooked shallots and bacon, the sugar and the wine, and the reserved marinade. Cover, and cook over medium-high heat, turning occasionally, until tender, 40 to 50 minutes. (If chicken begins to get too brown, reduce the heat.)

5. Meanwhile, melt the remaining 1 tablespoon butter in a small skillet over high heat, and sauté the mushrooms until golden, 4 to 5 minutes.

6. Transfer the cooked chicken to a heatproof serving platter, and cover it with the mushrooms. Keep the chicken warm in a low (225° F) oven while making the sauce.

7. Remove all but 1 tablespoon drippings from the skillet. Add the chicken stock and cook over high heat for 1 minute, scraping the sides and bottom of the pan. Stir in the cream and lemon juice; cook 2 minutes. Remove the skillet from the heat. Whisk ¼ cup of the sauce into the egg yolks, and then slowly beat this mixture back into the rest of the sauce. Cook over low heat, stirring constantly, for 2 minutes (do not boil). Pour the sauce over the chicken, garnish with the parsley, and serve.

Serves 4

S T .   B R I D E
S H O R T B R E A D

brought tins and tins of shortbread back from Scotland as souvenirs. The best keepsake of all, however, is the recipe itself. But judge for yourself.

1 cup (2 sticks) unsalted
   butter, at room
   temperature
½ cup sugar
1 egg yolk
2 tablespoons heavy or
   whipping cream

1½ teaspoons vanilla extract
¼ teaspoon grated orange zest
2½ cups all-purpose flour
½ cup rice flour

1. Preheat the oven to 325° F.

2. Beat the butter with the sugar in a large bowl. Beat in the egg yolk. Then add the cream, vanilla, and orange zest; mix well.

3. Combine the flours, and work them into the butter mixture with your fingers. Knead lightly and form into a ball.

4. Invert a 9-inch round cake pan; butter and flour the underside of the pan. Press the dough ball onto the surface to form a smooth 9-inch round. Sprinkle a baking sheet with flour; invert the dough onto the sheet, loosening it from the cake pan with a metal spatula if necessary. (Or make it in a shortbread mold if you have one.) Smooth the top, and press the edges decoratively with the tines of a fork. Bake for 10 minutes.

5. Remove the shortbread from the oven. Lightly score (⅛ inch deep) the shortbread into 8 to 12 wedges, using a pastry wheel or serrated knife. Return it to the oven and bake until the edges begin to brown, about 40 minutes. Cool on a wire rack.

Serves 8 to 12

AN INVITATION TO ROMANCE

*P*aris: Ever the vigilante of the American food scene, I note a trend in eating places across the nation to eschew the "Nouvelle Anonymous" dishes that have preoccupied chefs for over a decade in favor of much simpler, heartier fare—what I tend to think of as bistro food.

But then, to me *bistro* is the most aromatic word in the culinary vocabulary. Say *bistro* to anyone who's ever been to France and the free association will be unflaggingly the same: cramped quarters, dark smoky wood, frosted glass, and potted palms. In short, a clandestine, romantic hideaway in a very public place, where calories take the place of sex!

I must confess I never knew the privilege of this congenial consumption until I was past forty and in Paris for the first time. The bistro I was taken to was a Belle Epoque establishment named Chez Joséphine or Chez Pauline—not far from Montparnasse. And while I can no longer remember which Bonaparte lady the restaurant honored, I will never forget the food (so honest and so ample) and the wine (a Beaujolais so fresh it made me sneeze at the first sip)!

What I remember best of my first bistro is the clientele, an extraordinary cross-section of Parisian society: chic ladies, rough-and-tumble motorcyclists, and wan unisex couples. All of whom greeted each new arrival (coming from the kitchen or the street— with arias of breathy pleasure and what appeared to be a constant tableau of wine goblets held aloft. I did not speak the language well enough to understand their salutes at the time, but now I think that they rose and toasted one another with such frequency for one reason alone—to escape the searing calligraphy of the ancient and thorny bentwood chairs that pressed hard against both the shoulder blades and the knees. Certainly the marble-topped tables offered no accommodation for the rest of their bodies, as none was large enough to hold more than a third of the dishes that appeared (along with fresh carafes of wine) in endless relays from the moment one was seated.

This bistro's bill of fare was a scrawl of violet ink on blurry paper—as indecipherable as an Egyptian papyrus to me, so I ordered blindly. How I came to eat so well I will never understand, but the snowy plates were swabbed as clean at the end of the meal as they had been when the mustached *garçon* laid them out hours before. And the phenomenon seemed not unusual in the least, as platter after platter of intoxicating dishes—melting soups, gold-roasted birds with skins as crisp as tree bark, and pale, herb-scented veal stews whose perfume virtually took your breath away—were spooned, carved, and ladled forth to the hostelry's voracious customers.

That was my first bistro meal. There have been hundreds (perhaps thousands) eaten in the interval since. And while not every attempt at what the French call *la cuisine de famille* (familiar cookery) whets my tastebuds equally, I have never had a bad bistro meal yet.

I am knocking wood (the dark and smoky kind, of course) to keep the record unblemished.

VEAL IN A
GREEN SAUCE

ॐ

My favorite bistro food is stew; here's the recipe for the best one in my Francophile repertory. Serve it with rice, noodles, or over toast.

BOUQUET GARNI
1 bay leaf
Pinch of dried thyme
3 sprigs fresh parsley
1 scallion (green onion)
1 clove garlic, crushed

4½ tablespoons unsalted
  butter
3½ pounds boneless stewing
  veal, cut into 2-inch cubes
2 tablespoons all-purpose
  flour

¾ cup homemade chicken or
  veal stock or canned broth,
  heated
¾ cup dry white wine
1 teaspoon salt
½ teaspoon freshly ground
  black pepper
1½ pounds fresh spinach,
  rinsed
4 egg yolks
⅓ cup heavy or whipping
  cream

1. Place all the bouquet garni ingredients on a doubled square of cheesecloth, and tie it up to form a bag. Set it aside.

2. Melt the butter in a Dutch oven over medium heat. Add the meat and cook, stirring constantly with a wooden spoon, until all the pieces are coated with butter and have turned slightly golden, 5 to 6 minutes. Sprinkle with the flour; cook and stir 3 minutes longer. Add the hot stock, the wine, and the bouquet garni. Cook over medium-low heat for 45 minutes, turning the meat frequently. Stir in the salt and pepper.

3. Meanwhile, cook the spinach in boiling salted water for 1 minute. Rinse it immediately under cold running water, and drain. Press out all the liquid through a fine-mesh sieve, and chop coarsely.

4. Remove the bouquet garni from the Dutch oven, and stir the spinach into the meat. Beat the egg yolks with the cream; gradually stir into the Dutch oven over very low heat. Do not allow the mixture to boil. Cook, stirring, until the sauce is thick enough to coat a spoon, 3 to 4 minutes.

Serves 6

G A T E A U   B R E T O N

here are certain cakes I would willingly include in my last meal on earth. The following bistro meal-ending from Brittany is one of that variety. It is a dry vanilla-and-butter-flavored torte, very crumbly to the fork and so sensual it resembles an unexpected kiss. Can any confection offer a diner more?

1¼ cups (2½ sticks) unsalted
butter, at room temperature
¾ cup granulated sugar
1 egg
2 egg yolks
⅓ cup ground blanched
almonds

2 teaspoons kirsch
1½ teaspoons vanilla extract
1¾ cups all-purpose flour,
sifted
1 egg, lightly beaten
Confectioner's sugar
Fresh violets (optional)

1. Preheat the oven to 350° F. Butter a 9 x 1½-inch fluted tart pan with removable bottom; set it aside.

2. Beat the butter and the granulated sugar in a large bowl until light and fluffy. Add the egg and egg yolks, one at a time, beating well after each addition. Beat in the almonds, kirsch, and vanilla. Fold in the flour. Spoon the batter into the prepared tart pan, and spread it evenly. Brush with the beaten egg. Bake until the top is golden, about 30 minutes. Allow the tart to cool in the pan on a wire rack.

3. Remove the tart pan rim. Dust the cake lightly with confectioner's sugar, and decorate it with violets if desired.

Serves 8 to 10

Note: This cake improves in texture and flavor if allowed to stand at room temperature, covered, overnight.

*F*ort Worth: Cooking on TV may garner a cookbook author a few partisan fans across the nation, but the major residual, as far as I am concerned, is gray hair!

On a publicity tour of Texas I was booked to appear on four different television shows in a week, with a separate time allotment for each program ranging from two to twelve minutes.

What's the TV chef to do? Prepare a different dish on each program, obviously.

For the first show, a six-minute guest spot in Fort Worth, I decided to whip up an exemplary dessert that I dubbed "Impossible Pie." It takes less than two minutes to throw the ten ingredients into a blender; two more to whip them to a froth; and a scant ninety seconds longer to pour the mixture into a buttered pie plate and get it to an oven—where in the best of all possible worlds, the components bake to a gold-crusted, orange-scented coconut pie in an hour flat!

Minutes are no problem to a practiced TV cook, but the hour's baking time was thorny. After much deliberation, I concluded that the only way I could extract a finished pie from an oven was to bring one baked in advance. Transporting an Impossible Pie from Greenwich Village to Fort Worth required the cooperation of a sturdy cardboard box, a careful taxi driver, the ministrations of a lovely Delta flight attendant who dexterously strapped the confection into a seat belt, and the pilot who flew it to Texas without spilling a crumb.

A pie that crosses six state lines is only half the tale. At the TV studio the next day, there was yet another cliff-hanger. The producer, somehow expecting me to talk rather than cook, had provided only a low sofa and coffee table as props. Even half-baked, no pie could possibly be forthcoming from me in the lotus position, so a kitchen set had to be hastily improvised. The sound of hammering was still going on when the lights flashed ON THE AIR.

Tension was certainly palpable on that program. As there was no oven, my uncooked pie had to be lowered from countertop to a flimsy shelf below, where it dripped on my shoes, on my apron, and almost on the finished product, waiting to be proudly displayed. The New York–baked pie was finally held aloft, however, and then sliced, tasted, and pronounced perfect by a voluble host.

So why the gray hair, you ask? Well, as he chomped away, this interviewer turned and, looking me straight in the eye, inquired, "Did you-all *really* bake this de-licious pie this mornin'?"

I try to be a truthful cook always, but sometimes the flesh is weak. Before I could shake my head yea or nay, a satellite weather map happily replaced us both.

I M P O S S I B L E
P I E

〰〰

*T*he story has a sequel. At the San Antonio airport two days later, a distinguished gray-haired lady approached me at the baggage carousel. "Pardon me, sir." She smiled. "But there is something I have to know. Are you or are you not the man who made an Impossible Pie on TV in Fort Worth?" When I admitted I was, she absolutely beamed with delight.

"Wonderful! You see, I didn't have a pencil at the time. So just tell me those ingredients again . . ."

3 eggs
4 tablespoons (½ stick) unsalted butter, cut into bits
½ cup all-purpose flour
1 cup sugar
2 cups milk
¼ teaspoon salt

½ teaspoon baking powder
1 teaspoon vanilla extract
2 tablespoons orange liqueur
1 cup grated fresh coconut

1. Preheat the oven to 350° F. Lightly grease a 10-inch ceramic quiche pan or glass pie plate.

2. Place all the ingredients, in the order given, in a blender. Blend at low speed for 30 seconds, then at high speed for 2 minutes.

3. Pour the mixture into the prepared pie plate, and bake for 1 hour. Cool completely on a wire rack.

Serves 8 to 10

EATING IN 3-D

San Antonio: Having read and interpreted the signs and portents in the culinary wind for some time, I am about to make a small but sportive food prediction. The dish that is waiting in the wings for a full-scale prandial revival: *the triple-decker sandwich!*

Now, you may retort that the triple-decker has never left the food scene, but you would be wrong. A small survey of leading "gourmet deli's" and high-tabbed soda fountain–luncheonettes around the country revealed that sales of overstuffed sandwiches as a whole have been on a steady decline since the mid-1970s; and the sale of sandwiches based on heavy bread use (like the bespoke triple-decker) have plummeted even further in the '80s as lunching Americans opted for fitness over heavy duty feasting every time.

If that is the case, you are probably wondering, why a full-scale sand-wich revival now?

By and large, food fads and "trendy" dishes are cyclical. At the present time a whole new cadre of nutritionists, working in the field of complex carbohydrates, have come up with dietary programs for busy execu-tives that not only permit but actually insist on high starch consumption for two out of every three meals per day. That's one thing!

Another is the emotional charge of "comfort food" on our psyche.

I first suspected rumblings on the sandwich scene when Hellmann's–Best Foods held an informal "olympics" between top sandwich makers in New York last September. Every single entry in this "Deli Challenge" was a triple-decker!

On a more personal note, I was asked to architect and develop what was described as "the ultimate bacon, lettuce, and tomato sandwich" recently, as part of an urban renewal program in San Antonio, Texas.

To this southwestern city's credit, a private landmarks group, with local government support, has undertaken a massive project to upgrade and revitalize a somewhat seedy downtown area known as Houston Street. To kick off the rehabilitation of Houston Street, a huge three-story Art Deco Antique Sampler Mall opened not too long ago. One of the side-light attractions of the mall is a gorgeously overblown (1930s-style) luncheonette known as B.L.T.'s. My sandwich was designed to be its top-of-the-line offering.

When you glance at the recipe for this super-munch, you may suspect I went a little hog-wild. I won't deny it. Greene's B.L.T. is, for instance, a triple-decker served not on toast but rather on grilled home-baked whole-wheat batter bread. The sandwich's major upholstery is two kinds of bacon (Canadian-style and thick-cut too), layered with ripe tomato, crisp lettuce, and in Texas' honor, shavings of pickled jalapeño peppers.

WHOLE-WHEAT BATTER BREAD

🌀🌀🌀

1½ cups lukewarm water	1 teaspoon salt
1 package dry yeast	2 tablespoons unsalted
2 tablespoons honey	butter, at room
2 cups whole-wheat flour	temperature
1 cup all-purpose flour	

1. Place the water in the large bowl of an electric mixer. Sprinkle it with the yeast, and stir in the honey. Let the mixture stand until foamy, about 5 minutes.

2. On medium speed, beat in 1 cup of the whole-wheat flour, ½ cup of the all-purpose flour, the salt, and the butter. Beat 2 minutes, scraping the sides of the bowl often. On low speed, beat in the remaining 1 cup whole-wheat and ½ cup all-purpose flours. Cover with a tea towel, and let rise in the bowl in a warm place until doubled in volume, about 1 hour.

3. Meanwhile, grease a 9 x 5 x 3-inch loaf pan.

4. Stir the dough down by beating 25 strokes with a wooden spoon. Spread the dough in the prepared loaf pan, and cover it loosely with a flour-rubbed tea towel. Let it rise in a warm place until the dough reaches the top of the pan, about 1 hour.

5. Meanwhile, preheat the oven to 400° F.

6. Bake until the bread is golden brown and sounds hollow when tapped with your finger, about 30 minutes. Remove it from the pan and let it cool on a rack.

Makes 1 loaf

SUPER BACON, LETTUCE, AND TOMATO SPECIAL

*3 slices Whole-Wheat
Batter Bread, about
½ inch thick (see
page 209)
Unsalted butter, at room
temperature
1 to 1½ tablespoons best-
quality mayonnaise
1 pickled jalapeño pepper,
seeded, thinly sliced
lengthwise*

*3 slices Canadian bacon,
sautéed
2 large leaves Boston or
butter lettuce
1 small ripe tomato, thinly
sliced
2 strips thick bacon, fried
crisp*

Grill (or toast) the bread, and lightly butter the slices. Spread one
buttered side with mayonnaise. Arrange the jalapeño strips on the mayonnaise, and cover them with the Canadian bacon. Top with a second
slice of bread. Spread on more mayonnaise, then add the lettuce, tomato,
and finally, the bacon. Spread more mayonnaise over the top if desired,
and cover with the remaining bread slice.

Serves 1 hearty appetite

SPICES THAT GLOW IN THE DARK

St. Lucia: When things get really hot in my hometown, as they invariably do during the summer months, I bid all the local beach scenes (and the obligatory expressway gridlocks) a fond farewell . . . and make tracks for the blue Caribbean.

Why? Well, not to escape the heat, certainly, but to put it in its rightful place. For there is no place where I tan more evenly nor rewind with less emotional sweat than on a sparscly populated tropical island.

When I landed in St. Lucia several weeks ago, however, the first few hours in paradise appeared to be a mixed blessing. For starters, while the international airport in Vieux Fort is only forty miles from the capital city of Castries, the roads of St. Lucia are (to be kind) on the primitive side; so the trip, winding alternately through dense banana groves and along unexpected hairpin curves by the sea, took over an hour and a half to navigate. Moreover, when we arrived at the posh Cunard La Toc Hotel on a hundred acres of palmy shore, a power failure was in progress. All of Castries had been without electricity since noon. The tropical sun was setting fast, and the ice in the planter's punches that the thoughtful hotel management kept sending my way (as inner insulation) was melting even faster.

Now, if you think a New Yorker long accustomed to summer blackouts, brownouts, and beigeouts flips when the kilowatts kick over the traces in St. Lucia, you are dead wrong. He *dips* instead. This hotel sits practically at the water's edge, and even in the dark, the surf was easier to find than the bathtub's faucets. Oh yes, there is one other virtue to the absence of electricity: one may dine by candlelight without shaving, and no one is the wiser!

The fare at La Toc's elegant open-air dining rooms, and in most of St. Lucia in fact, is based on what the natives of the Caribbean island call "Creole cookery." A far cry from the Louisiana cuisine that goes by the same name, St. Lucia creole may have flourished under the kitchen stirrings of generations of French and English colonists, but the quintessential flavorings and unusual ingredients are purely local. And the culinary line goes straight back to the ancient Arawak and Carib Indians who settled this tiny archipelago between A.D. 200 and 400.

Like Martinique, which may be observed at the horizon line, and Grenada, its closest island neighbor, St. Lucia is a repository for most of the pungent spices that season Caribbean cookery. Nutmeg trees dot the landscape, and the brilliant scents of cinnamon, mace, and anise hang over the mountains at night like an exotic perfume.

Anywhere I go, my favored touch-down is the local marketplace on a Saturday morning. In St. Lucia, at the barn-red Central Market, the thermometer registers over one hundred degrees in the shade, but the sellers (from small farms and large plantations alike) do not seem to mind the heat. Under vast parasols, sucking long tubelike frozen "icicles" as they hawk their wares, they offer everything from mangoes and maubins (yellow-orange plumlike fruit) to baby goats for the night's dinner. Without a kitchen, I could only purchase food souvenirs: "red" garlic, bouquets of herbs, sticks of unsweetened rolled cocoa, West Indian limes, and vanilla pods still on the vine. Most of which, due to U.S. Customs restrictions, will never make the passage home. But what the heck! My luggage is imprinted forever with the fragrance of St. Lucia's cookery.

ST. LUCIA CHICKEN

〰〰〰

S t. Lucian cooks brown all fowl in a spicy golden caramel sauce that gives it a delectable flavor and an incredible hue. Serve rice alongside.

1 chicken (3½ to 4 pounds), cut into serving pieces	¼ teaspoon ground cumin
1 clove garlic, bruised	¼ teaspoon crushed coriander seeds
3 tablespoons sugar	¼ teaspoon ground turmeric
⅓ cup water	¼ teaspoon curry powder
1 rib celery, chopped	Salt and freshly ground black pepper
1 carrot, chopped	Chopped fresh parsley, for garnish
1 onion, chopped	
1 clove garlic, minced	
2 teaspoons chopped fresh parsley	
1 sprig fresh thyme, chopped	

1. Rub the chicken pieces well with the bruised garlic.

2. In a large heavy pot or Dutch oven, melt the sugar over medium-high heat, 5 to 6 minutes. When the sugar has melted and turned deep brown, reduce the heat to medium-low and slowly stir in the water. Stir until all sugar particles have dissolved, 2 to 3 minutes. Add the chicken to the pot, skin side down, in one layer. Then add the remaining ingredients through the curry powder. Cover, and cook for 15 minutes. Turn the chicken over, cover, and cook for another 15 minutes.

3. When the chicken is done, transfer it to a serving dish and keep warm. Boil the contents of the pot until slightly thickened, about 5 minutes. Add salt and pepper to taste. Pour the sauce over the chicken, sprinkle with the parsley, and serve.

Serves 4

BAKED PAWPAW

ॐ

awpaw is what St. Lucians call papaya, which is a tree melon of the passion-fruit family, and which I love passionately. The following recipe (which comes from a paperback cookbook sold on the island for the benefit of primary education in St. Lucia) calls for green papaya. I settled for unripe—and the dish was a hands-down winner in Manhattan!

2 strips bacon	3½ tablespoons unsalted
1 onion, chopped	butter
1 clove garlic, minced	Salt and freshly ground black
1 green bell pepper, cored,	pepper
seeded, and chopped	¼ cup fresh bread crumbs
1 medium tomato, peeled,	
seeded, and chopped	
1 unripe (or very firm)	
papaya, peeled, seeded,	
and cubed	

1. Preheat the oven to 400° F.

2. Sauté the bacon in a large skillet over medium heat until crisp. Remove the bacon with a slotted spoon, and drain it on paper towels. Crumble and set aside.

3. Add the onion to the bacon drippings; sauté 1 minute. Add the garlic, bell pepper, and tomato; reduce the heat to medium-low and cook for 5 minutes. Add the papaya and 2 tablespoons of the butter; cook for 3 minutes. Season with salt and pepper to taste, and transfer to a heatproof serving dish.

4. Melt the remaining 1½ tablespoons butter in a small skillet, and sauté the bread crumbs until golden, about 4 minutes. Spoon them over the papaya, and sprinkle with the bacon. Bake for 15 minutes.

Serves 6

CHILIED BANANAS IN ONION SAUCE

ॐ

long with cocoa beans and coconut, bananas are St. Lucia's chief export. They grow in rows on tall trees, with the fruit encased in bright blue polyethylene bags to protect it from insects and the like. This dish may be the banana's finest hour. Or its zestiest!

2 unripe bananas
2 tablespoons unsalted
  butter
1 teaspoon chili powder

1 medium onion, chopped
Juice of 1 large lime
Salt and freshly ground black
  pepper

1. Preheat the oven to 400° F. Peel the bananas and cut them in half crosswise; then cut them in half lengthwise.

2. Melt the butter in a large heavy skillet over medium-low heat. Stir in the chili powder and cook, stirring frequently, until it has dissolved. Raise the heat slightly, and sauté the bananas until lightly browned on both sides, 2 minutes per side. Transfer the bananas to an ovenproof serving dish.

3. Add the onion to the skillet and sauté until it is soft, about 5 minutes. Then add the lime juice, and salt and pepper to taste. Spoon the sauce over the bananas, and bake for 5 minutes. Serve immediately.

Serves 4

TRIAL BY FIRE

orning, New York: As a circuit-riding (or to be more accurate, jet-propelled) cooking teacher, I have stirred and sautéed at a heck of a lot of alien stoves in the line of duty. Some of the equipment encountered in my travels has been erratic, even makeshift at times, but I pride myself that I survive each new obstacle without complaint or cavil. And more to the point, always manage to whip up a passable soufflé in the process without undue egg on my face! Because that's what people pay hard cash to see all of us cooking teachers do: succeed in the kitchen without really trying.

As part of a seminar on American regional cuisine recently, Phillip Stephen Schulz (the bard of the barbecue) and I were prevailed upon to cook and teach at the open hearth of a Revolutionary-era kitchen fireplace. The event took place at the historic Benjamin Patterson Inn in Corning, New York. A museum restored to its original Spartan symmetry by the Corning Painted Post Historical Society to commemorate the Bicentennial of 1976, this inn is open to the public as a slice of late eighteenth- and early nineteenth-century life—including personnel garbed in homespun cotton and mobcaps.

Anachronistically, Greene and Schulz wore blue jeans rather than knee-britches beneath their aprons. But we did cook by candlelight.

Unsteadily, it must be noted, since the room was so thick with smoke from the wood fire that it was impossible to tell ingredients from utensils. Also, somewhat eccentrically, we were forced to teach from a prone position, as brick hearth cooking must be performed on bended knee.

The kitchen we taught in was large by colonial standards, but no quarters for the hundred students enrolled in the class. Of a consequence, dishes had to be prepared, then prepared again, in relays for twenty students at a time—all of whom held handkerchiefs pressed against their nasal passages as the fire was stoked, and restoked, expectantly.

Whipping up a dish from start to finish in approximately a quarter hour, and for a clutch of coughing standees whose only good view of the proceedings was the instructors' prominent rear ends, presented a real problem. The solution? Fast food, New England–style. Cheddar pancakes for me, mixed together quickly in the gloom and spooned awkwardly onto a swinging, sizzling griddle, inches above the coals. My partner Schulz opted for burnished shrimp, barbecued on an antique gridiron.

Speaking of fire, as we must, I will tell you my pancakes were only slightly singed in the translation from range top to open hearth. However, my helper—a lovely, utterly dedicated museum worker named Maxine—was almost immolated when a ruffle on one of her petticoats was set aflame by a stray bit of white-hot ash.

"Is there a fire extinguisher in the house?" I murmured in mute horror.

Maxine merely laughed and stamped on her skirt-end with a firm tread. "Not to worry," she said. "It happens all the time when you cook in a fireplace."

For the record, it was a great experience. But I have no plans for a return incendiary engagement.

C L O A K E D   S H R I M P

*T*his is a Phillip Schulz outdoor specialty, adapted from his book *Cooking with Fire and Smoke* for indoor cooking. What cloaks the shrimp? A spicy sauce dappled with a smidgen of bitter chocolate.

2 tablespoons unsalted butter or vegetable oil
1 large onion, finely chopped
¾ cup ketchup
¼ cup water
3 tablespoons Worcestershire sauce
3 tablespoons dark brown sugar
1 tablespoon distilled white vinegar

1 tablespoon tomato paste
¼ teaspoon dry mustard
Dash of hot pepper sauce
1½ tablespoons unsweetened cocoa powder
½ tablespoon unsalted butter, at room temperature
16 large shrimp, shelled and deveined
16 strips lean bacon, each 2½ inches long

1. Melt the butter in a medium-size heavy noncorrodible saucepan over medium heat. When the foam subsides, add the onion; sauté until soft, 5 to 6 minutes. Then add the ketchup, water, Worcestershire sauce, brown sugar, vinegar, tomato paste, mustard, and hot pepper sauce. Heat to boiling. Reduce the heat and simmer until thickened, about 20 minutes.

2. In a small bowl, combine the cocoa and the softened butter. Mash with the back of a spoon until a paste is formed. Add the paste to the barbecue sauce, and stir until smooth. Remove from the heat.

3. Dip each shrimp into the sauce, and arrange them on a plate. Let them stand for 20 minutes.

4. Meanwhile, preheat the broiler.

5. Wrap each shrimp in a piece of bacon, and place them on a broiler tray. Broil 4 inches from the heat until the bacon is crisp, about 4 minutes on each side. Serve immediately, accompanied by the remaining sauce.

Serves 4 as an appetizer

NEW ENGLAND "PANNYCAKES"

❧

*T*his recipe is a church supper entrée that makes a splendid brunch, lunch, or teatime item when other pickings are slim. Easy to make, they may be prepared in advance and reheated in a 350° F oven for 10 minutes prior to serving. I offer them with sour cream, and sometimes applesauce, on the side.

¼ cup coarsely grated mild Cheddar cheese
2 tablespoons all purpose flour
½ teaspoon baking powder
⅛ teaspoon ground allspice
½ teaspoon finely grated lemon zest
1½ tablespoons finely chopped fresh parsley

¼ teaspoon salt
Pinch of freshly ground black pepper
Pinch of cayenne pepper
½ cup sour cream
2 egg yolks
Sour cream, for serving
Chopped fresh chives, for garnish

1. Combine the cheese, flour, baking powder, allspice, lemon zest, parsley, salt, and peppers in a medium-size bowl. Toss well. Beat in the ½ cup sour cream and the egg yolks until smooth.

2. Lightly grease a cast-iron griddle or skillet, and place it over medium-high heat until hot but not smoking. Drop the batter onto the hot griddle by large tablespoonsful—no more than 4 at a time. When the surface bubbles, after 2 minutes, carefully turn the pancakes over with a spatula and let them cook for about 30 seconds to lightly brown the other sides. Transfer to a serving platter and keep warm while cooking the remaining cakes. Serve hot, with sour cream sprinkled with chives.

Serves 4

A SNAG IN YOUR DILLY?

COOK IT

Melbourne: Wandering around a greengrocer's or a supermarket in this city, the acknowledged epicurean hub of Australia, can be a totally mystifying experience to an able-bodied American cook. Even to one like myself, whose culinary wanderlust has led to many an alien checkout counter over the years.

Grocery shopping in Rome, Paris, Madrid, or even Moscow can be a breeze if you have a pointing finger on one hand and a useful phrase book in the other. Not so "down under," however, where things are seldom what they seem to be, according to the hand-lettered placards that adorn most of the merchandise for sale. To be specific: In an Aussie butcher shop, a chicken is always tagged a "chook," just as a sausage is known as a "snag." Worse yet for the uninitiated consumer, both are weighed off in kilos rather than pounds.

Browsing for foodstuffs in the famous indoor Prahan Market of Melbourne at 6:00 A.M.—the hour when the *fair dinkum* (really savvy) shoppers arrive to fill up their *dillys* (shopping bags)—I was utterly mystified by the unfamiliar names ascribed to ordinary run-of-the-mill comestibles. At least until my gastronomic guide, the estimable Australian cookbook author and teacher Beverly Sutherland-Smith, arrived to make the appropriate translations.

"It's reverse nationalism, actually," she explained. "Since Australians have only a borrowed cuisine, they tend to highly personalize ingredients. Often with slang. Probably so the rest of the world is forced to ask, 'Now what the devil is that?' "

It really is not too hard, once you get the hang of it, to think of peas as "pods," or a bunch of beets as "beetroot," or a rutabaga as a "swede," or even mushrooms as "mushies." But I draw the line at calling green onions "shallots," particularly when a peck of actual shallots within arm's reach are labeled "eschallots."

Australians also have the very odd notion that "pumpkin" is an umbrella name for every form of winter squash—whether it be a Hubbard, butternut, turban, or green acorn that comes to hand. Which probably explains why good old-fashioned pumpkin pie has never become a very popular dessert in this country!

Another curious indigenous ingredient, at least to my palate, is Australian tomato (always pronounced toe-MAH-toe) sauce. Unlike its rough-textured counterpart found in kitchens elsewhere, this stuff is a fairly liquid bottled condiment. Not ketchup, exactly; it's less spicy. But like enough so that Australians pour it indiscriminately over their burgers and chips (fries) the way their American cousins do ketchup.

When I was doing an in-store demonstration in this city recently, I requested a bottle of ketchup. It turned out to be Heinz. But when I added some to a sweet-and-sour sauce I was stirring up for avocados, its presence was greeted with smiles of polite derision.

"Why not use tomato sauce instead?" one watcher finally asked.

"Frankly, because I've never tasted the stuff," I replied.

"You should. I'll give you my mum's recipe," she said. And did, with the following postscript added: "This sauce can be very addictive. But it's a good drop of work. Perhaps you should sample the commercial variety as well."

I did. But as they say in Australia, even a *drongo* (fool) would know the winner!

AUSSIE-STYLE TOMATO SAUCE

This sauce must either be refrigerated or sealed and stored in sterilized glass jars.

12 large ripe tomatoes, peeled, seeded, and coarsely chopped
1 medium onion, chopped
1 clove garlic, chopped
1 cup malt vinegar
1½ tablespoons salt
2 teaspoons crushed allspice berries

½ teaspoon freshly grated nutmeg
½ teaspoon ground ginger
½ teaspoon ground cloves
1 teaspoon cayenne pepper
2 teaspoons baking soda
1 cup light corn syrup

1. Place the tomatoes, onion, and garlic in a large noncorrodible pot, and cook over medium heat, stirring often, until smooth, about 30 minutes. Cool slightly, then purée in a food processor or blender until smooth. Strain.

2. Return the strained mixture to the pot, and add all the remaining ingredients. Heat to boiling. Reduce the heat and cook over medium-low heat, stirring occasionally, for about 2 hours. The mixture should be thick and smooth. Cool slightly and refrigerate, or can in sterilized jars according to the manufacturer's directions.

Makes about 5 cups

JODY GILLIS'S SWEET-AND-SOUR AVOCADOS

*T*he most popular dish that I demonstrated in Australia is the following appetizer (which is known for some bizarre reason in that country as an entrée). The recipe comes from a good cooking friend from Santee, California, who now enjoys a certain culinary reputation across the Pacific as well. I always make Jody's avocados with ketchup, but any intrepid soul who is ready and able might be willing to put Aussie-Style Tomato Sauce to the ultimate test.

8 strips bacon	*¼ cup red wine vinegar*
4 tablespoons (½ stick)	*1 tablespoon soy sauce*
unsalted butter	*3 ripe avocados*
¼ cup sugar	*Juice of 1 lemon*
¼ cup ketchup	

1. Sauté the bacon strips in a heavy skillet until crisp. Drain on paper towels, crumble, and set aside.

2. Melt the butter in a small saucepan, and add the sugar, ketchup, vinegar, and soy sauce, stirring over low heat until the sugar dissolves, 2 to 3 minutes. Keep warm.

3. Cut the avocados in half lengthwise. Remove the pits, and sprinkle the flesh with the lemon juice.

4. Divide the crumbled bacon into six portions, and place some in each avocado cavity. Spoon the warm sauce evenly over the avocados, and serve immediately.

Serves 6

CUTTING THE MUSTARD

$\mathcal{S}$onoma County California: In California's wine country this spring, there is a haze of bright yellow plants, thick as hedges, growing among the unbudded grape vines. Even to an uneducated seedsman's eye, the foliage appears to be mustard.

As a wildflower, mustard has a slightly tangy scent that sets bees off their course. Its ferny stalks hold literally thousands of blooms, not unlike miniature buttercups, that turn street pavements and barn sides and everywhere else they alight bright gold, for the blossoms drop off like confetti.

Mustard is very familiar to me. I have fought this weed with hoe and trowel for most of my life, and I will testify that it has a root tenacity akin to crabgrass. So, I decided at first sight, the mustard I saw flowering in Sonoma County could not possibly have any relation to the mustard I flay in Amagansett. Since wine is a natural confederate in mustard-making, I reckoned it was some agricultural marriage made in heaven.

And I congratulated Sonoma's most distinguished resident, the writer M.F.K. Fisher, on the happy alliance in her backyard.

"Oh pooh!" the lady declared with a touch of asperity. "That is not the kind of mustard that will ever end up on a hot dog. It's wild mustard. Local growers decided that 'controlled' weed planting would make the best crop rotation for the soil of the root stock. So now we have wild mustard, *everywhere!*"
"It's pretty . . ." I said lamely.
"Pretty dumb," announced my friend Mary Frances. "Because I'll tell you a secret: wild mustard is uncontrollable."

The kind of mustard plants that grow on the hills of Dijon (where M.F.K. Fisher spent many fruitful years) produce pungent seeds when their petals fall. Crushed and steeped with vinegar, oil, sour must of wine, and seasonings, these seeds transform into the most intoxicating unguent known to the human tongue. Wild mustard, however, just produces more wild mustard.

"But both plants *do* look alike," M.F.K. Fisher allowed. "Some years ago, I had a funny experience on a train from Burgundy to Paris. I was seated behind two highly prejudiced American lady tourists who had not one good word to say about the French. They hated French food, and detested French wine, and mistrusted all Frenchmen too. At one point, the more opinionated of the two pointed out the window, where the famed mustard fields of Dijon were in full golden bloom. 'Look at that,' she cried. 'Isn't that typical of the French mentality—to allow good farmland to go to waste, growing nothing but wild mustard!' I never said a word. So I guess they spent their lives believing in the profligacy of the French!"

If there's a moral to be gleaned from all this, perhaps it is that we shouldn't judge the profligacy of wild mustard in a vineyard either—at least until the grapes are harvested.

MINCED BEEF DIJON-STYLE

❧

*W*hat you will need for this dish—aside from good Dijon mustard and white wine—is some leftover pot roast or roast beef. This dish is *not* hash, but it *is* heavenly.

5 small baking potatoes
3 tablespoons unsalted
* butter*
2 tablespoons Dijon mustard
2 cups minced onions
1 pound leftover cooked
* pot roast, thinly*
* sliced and chopped*
* (about 2 cups)*

1 clove garlic, minced
Pinch of ground allspice
Salt and freshly ground black
* pepper*
1½ tablespoons red wine
* vinegar*
¼ cup dry white wine
Chopped fresh parsley, for
* garnish*

1. Cook the potatoes in boiling salted water until just tender, about 15 minutes. Rinse under cold running water until cool, and drain. Cut into ¼-inch-thick slices.

2. Melt the butter in a large heavy skillet over medium-low heat. Stir in the mustard, and then the onions. Cook, stirring occasionally, until the onions are tender, about 10 minutes. Lightly toss in the potatoes.

3. Add the meat to the potato mixture. Sprinkle with the garlic and allspice, rubbing the seasonings into the meat with a knife. Cook, tossing gently, for 10 minutes. Add salt and pepper to taste, and sprinkle with the vinegar and wine. Continue to cook for 3 to 4 minutes. Sprinkle with parsley, and serve.

Serves 6

MUSTARD BAKED SHRIMP

ᗡᗒᏩ

Another Francophile specialty, this makes a welcome first course when the mustard is Dijon and the wine a Sonoma sauvignon blanc. The French bake this dish in scallop shells, but any ovenproof ramekins will do.

3 tablespoons unsalted butter
2 tablespoons all-purpose
   flour
1 cup milk, heated
⅛ teaspoon freshly grated
   nutmeg
Pinch of cayenne pepper
½ teaspoon salt
¼ teaspoon freshly ground
   black pepper
1½ tablespoons minced
   shallots

2 tablespoons chopped fresh
   parsley
¼ cup dry white wine
3 tablespoons Dijon mustard
1 small egg yolk
1¼ pounds small shrimp,
   shelled and deveined
2 tablespoons freshly grated
   Parmesan cheese

1. Preheat the oven to 450° F.

2. Melt 2 tablespoons of the butter in a heavy saucepan over low heat. Stir in the flour; cook, stirring constantly, for 2 minutes. Whisk in the hot milk. Add the nutmeg, cayenne, salt, and pepper. Cook, stirring occasionally, for another 10 minutes.

3. Melt ½ tablespoon of the butter in a skillet. Add the shallots; cook over medium heat for 1 minute. Add the parsley and wine; cook over high heat until almost all the wine has evaporated, 2 to 3 minutes.

4. Add the shallot mixture to the sauce, and cook for 5 minutes. Remove the pan from the heat, and stir in 1½ tablespoons of the mustard and the egg yolk; set the pan aside.

5. Wipe out the skillet the shallots were sautéed in, and add the remaining ½ tablespoon butter. Sauté the shrimp over medium heat, stirring constantly, until they turn pink, about 3 minutes. Stir in the remaining 1½ tablespoons mustard. Remove from the heat and add one third of the sauce.

6. Divide the shrimp mixture among 4 ramekins or scallop shells; spoon equal amounts of sauce over the shrimp. Sprinkle ½ tablespoon cheese over each. Bake until bubbly and light brown, 12 to 15 minutes. Let stand for 5 minutes before serving.

Serves 4

RECIPES FROM BEEF COUNTRY

Bismarck: I have just tied a strip of genuine cowhide 'round my finger to remind myself *never* to accept the honor of judging another food contest in the fall—unless it happens to take place in a warm climate!

I came to Bismarck, North Dakota, from New York, where the temperature was unseasonably torpid (in the high eighties), only to discover that the first snowfall had already descended upon North Dakota. While most of the community was sensibly attired in windbreakers and parkas, judges from the Northeast (like me) were still wearing safari suits. Aside from the weather, however, my trip to "the Badlands" was the most fun I've had since a recent visit to Disneyland, for the hospitality of cattlemen in general, and the CowBelles (their wives, who sponsor the National Beef Cook-Off along with the Beef Industry Council) in particular, is legendary. As tenderfoot tourists we were treated to a "Whoop-Up Wingding"; a livestock auction; a "pitchfork beef fondue"—and more prime beef than I can remember chomping at one clip since the day when meat rationing ended after World War II.

For me, acting as judge at this tenth annual event was more rewarding then being one of the top money winners, for I got to sample some extremely inventive recipes submitted by contestants from forty-eight states, each hoping to become the nation's number-one amateur beef chef.

Rules required the entrants to submit recipes using only economical cuts of meat: chuck, round, rump, brisket, plate, shank, or ground beef. After tasting each dish, I must confess a higher regard for the future of American ingenuity than ever before!

The prize-winners, selected by a panel of dedicated food editors, TV personalities, and columnists, were rated on taste, appearance, originality, ease, and practicality. It was not easy to select a winner, and an awful lot of soda water, black coffee, and apple slices (for cleansing the palate) were consumed while we "beefed" over which dish would take the honors. Cash prizes totaling $10,000 were awarded to the three top finalists and five honorable mentions, so you will understand why the deliberations took eight hours to come up with the 1983 champion. With no lunch break, either!

During the course of endless samplings, I was very often drawn to dishes that did not pass muster (even as runners-up) because of some odd, hard-to-find ingredient or curious cooking crotchet on the part of the contestant. Therefore, as a minority report, I am saluting not only the top winner (for a highly unusual version of *steak au poivre* made with round steak in lieu of sirloin) but two other entries that neither won, placed, nor showed anything except a darn good idea for beef cookery.

These recipes are a residual of the Tenth Annual National Beef Cook-Off in Bismarck. Along with an unanticipated souvenir: the worst cold I have had in years!

EMILE J. FERRARA'S "TOP ROUND AROMATICA"

〰〰

Mr. Ferrara, an art instructor from Bristol, Rhode Island (and the second male to win the National Beef Cook-Off), took top prize for a pan-broiled creation that can be whipped up in 30 minutes flat.

1 beef top round steak, 1 inch thick (2 pounds)
1 tablespoon black peppercorns, crushed
1 tablespoon unsalted butter
1 small clove garlic, crushed
1 tablespoon vegetable oil
¼ cup dry red wine

2 tablespoons cognac
½ cup heavy or whipping cream
2 tablespoons chopped fresh parsley
Salt
Chopped fresh parsley, for garnish

1. Pat the meat dry with paper towels.

2. Combine the peppercorns, butter, and garlic in a small bowl; mix well. Spread this evenly over both sides of the steak.

3. Heat the oil in a heavy skillet over medium-high heat. First brown the edges of the steak; then cook until well browned on both sides, about 4 minutes per side for medium-rare. Transfer the steak to a serving platter; keep warm.

4. Add the wine and cognac to the skillet, and cook over high heat for 1 minute. Reduce the heat, stir in the cream and 2 tablespoons parsley, and cook for 2 minutes. Season with salt to taste.

5. Carve the steak on the diagonal, and spoon the sauce over the top. Garnish with parsley, and serve.

Serves 4 to 6

"*BEEF STIK SNAX*," *TEX-MEX-STYLE*

he original version of this non-winning dish, submitted by Thelma Herbert of Ohio, served the tender-fried beef strips with a sauce of packaged onion soup and sour cream. The judges nixed it. On my own, I substituted salsa, added tortillas and shredded lettuce, and came up with a Tex-Mex kitchen winner!

1 pound beef top round steak
¼ cup ground almonds
¼ cup all-purpose flour
1 teaspoon chili powder
½ teaspoon seasoned salt
*¼ teaspoon freshly ground
   black pepper*
Pinch of dried oregano

½ cup vegetable oil
½ cup sour cream
½ cup prepared tomato salsa
*1 teaspoon chopped fresh
   cilantro (Chinese parsley)*
*8 to 10 flour tortillas,
   warmed*
Shredded iceberg lettuce

1. Using a fork, pierce the steak on both sides at ½-inch intervals. Cut it into 3 x ½ x ½ -inch strips.

2. Combine the almonds, flour, chili powder, seasoned salt, pepper, and oregano in a shallow bowl. Mix well. Roll the beef strips in this mixture so that they are well coated.

3. Heat the oil in a heavy skillet. Sauté the meat strips over medium heat, a few at a time, about 30 seconds per side. Keep warm.

4. Combine the sour cream, salsa, and cilantro in a bowl.

5. To serve, place a few beef strips on a tortilla. Spoon some of the sour cream sauce over the top, sprinkle with shredded lettuce, and roll up.

Serves 4

PLUM GOOD
BEEF BRISKET

ଓচে

*T*he following fruity dish, submitted by Katharine Moss of South Carolina, was ankled out by the second-prize winner (a traditional tzimmes pot roast from Vermont). Miss Moss used only a plum sauce to season the finished dish. With a deep bow to the creator, I added some meat juices as well. It's plum better!

¼ cup soy sauce
1 medium-size onion, sliced
1 beef brisket (2½ to 3 pounds)
2 cans (16 ounces each)
  purple plums
2 tablespoons honey
2 tablespoons fresh lemon
  juice
3 tablespoons fresh orange
  juice

2 tablespoons sugar
½ teaspoon Worcestershire
  sauce
¼ teaspoon grated orange zest
¼ teaspoon ground cinnamon
Chopped fresh parsley, for
  garnish

1. Preheat the oven to 350° F.

2. Place the soy sauce in a small skillet, and sauté the onion in it until tender, about 5 minutes.

3. Place the meat in a Dutch oven, fatty side down, and pour the onion mixture over it. Drain the plums, and add all but ¼ cup of the syrup to the Dutch oven. Cover, and bake until tender, about 2 hours.

4. Meanwhile, force the plums through a sieve into a medium-size saucepan. Add the reserved ¼ cup syrup and the honey, lemon juice, orange juice, sugar, Worcestershire sauce, orange zest, and cinnamon. Bring to a boil. Reduce the heat and simmer for 10 minutes.

5. Just before serving, stir ¼ cup of the cooking juices into the plum sauce. Spoon some of the sauce over the meat, and sprinkle with parsley. Pass the remaining sauce.

Serves 6

I DON'T MEAN TO CRAB, BUT...

San Francisco: I love San Francisco, even though a lot of very strange culinary goings-on take place there from time to time. Like what? Well, like chocolate-covered garlic buds, blue corn sorbet, and cactus salad, for starters. I could name more but I won't, because I *do* love the place.

However, there is one San Franciscan tradition of which I heartily approve, and that's the Annual Crab Festival held on Pier 39, adjacent to Fisherman's Wharf and smack across the water from Alcatraz Island.

I hold the Crab Festival (which is actually a crab cooking competition) in very high esteem. Although in all candor, I must admit that the bulk of my admiration is reserved for the panel of gastronomic stalwarts who taste and select the winning entries (or entrées) rather than the teams of bright-faced chefs who prepare them. Why? Out of sheer, undying empathy. Because I was once a judge at the crab olympiad myself, a few years back, and my alimentary canal has never been quite the same since!

The sequence of the contest is, at this writing, a kind blur, but I recall that I was exhorted to fly from New York, with all expenses paid and the promise of some "extraterrestrial crab cuisine!" Which proved to be an accurate assessment.

The actual judging took place in an elegantly appointed room. As the panelists were ushered in, we were teamed up in pairs by a random selection of names chosen from two baskets.

I was paired with a portly writer from Seattle. Together, equipped with pencils and forks, we worked our way through the room, tasting twenty-nine variously seasoned versions of spiced crab in half an hour.

My partner watched as I sampled the first.

"Like it?"
"Not really. Too bland."

He narrowed his eyes. "Have you ever judged one of these food contests before?"
"Never." I shook my head.
"Well." He looked sage. "Don't low-rate that dish until you taste at least ten or twelve others. You'll be surprised how delicious it will seem in retrospect."

He was dead right, of course. After Spiced Crab I was assigned a new partner and another category: Chef's Choice, dishes that ran the culinary spectrum from crab pie to nouvelle crab fingers. One entry, a warm porringer of Dungeness crab swimming in cream and cheese, particularly struck my taste buds. I was about to slurp a second helping when my partner (the food editor of a large newspaper) whispered, "Stop!" She took my arm firmly. "Aside from the calories in that dish—which frankly, my dear, you do not need—it will make you sick!"

I wish I'd heeded her advice, but I did not. Instead I licked the spoon and then volunteered to judge the twenty-five remaining Crab Louis salads on my own. Speak of gastronomic collision courses!

When the winners were finally tallied, called in, and toasted, every jurist but one raised a tulip of Champagne. I, greener than my name, made my congratulatory sip with Alka Seltzer.

S P I C E D   C R A B

❧

*T*he spiced crab entry from Chef Mario Rotti of Princess Cruises won the grand prize (Maître Chef de Cuisine), and it deserved every kudo it received.

1¼ pounds king crab legs, cooked

3 tablespoons white wine vinegar

1½ tablespoons English dry mustard

½ cup dry bread crumbs

1 small clove garlic, minced

¼ teaspoon dried oregano

½ teaspoon hot pepper sauce

¼ teaspoon salt

¼ teaspoon freshly ground black pepper

1 teaspoon chopped fresh parsley

½ cup (1 stick) unsalted butter, melted, for serving

1. Preheat the oven to 400° F. Lightly butter an ovenproof serving dish.

2. Using sharp heavy scissors, carefully cut the crab legs lengthwise, trying not to pierce the meat. Remove the crabmeat in one piece. Cut it into 2-inch-long segments.

3. Combine the vinegar and mustard in a small bowl, and mix well.

4. Combine the bread crumbs, garlic, oregano, hot pepper sauce, salt, pepper, and parsley in a medium-size bowl. Mix thoroughly.

5. Lightly coat the crab pieces with the vinegar-mustard mixture, then roll them in the bread-crumb mixture. Arrange the crab pieces in the prepared baking dish, and bake for 10 minutes. Serve with melted butter on the side.

Serves 4 as an appetizer

CRABMEAT AU GRATIN

C rab au gratins come and go, but you will never taste a better version than the following handiwork of L.A. chef Raymond Marshall.

2 tablespoons unsalted butter
¼ cup chopped scallions
   (green onions)
1 small clove garlic, minced
4 ounces mushrooms,
   sliced
1 teaspoon chopped fresh
   cilantro (Chinese parsley)
¼ teaspoon freshly ground
   white pepper
1¼ cups crème fraîche
   (see Note)

2 tablespoons unsalted
   butter, at room
   temperature
1 tablespoon all-purpose
   flour
1 pound cooked crabmeat
½ cup coarsely grated
   Monterey Jack cheese
2 tablespoons freshly grated
   Parmesan cheese

1. Melt the butter in a medium-size saucepan over medium heat. Stir in the scallions; cook 1 minute. Add the garlic, mushrooms, and cilantro. Cook, stirring often, for 5 minutes. Then stir in the white pepper and the crème fraîche.

2. Mix the softened butter with the flour in a small bowl until smooth. Stir this into the crème fraîche mixture, and simmer over medium heat until thickened, about 4 minutes.

3. Meanwhile, preheat the broiler.

4. Stir the crabmeat into the crème fraîche mixture. Cook over medium-low heat, stirring occasionally, until the crab is heated through, about 8 minutes.

5. Transfer the crab mixture to a 1-quart casserole or individual ramekins. Sprinkle with both cheeses, and cook under the broiler until lightly browned, 45 seconds. Serve immediately.

Serves 4 to 6

Note: Crème fraîche is available (at a steep price) in most fancy food shops. However, you can make your own: Combine 1¼ cups heavy cream with 2 teaspoons buttermilk (do not use ultra-pasteurized for either), and heat until lukewarm (90° F). Pour into a sterilized jar, leaving the top loose. Cover with a towel, and let stand until thickened, 10 to 12 hours in warm weather, 20 or more in cold. Store, tightly covered, in the refrigerator. It will keep for about 2 weeks.

BERT ON BERT

CHAPTER FIVE

DEAR BERT MAIL

am an assiduous letter writer and an equally devoted recipient of mail. As a small child, I used to affix my name to every advertising coupon and circular that appeared in my mother's consignment of monthly magazines, just to encourage an active correspondence. And the postman on our Humphrey Street route (in Queens) not only rang twice—he got to know my name very, very well from the intense volume of replies.

In later life fan letters, happily, take up the slack. I cannot speak for any other recipe givers 'round town, but Greene's mailbox on West Twelfth Street fairly bulges with a wealth of letters weekly.

Needless to say, I answer them all. Although to be truthful, missives from public relations firms truly test my letter-writing mettle. Not long after I wrote about my predilection for using a splash of Coca Cola in cookery, I was approached by four separate flackpersons, ostensibly complimenting me on my "foray into *new wave* cuisine" but wishing heartily that I would be tempted to take similar recipe flyers with such diverse ingredients as 7-Up, frozen yogurt, apple juice, and domestic Champagne.

Most of the letters I receive are compliments for the chef. Sometimes, however, something written stirs a reader's memory. The following (edited) note and answer speak for themselves.

Dear Mr. Greene,

Your tribute to teacher Dione Lucas brought to mind a very brief, happy encounter. Over twenty years ago, I worked on the TV production of *Omnibus*. During the Christmas season, they presented a segment of famous people doing their thing with toys—an architect built a bridge with a child's erector set; a band leader used toy instruments, etc. I do not remember most of their names, but I do remember Dione Lucas because during rehearsal, she made little mushroom omelets which she offered to a fortunate crew. The taste was so incredibly delicious that all I could do was stare in awe at this lovely lady standing on stage cooking at a toy stove . . . thinking she must be a magician.

Ever since I have always looked through cookbooks—hoping to find her recipe for those omelets. Perhaps you might be able to give me one since you worked so closely with her.

R.D.
Westbury, New York

Dear Miss D.,

I knew Dione Lucas's omelet repertoire very well. Unfortunately, my close relationship with the lady took place almost thirty years ago—so my memory is not as green as I would wish.

She was my first (and only) teacher, and the recipe for a classic unfilled omelet that I teach today is the one she taught me.

Mushroom filling I remember well as to ingredients. The proportions may be slightly off, but I don't think so. Dione was a strong believer in lemon juice as a flavoring, with the liquid almost absorbed in the cookery but the wonderful bouquet intact.

Try this devise. I hope it strikes your verdant memory.

Bert Greene

P.S. I think Dione sprinkled her mushroom omelet with chopped parsley too!

DIONE LUCAS'S MUSHROOM OMELET

4 ounces mushrooms

4 tablespoons (½ stick) unsalted butter

1 tablespoon finely chopped shallot

1 teaspoon fresh lemon juice

4 eggs

2 tablespoons cold water

Salt and freshly ground black pepper

1 teaspoon unsalted butter, at room temperature

Chopped fresh parsley, for garnish

1. Reserve 2 unblemished mushroom caps. Cut the remaining mushrooms into ⅛-inch-thick slices.

2. Melt 3 tablespoons of the butter in a small skillet over medium-low heat. Add the shallot; cook 1 minute. Raise the heat slightly, and add the sliced mushrooms and reserved caps. Sauté until lightly golden, about 4 minutes. Stir in the lemon juice, and cook 2 minutes longer. Remove the skillet from the heat. Set the mushroom caps aside.

3. Beat 2 of the eggs with 1 tablespoon of the cold water in a large mixing bowl until frothy. Add half the sliced mushroom mixture.

4. Place an omelet pan (I prefer nonstick) over medium-high heat until hot. (When the pan is ready, a speck of water dropped in the center will sizzle.) Add 1½ teaspoons butter. When the foam subsides, tilt the pan to coat the bottom and sides with butter. Stir in the egg mixture and scramble vigorously two or three times until the eggs barely set. Sprinkle with salt and pepper to taste. Turn the omelet out onto a warm serving plate and dot it with ½ teaspoon of the softened butter. Decorate with 1 reserved mushroom cap.

5. Repeat the process with the remaining eggs and mushrooms. Sprinkle both omelets with parsley before serving.

Serves 2

SARAH ECKSTEIN'S CINNAMON CAKE

❦❦❦

When I noted in print some while back that what I truly longed for was a recipe similar to my mother's buttery two-egg cake, the mail trebled. From the onslaught, have this flavorsome benefi-cence. The recipe was sent by Mrs. Sarah Eckstein. The cake was her mother's formula and, while nothing like my parent's creation, is a prize-winner quite on its own. Mrs. Eckstein has kindly allowed me to share it with you.

8 tablespoons (1 stick) unsalted butter, at room temperature	3½ teaspoons baking powder ⅛ teaspoon salt
½ cup plus 2 tablespoons sugar	1 cup milk 1 teaspoon vanilla extract
2 eggs	½ teaspoon ground cinnamon
2¼ cups sifted all-purpose flour	

1. Preheat the oven to 350° F. Grease and flour a 9-inch springform pan. Set aside.

2. Beat the butter in a large mixing bowl until light and fluffy. Slowly beat in ½ cup sugar. Then add the eggs, one at a time, beating thoroughly after each addition.

3. In a medium-size mixing bowl, sift the flour with the baking powder and salt. Combine the milk and vanilla in another bowl. Add the flour mixture to the butter mixture in thirds, alternating with thirds of the milk mixture. Pour the batter into the prepared springform pan.

4. Combine the remaining 2 tablespoons sugar with the cinnamon and sprinkle over the batter. Bake until a toothpick inserted in the center comes out clean, about 45 minutes. Cool completely on a wire rack before releasing the pan.

Serves 8 to 10

AND NOW FOR AN ENCORE...

Will Rogers once declared that "leftovers are the kind of foods that are here today—and here tomorrow, too!"

Speaking for myself, I disagree. I believe the reason that most leftovers are held in such ill contempt is the name alone. For a *leftover* implies a mess of undesired (and certainly unlamented) victuals to most diners. Webster defined the word in even less appetizing terms. He dubbed leftovers "unused remnants," aligning them with other "stumps, butts, and parings." And plainly nothing to work up an appetite over!

As a longtime lover of kitchen remnants, however, I warrant that Mr. Webster never tasted a skillet of properly seasoned roast beef hash, or thrust a fork into a golden-crumbed chicken croquette, before he made that evaluation.

Old prejudices die hard—in and out of the oven. And bad names only get worse.

If I were a public relations man, I would propose an extensive campaign to upgrade the leftover image and emancipate them from pejorative associations. As I am not, I will simply suggest a new moniker instead: *redivivus*.

You must admit it's classy, and Latin into the bargain. More to the point, it means *having a new life or being restored*. And that's the best thing anyone can ever say about a leftover.

The redivivus I have in mind is a culinary union: the stuffing of tender cabbage leaves with chopped "unused remnants" of pork and ham.

Besides its brand-new name, this is a very special treat. Unlike most Middle European cabbage dishes you are used to, this one comes from France. It cooks in a mere 30 minutes and is blanketed with a creamy horseradish sauce.

To produce *Chou Farci* for tomorrow night's dinner, however, you must dine on roast pork tonight!

From Greene's copious collection of *rôti*, here's the formula for one of my favorites. This dish, to be utterly truthful, is the very first roast of pork I attempted when I was a young kid in the kitchen. I cannot even remember the original culinary source, but I have made it so often and with such gratifying results that I tend to think of it as mine alone. The secret (for those cooks into secrets) is the topping of chopped fresh vegetables that keep it both moist and aromatic at one and the same time.

Enjoy it with my benediction and the knowledge that the next night's dinner will be *even better*.

CARAWAY ROASTED LOIN OF PORK

ᗺᗺᗺ

Caraway seeds and roast pork are a match made in culinary heaven. Be sure that your seeds are fairly fresh—they lose their fragrance quickly once out of the jar.

1 pork loin roast (4 pounds; see Note)
1 clove garlic, crushed
Salt and freshly ground black pepper
¼ cup Dijon mustard
4 tablespoons (½ stick) unsalted butter

1 onion, coarsely chopped
1 carrot, coarsely chopped
3 tablespoons caraway seeds
1 sprig fresh thyme, or ¼ teaspoon dried

1. Preheat the oven to 350° F.

2. Tie the roast with string, and pat it dry with paper towels. Rub the entire roast well with the garlic, and with salt and pepper to taste. Spread the mustard evenly over the top and sides. Place the roast on a rack in a roasting pan.

3. Melt the butter in a small skillet over medium-low heat, and sauté the onion and carrot until soft, 8 to 10 minutes. Spoon the vegetables over the roast. Sprinkle it with the caraway seeds, and lay the thyme sprig on top. Roast for 2 hours (30 minutes per pound), basting with the pan juices every 15 minutes. Let the roast stand for 15 minutes before carving and serving.

Serves 4 to 6

Note: For easier carving, have your butcher cut through the shin bone.

CHOU FARCI

W hat puts the savor in a plate of *chou farci?* A mystery ingredient sprinkled on the green envelopes just before they gently poach—namely, a little whiff of gin.

2 cups chopped leftover
  cooked pork
4 ounces sliced boiled ham,
  chopped (about 1 cup)
1½ cups cooked rice
1 small onion, finely
  chopped
1 clove garlic, minced
1 tablespoon finely chopped
  fresh dill
⅛ teaspoon ground allspice
⅛ teaspoon freshly grated
  nutmeg
¼ teaspoon hot pepper sauce
2 eggs, lightly beaten

Salt and freshly ground black
  pepper
1 medium-size Savoy
  cabbage, leaves separated
2 cups homemade chicken
  stock or canned broth
1 tablespoon dry gin
2 teaspoons unsalted butter
2 teaspoons all-purpose flour
1 teaspoon prepared
  horseradish
1 egg yolk
¼ cup heavy or whipping
  cream
Fresh dill sprigs, for garnish

1. Combine all ingredients through the 2 eggs in a large bowl, and mix well. Add salt and pepper to taste, and set aside.

2. Cook the cabbage leaves in boiling salted water just until slightly wilted, about 1 minute. Drain.

3. Place ⅓ to ½ cup of the filling on each leaf (depending on the size of the leaf), and roll up the leaf, tucking the edges underneath. Arrange the rolls in a skillet or heavy saucepan large enough to hold them in a single layer. Add the chicken stock, sprinkle with the gin, and bring to a boil. Reduce the heat, cover, and simmer until tender, about 30 minutes.

4. Using a slotted spoon, remove the cabbage rolls; keep them warm, covered, in a low (225° F) oven. Raise the heat under the cooking liquid, and boil it for 3 minutes. Reduce the heat to low.

    5. Mash the butter with the flour in a small bowl until smooth. Stir this into the sauce. Add the horseradish, and cook until the sauce is slightly thickened, 4 to 5 minutes. Combine the egg yolk with the cream, and stir into the sauce. Cook until warmed through, about 1 minute; do not boil. Spoon the sauce over the cabbage, top each roll with a sprig of dill, and serve.

    Serves 6

JUST PLAIN BERT

*E*ver hear of a culinary busybody? No? Well, I guess I am the prototype, for I have been nosy all my life! When I was younger, my parents rationalized this trait as "the burden of an inquiring mind." I think they assumed I would write famous novels someday, although I was, as Christopher Isherwood so nicely put it, merely "a camera with its shutter open, quite passive, recording but not thinking."

When the long-awaited tomes did not materialize, they put my overweening curiosity down to some genetic flaw.

"He takes after your side of the family," my father would fulminate darkly. "Always wanting to know what is none of his business."
"My family? Your family!" My mother would shrug. "Let's face it—the kid is a *buttinsky*!"

That should have been the last word on the subject, but it wasn't. Neither parent recognized the fact that I was simply emulating a favored radio soap opera character of the day, *Just Plain Bill*. Bill was a kindly old duffer, but we shared a personality problem: an irresistible urge to iron out the lives of everyone within a five-mile radius, even when there was no pressing need.

Just Plain Bill's score of orphans protected, divorces averted, and prodigal sons reconciled was a heck of a lot better than Just Plain Bert's, obviously. So over the years I redirected my meddling impulses from psyches to shopping bags!

Almost against my will, I still find myself sidling up to perfect strangers in supermarkets to check out the contents of their carts.

"That's awfully tired broccoli," I will cluck. "Cauliflower is a better buy, if you haven't noticed." And I will receive the kind of withering glance usually reserved for subway flashers for my efforts.

Clearly I cannot restrain my urges to tell shoppers not to buy underripe melons or overaged bananas, but I expect small thanks for the gratuitous advice. Culinary busybodies, you see, always get the short end of the conversation.

At a towering display of seasonal apples at the greengrocer's last week, I attempted to strike up an avuncular conversation with a nice young couple, who were seriously weighing rosy McIntoshes.

"Those won't make a very good pie." I winked.
"Really?" The young man smiled wanly at the lady by his side. "Tell us what will."

As this appeared to be a gilded opportunity, I instantly went into my song and dance, a discourse on Russets, Pippins, Northern Spies, and Granny Smiths—all the apples of choice, as a matter of fact.

"That's wonderful information," the young man said, "but we don't really know anything about making pastry."

"Well, that's easy as pie . . ." I began. And would have gone further if they hadn't vanished behind a convenient pyramid of pumpkins. So *you* have the advice, instead. Like Just Plain Bill, I am not only nosy, I am persistent as well!

TWELVE-APPLE PIE FOR TWELVE PEOPLE

♋♒♌

*J*he sage advice in today's episode of Just Plain Bert is "holidays are coming up." So skip the commercial and clip this recipe for the best apple pie in his book. It makes a super end to the super dinner of your choice.

1 package (6 ounces) dried apricots
1 cup fresh orange juice
¾ cup granulated sugar
1 curl orange zest (about 4 inches long)
Darlene Schulz's Pie Pastry (recipe follows)
12 tart green apples

2½ tablespoons all-purpose flour
1¼ cups (packed) light brown sugar
1 teaspoon vanilla extract
1 teaspoon grated lemon zest
3 tablespoons unsalted butter
1 egg, beaten

1. Preheat the oven to 425° F.

2. Combine the apricots, orange juice, granulated sugar, and orange curl in a medium-size saucepan. Heat to boiling, stirring constantly. Reduce the heat and simmer over medium-low heat until the apricots are tender, about 20 minutes. Set aside to cool. Finely sliver the orange zest.

3. Roll out half the dough to form a 12-inch round and line a 10-inch ceramic or glass pie plate with it. Trim the edges.

4. Pare and core the apples; cut them into ½-inch-thick slices. Place them in a large bowl, and toss with the flour. Add the brown sugar and vanilla. Stir in the cooled apricot mixture and the slivered orange peel. Mix well.

5. Arrange a third of the apple mixture in the pastry shell. (Do not let the slices sit until syrupy.) Sprinkle with ½ teaspoon of the lemon zest, and dot with 1 tablespoon of the butter. Arrange another third of the apple mixture in the shell. Sprinkle with the remaining ½ teaspoon lemon zest, and dot with 1 tablespoon of the butter. Add the remaining apple mixture, piling the apples high in the center. Dot with the remaining 1 tablespoon butter.

6. Roll out the remaining dough, place it over the apples, and seal and flute the edges. Using a sharp knife, cut 4 slits in the top of the pie to allow steam to escape. Brush the pastry with the beaten egg.

7. Place the pie on an aluminum foil–lined baking sheet, and bake for 15 minutes. Reduce the temperature to 350° F and bake for another 45 minutes.

Serves 12

DARLENE SCHULZ'S
PIE PASTRY

Darlene Schulz is an amazing homemaker/pie-baker who lives in Brownsville, Wisconsin—which is as old-timey and small town as one can get these days (population 340). Unfortunately Darlene recently converted her family to natural foods, so she never makes this famous crust anymore. Now that's real soap opera stuff!

2 cups plus 2 teaspoons all-
    purpose flour
2 teaspoons sugar
1 teaspoon salt
¾ cup lard

1 egg, beaten
1½ teaspoons red wine or
    cider vinegar
2 tablespoons cold water

1. Sift 2 cups flour with the sugar and salt into a large bowl. Cut in the lard, blending with a pastry blender until the texture resembles coarse crumbs.

2. Combine the egg, vinegar, and water in a small bowl. Using a fork or knife, cut this into the flour mixture to form a soft dough. (Do not overwork it.) Sprinkle with the remaining 2 teaspoons flour, wrap well, and chill for 1 hour before using.

Makes pastry for one 10-inch double-crust pie

HOLD THAT GARNISH

To my easterner's frame of mind, Southern California is the most seductive slice of geography in the Union. The even-tempered climate, extra-lush topography, and (may as well admit it) perpetually tanned, overexposed inhabitants cruising the freeways in convertibles frankly turn me on!

Not everyone shares my enthusiasm. Take my cousin Bunny, for example. A happily married lady of independent thought, my cousin adamantly refuses to even consider crossing the Sierras for a look-see.

"Why would I go?" she asks rhetorically, "when every awful thing that has affected this country in the past fifty years started there! Just think about it! McDonald's! Drag racing! Divorce! Farrah Fawcett hairdos . . . and *Reagan*! All started in California!"

Bunny and I do not agree on everything, but her premise certainly gave me pause. Thinking it over, in fact, occasioned a negative addition of my very own: *Fruit!*

Now, before the California Fruit Growers get their groves in an uproar, let me state unequivocally that I have no quarrel whatsoever with produce in its rightful place—on a dessert trolley, or in the breakfast bowl for that matter. What I abhor is the recent practice of placing gratuitous garnishes (orange, pineapple, strawberry, melon, and kiwi slices) on plates of utterly ill-matched scrambled eggs, cheeseburgers, French toast, and even spaghetti on occasion.

The added touch of fresh fruit springs directly from a recent American food style known as "California cuisine." And, since most of that is restaurant fare microwaved prior to serving, the fruit is often served up warmer than the *plat du jour*. My argument with the use of fruit as a garnish is not merely aesthetic, for it is also the most glaring example of conspicuous consumption on record.

Many diners (like myself) merely fork this untasted fruit to one side of their plates, where it is eventually consigned to a garbage pail or disposal system—in a nation where (at the most recent estimate) a fifth of the population is ill fed and over a million are actually starving!

Without wishing to sound like a national scold, I beg the nation's restaurateurs, chiefs, and food stylists to rethink this policy of wanton waste at the dinner table. For, believe you me, the profligate exercise will get worse unless we the people put a stop to it! On my plate, let there be parsley or let there be nothing at all!

Despite my cousin Bunny's admonitions, I still have a furtive letch for Southern California. And if you assume I am anti-fruit at meals, you are dead wrong—as you can see in the following alliances of my own, neither of which requires any garnish other than a knife and fork!

RUSSIAN VEAL AND CHERRY STEW

C herries and veal may appear to be a mismatched pair of ingredients for a stew pan, but outward appearances are often deceiving—as evidenced by the following dish, Moscow-inspired. If you are using fresh cherries, you may wish to add a drop of red wine vinegar before serving; the stew should be sour/sweet.

6 tablespoons (¾ stick) unsalted butter

1 teaspoon vegetable oil

2 pounds boneless veal, cut into 1-inch cubes

2 tablespoons all-purpose flour

4 large scallions (green onions), trimmed and finely chopped

2 cups pitted Morello or other sour cherries

⅓ cup seedless golden raisins

⅔ cup homemade chicken stock or canned broth, heated

¾ cup port wine

1 cardamom pod

Salt and freshly ground black pepper

8 to 10 small white onions, peeled, a small cross cut into the root end

Pinch of sugar

3 tablespoons kirsch

5 cups cooked rice, heated

1. Heat 4 tablespoons of the butter with the oil in a heavy skillet over high heat. Brown the meat on all sides, a few pieces at a time. It will take 6 to 8 minutes. Transfer to a Dutch oven.

2. Sprinkle the flour over the meat; cook over low heat for 1 minute. Add the scallions, cherries, raisins, stock, and ½ cup of the port. Stir well.

3. Open the cardamom pod with a sharp knife; remove and crush the seeds. Add them to the meat, and season with salt and pepper to taste. Bring to a boil. Reduce the heat, cover, and cook over very low heat, stirring occasionally, until the meat is tender, 1½ to 2 hours.

4. Meanwhile, melt the remaining 2 tablespoons butter in the skillet over medium-low heat. Add the onions and sauté until golden, 5 minutes. Sprinkle with the sugar and remaining ¼ cup port. Cook, covered, over medium heat for 5 minutes, shaking the pan occasionally. Then remove the cover, raise the heat, and cook until any liquid has evaporated. Add the onions to the meat during the last 30 minutes of cooking time.

5. Just before serving, stir in the kirsch. Serve with hot rice.

Serves 4 or 5

G R A P E F R U I T
A N D
T A N G E R I N E   S L A W

*J*he notion of citrus and onion together in a salad bowl dates back to the early 1930s. I discovered the next recipe in a pile of dusty newspaper clippings that I inherited from a New York evacuee who made tracks to the Sun Belt.

1 large grapefruit
2 medium-size tangerines
1 medium-size red onion,
     thinly sliced, rounds
     separated
Thinly slivered zest of
     1 orange
1 clove garlic, finely
     minced
½ teaspoon coarse salt
1 teaspoon Dijon
     mustard

Juice of 1 lemon
½ cup olive oil
Juice of 1 orange (about
     ¼ cup)
Freshly ground black
     pepper
1 bunch watercress
     leaves, large stems
     removed

1. Peel the grapefruit and tangerines. Using a very sharp knife, remove all the pith. Slice the fruit crosswise into rounds about ¼ inch thick. Cut the segments apart. (There should be about 3 cups fruit.) Place the fruit in a serving dish, and top it evenly with the onion rounds. Sprinkle with the slivered orange zest.

2. Using the back of a spoon, mash the garlic with the salt in a medium-size bowl. Stir in the mustard and lemon juice. Very slowly whisk in the oil. The mixture will be quite thick; thin it with the orange juice. Pour the dressing over the salad, and sprinkle with pepper. Cover and chill thoroughly.

3. Just before serving, garnish the dish with the watercress. Toss the salad at the table.

Serves 4

DON'T BELIEVE EVERYTHING YOU READ

*T*o err may be human, but a blooper in a recipe is a crime against trusting cooks all over the world! Okay—will you settle for the metropolitan area?

Lately I have been the recipient of a healthy correspondence (happily more *fan* than *pan* mail) from readers who politely write to inquire why an elusive ingredient in my recipe's listing does not appear in the procedure steps that follow. The answer to that query, my friends, is an outdated expression, still current in my circles: *Snafu*.

One of a breed kindly dubbed as "tardy writers," I do not get ideas quickly. Indeed I barely manage to start the creative juices flowing until a day before my deadline. This column therefore is often sent to the copy desk hours before press time, or at that penultimate moment when the die (or at least the type) is on its way to being cast—so there is little time for editorial niceties like remedial proofreading or author's alterations. One slip and all hell breaks loose. In last week's prescription for an otherwise airy *quiffle,* for instance, an omission left that half quiche/half soufflé practically cheeseless at the oven door.

The correct procedure would have added a tablespoon, not a teaspoon, of Parmesan cheese to the egg yolk mixture, with the remaining three tablespoons sprinkled on top just prior to baking.

The worst goof in this column so far happened at the beginning of the year. Among my resolutions for 1981, I included a formula for a favored thinning dish: a cold lima bean and Gruyère cheese salad that is heavily peppered—but never so heavily as in the recipe that appeared in this newspaper. Have a glance at just one of the subsequent letters that arrived (edited to protect the innocent)!

Dear Editor:

Your paper just killed my mother-in-law.

She came to stay with us a few days ago. We prepared for her supper Bert Greene's "Salad of Beans with Black Pepper," printed on Wednesday, January 7, 1981. The recipe, as you printed it, called for "3 tablespoons freshly ground black pepper."

When my mother-in-law took her first mouthful of this salad, she was shaken by such a violence of uncontrollable coughing that she went into a heart attack and died.

After the funeral, I began investigating the recipe. . . . It turns out it was taken from Bert Greene's book *Kitchen Bouquets,* on page 275. One glance shows the monstrosity of the typographical error. While typing the ingredients, the typist must have dozed off! On one line "3 tablespoons of vinegar" were converted into "3 tablespoons of pepper." On the next line "½ teaspoon of pepper," together with the vinegar, was thrown out the window.

Had the death been of any other member of my family, I would, by now, obviously be suing the *Daily News* for twenty million dollars in damages. But in fact, I am so delighted to be rid of my mother-in-law that, if you will send me the name of your favorite charity, I will be glad to make a contribution.

[Name Withheld]

Now if you think I didn't take that note to heart, you don't know your chickens! Speaking of which, another recipe . . .

CHICKEN TARRAGON ALPINE

෪

*T*his is a casserole dish I invented many, many years ago for The Store in Amagansett. Through the years the formula weathered a few changes of ingredients, but it still goes well with an accompaniment of rice.

1 chicken (3½ pounds), cut
　　into pieces
1 clove garlic, bruised
Juice of 2 lemons
1 teaspoon salt
½ teaspoon freshly ground
　　black pepper
6 shallots, minced
1 cup (2 sticks) unsalted
　　butter (approximately)
¾ cup dry white wine
1 teaspoon chopped fresh
　　tarragon, or ½ teaspoon
　　dried
2 medium-size onions,
　　chopped
1 small green bell pepper,
　　cored, seeded, and finely
　　chopped
2 tomatoes, seeded and
　　coarsely chopped

12 mushroom caps
1 medium-size zucchini,
　　cut into ¼-inch-thick
　　rounds
18 small white onions
1 teaspoon sugar
4 strips bacon, cooked crisp
　　and crumbled
2 tablespoons all-purpose
　　flour
½ cup strong homemade
　　chicken stock or canned
　　broth (see Note)
1 egg yolk
¼ cup heavy or whipping
　　cream
1 teaspoon cognac
Chopped fresh parsley or
　　tarragon, for garnish

1. Preheat the oven to 350° F.

2. Rub the chicken pieces well with the garlic. Arrange the chicken in a baking pan, and sprinkle it with the juice of the lemons and the salt, pepper, and shallots. Dot with 4 tablespoons of the butter. Bake for 30 minutes, basting every 10 minutes with ½ cup of the wine.

3. Turn the chicken pieces over and sprinkle with the tarragon and 4 tablespoons of the butter, cut into bits. Bake another 30 minutes, basting every 10 minutes. Transfer the chicken to a broiler tray. Strain and reserve the juices.

4. Heat the broiler, and broil the chicken until brown, 2 minutes. Keep it warm while you prepare the vegetables.

5. Melt 4 tablespoons of the butter in a skillet over medium heat, and sauté the chopped onions and bell pepper until the onions are golden, 5 minutes. Transfer the vegetables to the dish in which you will serve the chicken. In the same skillet, sauté the tomatoes over medium heat until slightly cooked, 3 to 4 minutes. Add them to the onion mixture in the dish.

6. Again using the same skillet, sauté the mushrooms over medium-high heat, adding butter as needed, until golden, 4 to 5 minutes; set them aside. Then quickly sauté the zucchini over medium heat for 2 to 3 minutes; set it aside.

7. Using a sharp knife, cut a small cross in the root end of each white onion. Sauté over medium heat until golden brown, 4 to 5 minutes. Then pour the remaining ¼ cup wine over them, and sprinkle with the sugar. Cook over high heat until all the liquid has been absorbed, 3 to 4 minutes.

8. Arrange the chicken on the bed of vegetables. Garnish with the bacon and the mushrooms, zucchini, and white onions. Keep warm.

9. Beat 2 tablespoons of the reserved juices with the flour until smooth. Heat in a saucepan over medium-low heat for 1 minute. Slowly beat in the remaining juices and chicken stock. Bring to a boil; remove from the heat.

10. Beat the egg yolk with the cream, and slowly add to the sauce. Return the pan to medium-low heat and cook until slightly thickened, 4 to 5 minutes (do not allow to boil). Season with salt, pepper, and cognac. Pour the sauce over the chicken, and return it to a 350° F oven to warm through, 10 minutes. Garnish with parsley or tarragon, and serve.

Serves 6

Note: To make strong stock or broth, simmer 1 cup until reduced to ½ cup.

SPRING GREENS FOR GREENE

ating out, I try to dine on whatever viand is in season whenever possible. In the kitchen, sad to say, I am usually a mite less demanding, often as not using hothouse (or hydroponically grown) tomatoes or frozen peas and artichokes whenever fresh are hard to come by. Not because I like the savor of these stovetop stand-ins, you understand, but simply to make do!

Shakespeare, who did not cook at all, said it much more succinctly than I could:

> At Christmas I no more desire a rose
> Than wish a snow in May's new fangled mirth.
> But like each thing in the season it grows!

Obviously I'm with *him* all the way to the greengrocer's. And if I seem somewhat uncivil toward the pile of tasteless strawberries and inelastic asparagus that have lined my supermarket's shelves all this past winter, so be it!

Happily, the calendar states that May is here once more. I would know it without that informant, for the juice is running in the maple trees and a whole new generation of robins (who never heard of Weight Watchers) is growing fat in my backyard on West Twelfth Street, where the worm supply is rumored to be the best in town.

Spring for a city dweller means that honest-to-goodness greens are practically on his table again. To celebrate an early harvest, this kitchen practitioner has been poking about in the windowbox between downpours. In premature high spirits, I purchased a flat of spiky young basil a few weeks ago, but every single seedling expired in the sudden April wind-chill factor. Hope, however, springs eternal where that ineluctable herb is concerned. More, hardier, basil will be set out tomorrow to enhance the first fuzzy fingers of zucchini when they appear.

Mint is my apartment enemy. First it takes over my sunniest windowsill, then it climbs like a philodendron up the kitchen telephone wire and frying pan handle and must be pinched back in retaliation. But why fight the march of nature? Particularly when there are green peas growing on poles somewhere, just to ameliorate this unruly wanderer.

Yes, spring is decidedly here. I have been eyeing some old shopping bags for a raid on Central Park's dandelion patch. If I do not get there, you will no doubt find me on Bleecker Street instead, seeking out the tenderest leaves I can find to ensure that a prized vernal recipe—Dandelion Bake—gets only the choicest ingredients.

The following are a special bequest from my spring kitchen, and will, I promise, give a winterized body a real lift!

DANDELION BAKE

❧

*T*he following homey recipe comes from a former boardinghouse keeper from Omaha, Nebraska. Her precept states that the greens should be no higher than a man's hand—which means a big mess of greens must be picked to add up to anything. But the finished dish is worth any calisthenics!

2 pounds dandelion greens
8 ounces arugula
3 tablespoons unsalted
   butter
2 tablespoons all-purpose
   flour
¾ cup milk, scalded

⅓ cup grated Swiss or
   Jarlsberg cheese
⅛ teaspoon freshly grated nutmeg
1 teaspoon red wine vinegar
Salt and freshly ground black
   pepper
¼ cup fine fresh bread crumbs

1. Heat the oven to 425° F. Lightly grease an 8-inch glass pie plate.

2. Wash the dandelions and arugula under cold running water. Remove the tough center ribs, and coarsely chop.

3. Bring a large pot of salted water to a rolling boil, and add the dandelions and arugula. Return to a rolling boil; then drain immediately, rinse under cold running water, and drain again thoroughly. Squeeze out all liquid with your hands.

4. Melt 2 tablespoons of the butter in a medium-size saucepan over low heat; whisk in the flour. Cook for 2 minutes. Whisk in the milk, and beat until smooth. Stir in the cheese, nutmeg, and vinegar. Season with salt and pepper to taste. Stir in the dandelions and arugula. Spoon the mixture into the prepared pie plate.

5. Melt the remaining 1 tablespoon butter in a small skillet over medium heat. Stir in the bread crumbs, and cook until lightly browned. Spoon the bread crumbs over the dandelion mixture and bake until bubbly, about 20 minutes.

Serves 4

SVENSKA ARTER

A bonus from a South Dakota kitchen—"at its best when the peas are picked no longer than one half hour before the dish is to be made," according to the Beaver Valley Church Bulletin, circa

1932. Scandinavian-Americans like their peas practically uncooked. With luck I get to the vegetable market on the same day that the dish is to be prepared. But even when the peas are not preternaturally fresh, Svenska Arter never fails to delight my table companions!

2 cups shelled fresh peas
    (about 2 pounds)
3 tablespoons unsalted butter
¼ cup water
½ teaspoon salt
¼ teaspoon freshly ground
    white pepper
¼ cup heavy or whipping
    cream

1 egg yolk
2 tablespoons chopped fresh
    mint
1 teaspoon confectioner's
    sugar
Pinch of cayenne pepper, or
    dash of hot pepper sauce

1. Place the peas in a saucepan, and add the butter, water, salt, and white pepper. Bring to a boil over high heat; reduce the heat and simmer for 3 minutes.

2. Combine the cream and egg yolk in a small bowl. Remove the saucepan from the heat, and stir the cream mixture into the peas. Return to low heat and stir until slightly thickened, about 3 minutes (do not boil). Add the mint, sugar, and cayenne pepper or hot pepper sauce to taste. Serve immediately.

Serves 4

COLD ZUCCHINI AND TOMATO SALAD

〰

*B*asil and tomato are more than just friends—I have noticed that tomatoes ripen redder in the garden when the herb is planted nearby. Now that must mean that something's up! Have a leaf from The Store in Amagansett's salad bar: cold zucchini (uncooked) tossed with tomatoes in a tart, mustardy vinaigrette that gives the greens a special meaning. This dish was a Store standby for eleven years. Try it on your kitchen counter as my guest!

3 to 4 zucchini, cut into ⅛-inch-thick slices (about 3 cups)
2 cups cherry tomatoes, halved
½ cup minced shallots
⅓ cup chopped fresh basil
¼ cup chopped fresh parsley
1 small clove garlic, mashed

½ teaspoon coarse salt
1 teaspoon Dijon mustard
Juice of ½ lemon
½ cup vegetable or olive oil
2 teaspoons red wine vinegar
⅓ teaspoon freshly ground black pepper

1. Combine the zucchini, tomatoes, shallots, basil, and parsley in a large bowl. Toss, cover, and chill well.

2. In a small bowl, mash the garlic and salt together with the back of a spoon until the mixture forms a paste. Stir in the mustard and lemon juice. Whisk in the oil, vinegar, and pepper. Toss the dressing with the zucchini-tomato mixture just before serving.

Serves 6 to 8

MAKE MY STACK HIGH

*P*ancakes (flapjacks, johnnycakes, griddle cakes, and the like) are a tried-and-true passion of mine. Though, sad to say, I have not set a fork to a stack in years.

Why? Dietary discretion, to be blunt. The mere sight of a plateful of these feather-weight, russet-edged confections, slathered with butter and awash with a river of syrup, is so utterly seductive that I am unable to exercise any willpower at all. The last time I was faced with a home-made pancake, I ate a dozen at one sitting!

Now that is a serious addiction, and the only reason I am not in the thrall of the terrible habit is snobbism. I am turned on only by honest-to-goodness real pancakes. Reasonably accurate facsimiles simply will not do!

Over the years I have become tempted less frequently because the art of pancake making has gone the way of gesso painting, woodworking, and topiary. The talented artisans who had been trained to perform these gratifying skills either retired or went to their eternal reward without instructing the next generation in the tools of their trade. For, goodness knows, the supposed experts—such as those culinary academy graduates who run the stylish brunch buffets at luxe hotels or fast-food pancake establishments—have no clue how to whip together (or flip) the kind of velvety flapjack that makes my temperature rise.

As a child (who knew no batter) I was weaned on Aunt Jemima's offerings, mixed up straight from the box by my expedient mother. When I grew up, however, I was taught the art by a wonderful woman who performed minor miracles with milk, eggs, flour, and a pinch of sugar, and I turned my back on packaged mixes forever after. Though I must confess, Aunt Jem's *oeuvre* did not seem quite so crease-resistant nor so downright tasteless in the old days as they do today. And let us not even speak of the additive-crammed frozen variety that carry her moniker on cartons in the supermarket.

What I cannot fathom for the life of me is why pancake making eludes American home cooks—forget chefs entirely! Flexible in nature, pancake batter may be whipped up in minutes, or made in advance by the chary and refrigerated overnight. The secret is to always keep the heat under the pan or griddle at the medium setting—and to work fast. High temperature will cause a golden cake to sear too quickly and turn blotchy rather than the shade of a perfect autumn leaf. Low heat, on the other hand, will result in a scrambled-egg-cake. So watch the flame, please!

Pancakes are at their best when they are consumed "straight from the griddle," but since that is the most conspicuous form of consumption, it is rarely put into practice. However, I find no great loss in either texture or taste when the pancakes are kept warm (though preferably unstacked) in a 200° F oven until the whole batch is ready for the greedy griddle-cakers to dig in.

What follows is my quintessential breakfast food, first in its classic style and then embellished with cottage cheese. Syrup and fruit are your option.

CLASSIC BREAKFAST PANCAKES

〰〰〰

*T*hese paradigm cakelets are compounded of buttermilk plus baking soda and a few choice ingredients. They are also the most divine mouthful I know—with or without the addition of raisins, blueberries, or crushed pecans.

3 eggs, separated
2 cups buttermilk
2 cups all-purpose flour
1 teaspoon baking soda
1 tablespoon sugar

1 cup raisins, blueberries, or
crushed pecans (optional)
4 tablespoons (½ stick)
unsalted butter, melted

1. Preheat the oven to 200° F.

2. Beat the egg yolks in a large bowl until light and lemon-colored. Slowly beat in the buttermilk.

3. Using a wooden spoon, stir the flour, baking soda, and sugar into the buttermilk mixture, being careful not to overwork the batter. The small lumps will disappear during the cooking. Stir in the fruit or nuts, if using, and the melted butter.

4. Beat the egg whites until stiff but not dry. Fold them into the batter.

5. Heat a griddle or cast-iron skillet over medium heat until hot. Rub it lightly with oil or butter, and pour about ⅓ cup batter for each pancake onto the griddle. Cook until bubbles form on top and the undersides are nicely browned, about 1 minute. Turn the pancakes over and brown the other side for 1 minute. Either serve at once or keep warm in the oven (unstacked) until the remaining cakes are cooked.

Makes about twelve 4-inch pancakes; serves 2 to 3

PHILLIP'S COLORADO SURPRISE PANCAKES

❧

*T*he formula for this yogurt and cottage cheese cake may be traced to Phillip Schulz's home state of Colorado, where no leavening was ever required because of the altitude. My friend Phillip says one half teaspoon of baking powder may be added for extra lightness, at your discretion. Though in all truth, I prefer them *sans* extra leavening, even at sea level.

4 eggs, separated
1 cup small-curd cottage cheese
1 cup plain yogurt
¾ cup all-purpose flour

2 tablespoons sugar
½ teaspoon baking powder (optional)
1½ teaspoons vanilla extract

1. Preheat the oven to 200° F.

2. Beat the egg yolks in a large bowl until light and lemon-colored. Slowly beat in the cottage cheese and yogurt. Mix thoroughly.

3. Using a wooden spoon, stir in the flour, sugar, and optional baking powder, being careful not to overwork the batter. The small lumps will disappear in the cooking. Stir in the vanilla.

4. Beat the egg whites until stiff but not dry, and fold them into the batter.

5. Heat a griddle or cast-iron skillet over medium heat until hot. Rub it lightly with oil or butter, and pour about ⅓ cup batter for each pancake onto the griddle. Cook until bubbles form on top and the undersides are nicely browned, 2 to 3 minutes. Turn the pancakes over and brown the other side for 1 minute. Either serve at once or keep warm in the oven (unstacked) until the remaining cakes are cooked.

Makes about twelve 4-inch pancakes; serves 2 to 3

STRUDEL THE NON-SCRATCH WAY

I am not a man easily given to shortcuts in the kitchen. Cake mixes and the like I dismiss entirely out of hand—frankly not so much because I suspect that danger lurks in the preservatives listed on every boxtop, but because the finished product always tastes so perfectly awful to my tongue. I eschew most other concentrates and frozen foods out of economic principle as well. The real stuff is usually cheaper.

So it will probably come as something of a shock when I confess that I have been experimenting with store-bought strudel pastry for the last few weeks.

The expedience is not totally capricious. With my longtime cooking associate, Phillip Schulz, I recently spent one whole day (from 8:00 A.M. to 8:00 P.M.) making strudel dough from scratch. The results, while not utterly dismal, were a far cry from the fragments of sunlit air I remember emerging from my grandmother's and cousin Rose's ovens. More to the point, my kitchen (and dining room table), where the dough had to hang and be slowly stretched, resembled a snowy battle zone. Every stick of furniture and every utensil was covered with a fine film of white flour from the copious dustings required to powder one's hands and the dough itself. Even my two cats bore traces of dried flour on their whiskers for days after.

I know that strudel-making requires time and patience, but for the moment I have put the acquisition of that special skill on hold, opting instead for the very best commercial dough I can buy. For, to be honest, the store-bought stuff out-crisped my "from scratch" attempts by a mile.

At the outset I must state, however, that even commercial strudel dough holds booby traps for a neophyte baker. Store-bought dough comes in rolled leaves that require deft stacking and rolling to achieve the gilded frangible layers that most perfectly surround a filling. Look for packaged varieties that clearly state "strudel leaves," not "phyllo pastry," on the box (Apollo and Poseidon are brands I have used with tonic success). Try to buy fresh leaves if possible. Frozen dough is often allowed to defrost on a supermarket shelf and then refreeze, which causes the fragile leaves to shred—or worse yet, disintegrate—when you attempt to separate them.

Working with strudel leaves requires a jot of serenity, so substitute Mozart for hard rock on the stereo. Be sure to place a damp towel on your work table first, then cover it completely with sheets of waxed paper. Carefully unroll the leaves from the package, and proceed with the recipe instructions below, brushing each leaf with melted butter and bread crumbs as directed. I generally use four leaves to create a perfectly delicate superstructure, but it must be noted that more demanding pastry chefs elect six rather than four to ensure extra crispness. If you choose to follow that maxim, remember to sprinkle the extra leaves with melted butter and bread crumbs as well.

What follows are two unique savory strudels that Phillip and I recently devised for brunch, lunch, or party fare. While not child's play, they are both manageable to prepare in advance. Even in a kitchenette!

SALMON AND CREAM CHEESE STRUDEL

*T*his is indubitably the quintessential strudel stuffing, even though it is borrowed from a lowly bagel. What gives it its fabulous savor is good-quality smoked salmon—the best choices are Nova Scotia or Scottish salmon. Make certain you allow the cream cheese to come to room temperature before whipping it, and use *fresh* dill, please.

4 ounces cream cheese, at room temperature
¼ cup heavy or whipping cream
½ teaspoon finely slivered lemon zest
Salt and freshly ground black pepper
4 strudel leaves

4 tablespoons (½ stick) unsalted butter (approximately), melted
1 tablespoon fresh white bread crumbs
4 ounces thinly sliced smoked salmon
1 tablespoon chopped fresh dill

1. Preheat the oven to 375° F. Spread a damp tea towel on your work surface, and cover it with waxed paper. Lightly butter a baking sheet.

2. Place the cream cheese in the bowl of an electric mixer, and beat until light. Slowly add the cream. Then add the lemon zest, and salt and pepper to taste.

3. Stack two strudel leaves on the waxed paper, with the long sides parallel to the edge of the table. Brush the top leaf with some of the melted butter, and sprinkle all the bread crumbs over it. Add the remaining 2 leaves of dough, and brush the top leaf with butter.

4. Using two knives, spread the cream cheese mixture over the bottom quarter of the dough, leaving an inch uncovered all around the edges. Cover the cream cheese with the smoked salmon, and sprinkle with the dill. With the aid of the towel, fold the side edges of the dough toward the center just enough to cover the filling by ½ inch. Brush the edges with butter and press them lightly so they do not unfold. Again with the aid of the towel, roll up the dough away from you and onto the prepared baking sheet, seam side down. Brush the surface of the dough with butter, and bake until crisp, about 25 minutes. Slide the strudel onto a rack to cool. Serve it slightly warm or at room temperature.

Serves 4 to 6 as a main course; more as an appetizer

B L A C K   F O R E S T
M U S H R O O M
S T R U D E L

◆◆◆

An adaptation of an Austrian classic, this delicate, aromatic hors d'oeuvre is at its best when wild mushrooms (shiitakes, pleurottes, or crimini) are its chief ingredient. If you are using the domestic button variety, increase the amount to 8 ounces and sauté them with only a little butter, to rid them of any excess juices.

2 tablespoons unsalted
   butter
1 shallot, minced
4 ounces wild mushrooms,
   chopped
4 ounces thinly sliced
   Black Forest ham,
   chopped
Salt and freshly ground black
   pepper
1 egg white, lightly
   beaten

4 strudel leaves
4 tablespoons (½ stick)
   unsalted butter
   (approximately), melted
2 tablespoons fresh white
   bread crumbs

1. Preheat the oven to 375° F. Spread a damp tea towel on your work surface, and cover it with waxed paper. Lightly butter a baking sheet.

2. Melt the 2 tablespoons butter in a large heavy skillet over medium heat. Add the shallot, and cook for 1 minute. Add the mushrooms, and sauté until lightly golden, about 3 minutes. Then add the ham, and cook 1 minute longer. Season with salt and pepper to taste, remove the skillet from the heat, and allow to cool. Stir in the egg white.

3. Stack two strudel leaves on the waxed paper, with the long sides parallel to the edge of the table. Brush the top leaf with some of the melted butter, sprinkle with 1 teaspoon of the bread crumbs. Add the remaining 2 leaves of dough, and repeat the butter and bread crumbs.

4. Spread the mushroom mixture over the bottom quarter of the dough, leaving an inch uncovered all around the edges. With the aid of the towel, fold the side edges of the dough toward the center just enough to cover the filling by ½ inch. Brush the edges with butter, and press lightly so they do not unfold. Again with the aid of the towel, roll up the dough away from you and onto the prepared baking sheet. Brush the surface of the dough with butter, and bake until crisp, about 25 minutes. Slide the strudel onto a rack to cool. Serve slightly warm or at room temperature.

Serves 8 as a first course; 4 as a main course

MY SIGNATURE DISHES

f I tell you I have recently had my culinary comeuppance, do me a favor—take it with a grain of salt!

Cases in point: two recent happenings where my ego was either battered or flattered—I still cannot rightly tell which! The first occurrence took place at a party I attended along with a hundred or so literary lions and show-biz shoguns, a social event crammed to the nines with not only the beautiful people but the brainy ones to boot.

Upon arrival at this event, I knew I was in trouble when I spotted three honest-to-gosh Pulitzer Prize honorees treading water at the bar, along with two Tony recipients and one Academy Awardee, reaching for plastic cups of white wine.

"You look familiar," a man I clearly recognized from his latest book jacket said to me, as I elbowed my way out of the crush. "Did you coach for Notre Dame?"

"No," I replied truthfully. "I write cookbooks and . . ."—my voice growing weaker—"appear on TV."

"Do people still do that?" he said, tossing down a glass of chardonnay. "I thought you people were all into catering now."

"No, no." I smiled thinly. "I used to be a caterer. But that was a long, long time ago."

"I knew you looked familiar," he went on enthusiastically. "You used to make a chicken dish my ex-wife really loved. Louise something-or-other . . ."

"Your wife?"

"No, your chicken!"

I made my way through the crowd, absolutely stunned. Because for all the success of the past decade since I stopped cooking for a living at The Store in Amagansett, Chicken Louisette was the only thing about me that this guy remembered. So, what price fame!

The other incident took place at a symposium of the Society for American Cuisine, in Charleston a week or so ago. I had flown there to deliver the keynote speech about American food.

When I was asked to speak, the society had requested that I submit three of my favorite recipes for a cookbook to be given to participants, compiled of all the speakers' preferred work. It was hard to choose which three out of the thousand recipes I'd devised over the years I wanted to represent me. In the end, I selected one each from what I consider to be my best books: *Bert Greene's Kitchen Bouquets, Honest American Fare*, and *Greene on Greens*.

After my speech, a couple made their way through the audience to the podium, to shake my hand. Or so I thought. Actually, they came to wag a finger instead.

"Bert! You didn't pick the right recipe for the Speakers' Collection." They smiled, but as they might at an errant child.

"Why? Which would you pick?" I asked.

The answer came back like a shot. "Lamb Shanks Provençale. From *The Store Cookbook*. After all, that's the recipe that made your reputation!"

With no argument from me, I present both those recipes here and now.

CHICKEN LOUISETTE

❧

I was often told that this dish, which I made perhaps ten thousand times when I was a storekeeper-chef, was named after Louisette Bertholle (one of the original co-authors of *Mastering the Art of French Cooking*), but it was neither proven nor disputed. It's still a satisfying party dish, because it may be made earlier and reheated just before serving. The essential toast points, however, must be freshly made and buttered.

7 to 8 tablespoons unsalted butter

2 chickens (2½ pounds each), cut up for frying

1 small onion, thinly sliced

Salt and freshly ground black pepper

4 ounces mushrooms, thinly sliced

2 tablespoons strong homemade chicken stock or canned broth (see Note)

3 tablespoons all-purpose flour

½ cup dry white wine

1 cup homemade chicken stock or canned broth

4 ounces cooked ham, chopped

4 slices white bread, crusts trimmed

Chopped fresh parsley, for garnish

1. Melt 4 tablespoons of the butter in a Dutch oven over medium-low heat, and brown the chicken pieces slowly, 12 to 15 minutes. Arrange the onion on top of the chicken, season with salt and pepper to taste, cover, and cook slowly for 30 to 40 minutes or until tender.

2. Remove the chicken pieces from the Dutch oven. Add 2 more tablespoons butter to the pot, and sauté the mushrooms over medium-high heat until lightly browned, about 5 minutes.

3. Remove the Dutch oven from the heat, and blend in the strong stock and the flour. Stir until smooth. Pour in the wine and the 1 cup stock, return the pot to the heat, and stir until the mixture comes to a boil. Add the ham, and simmer for 5 minutes. (The dish can be made ahead to this point. Return the chicken to the pot, cover, and refrigerate.) To finish the dish, return the chicken pieces, and simmer until they are heated through, about 10 minutes more.

4. Cut the bread slices into triangles. Heat 1 to 2 tablespoons butter in a skillet, and sauté the bread until golden brown on both sides. Arrange the chicken on a heated serving dish. Spoon the sauce over the chicken, arrange the toast points around the edges, sprinkle with parsley, and serve.

Serves 4

Note: To make strong stock or broth, simmer ¼ cup until reduced to 2 tablespoons.

LAMB SHANKS PROVENCALE

This dish came to The Store in Amagansett (and *The Store Cookbook*) as a residual of a long stay in the Village of Eze, France, back in the early 1970s. It is still an easy, earthy dish worthy of revival.

3 tablespoons all-purpose
    flour
Salt
Paprika
4 lamb shanks (about 1
    pound each)
2 tablespoons unsalted butter
2 tablespoons vegetable oil
1 large onion, thinly sliced

¾ cup dry red wine
1¼ cups water
¼ teaspoon chopped fresh
    rosemary, or a pinch of
    dried
Freshly ground black pepper
Chopped fresh parsley, for
    garnish

1. Preheat the oven to 375° F.

2. Season 1 tablespoon of the flour with salt and a little paprika, and lightly dust the shanks with the mixture. Heat the butter and oil in a deep heavy ovenproof saucepan over medium heat until hot but not smoking. Add the shanks and brown them on all sides, 8 to 10 minutes. Remove the shanks from the pan, lower the heat slightly, and lightly brown the onion in the pan. Return the meat to the pan; add the red wine, ¾ cup of the water, and the rosemary. Season with salt and pepper to taste. Cover the pan, transfer it to the oven, and cook until the meat is easily pierced with a fork, about 2 hours.

3. Remove the lamb shanks from the pan, and keep warm. Blend the remaining 2 tablespoons flour with the remaining ½ cup cold water, and add it to the pan juices. Place the pan on the stove, and stir over medium heat until the gravy thickens and comes to a boil, 4 to 5 minutes. Simmer for 2 to 3 minutes, then strain into a gravy boat.

4. Serve the shanks garnished with parsley. Pass the gravy separately.
Serves 4

GOING ONCE, GOING TWICE?

y father used to worry about my future. And rightly so I suppose, since I spent the better part of my adolescence unable to decide what I wanted to be.

"Remember," he would caution grimly whenever I showed signs of ambivalence, "a jack of all trades is the master of none!"

Sage advice—which I promptly ignored, for I had just heard the one about the "Renaissance man with more than one string to his bow."

But I must confess, my father's words haunted me a few weeks ago, after I made my professional debut as an auctioneer at a fund-raising event in Washington. The occasion was the recent annual convention of the International Association of Culinary Professionals. The auction, held at the close of the proceedings, was to benefit the organization's Culinary Advancement, Research, and Education Foundation, which is a source of scholarships and research grants for serious students of the culinary arts all over the world.

I suspect I was asked to be auctioneer at this outing because I am the tallest member of the Association who owns a tuxedo—and the one who has the loudest mouth to boot!

Whatever the reason for my selection, it turned out to be a popular choice. I lost my voice for a whole day after the proceedings, but my swollen ego easily made up for the lack. For through sheer willpower and derring-do, this budding auctioneer managed to rack up over $25,000 in less time than it took to peruse the catalogue of collectibles.

I must report that all the treasures up for grabs were donated by dedicated culinarians; and while the mix was eclectic to say the least—from the late James Beard's favorite shrimp tureen to a week of cooking classes at La Varenne in Paris, and including such diverse items as Gary Collins's TV apron and a night on the town with *New York Magazine*'s Underground Gourmet—all of the offerings went at banner prices, a fact that made Greene walk on air for weeks afterward. Everyone I met voiced the same sentiment: "If you ever decide to give up the stove, fella, there's a gavel in your future!"

The story has a coda—one that unfortunately bears out another of my father's admonitions: "Shoemaker, stick to your last." After my return from Washington I received a letter from a longtime pen pal whom I had never met. This woman just happened to be in Washington with her husband, a professional auctioneer, and witnessed my debut. In part her note reads:

> The auction was the most hysterical one we've ever seen. Actually, we were surprised we could even hear the bidding over the sound of rules crashing and breaking. I'm not saying you broke all the rules in the book—only 90% of them. The other 10% you either fractured or bent out of shape.

In case you're wondering, that was the end of my brilliant career as an auctioneer. But just to keep my hand in, here's a really priceless recipe. What am I bid for it?

TOMATO DEVIL'S FOOD CAKE

What makes a recipe a work of art? The right ingredients and non-fail directions. I'll stake my reputation on this rich, chocolatey dessert straight out of my book *Greene on Greens*.

FOR THE CAKE

2 large ripe tomatoes (about
　　1 pound)
4 ounces (4 squares) sweet
　　baking chocolate
1 cup (packed) dark brown
　　sugar
¼ cup milk
3 egg yolks
2 cups sifted cake flour
1 teaspoon baking soda
½ teaspoon salt
8 tablespoons (1 stick)
　　unsalted butter, at room
　　temperature
1 cup granulated sugar

1 teaspoon vanilla extract
2 egg whites

FOR THE FROSTING (see
　　Note)
1 medium-size ripe tomato
　　(about 4 ounces)
1½ cups (3 sticks) unsalted
　　butter, at room
　　temperature
4 extra-large egg yolks
1 tablespoon cognac
¾ cup confectioner's sugar

1. Preheat the oven to 350° F. Butter and flour two 9-inch cake pans.

2. Make the cake: Peel and seed the tomatoes. Place them in a blender, and blend until smooth. Measure off 1¼ cups tomato purée, and set it aside.

3. Place the chocolate, brown sugar, milk, and 1 of the egg yolks in the top of a double boiler. Cook, stirring occasionally, over hot water until smooth and slightly thickened, 10 to 12 minutes. Set aside.

4. Sift the flour with the baking soda and salt.

5. Beat the butter in a large mixing bowl until light. Slowly beat in the granulated sugar. Add the remaining 2 egg yolks, one at a time, beating thoroughly after each addition. Add the reserved tomato purée, the vanilla, and the chocolate mixture. Beat, then slowly stir in the flour mixture.

6. Beat the egg whites until stiff but not dry, and fold them into the cake batter. Pour the batter into the prepared cake pans. Bake until a toothpick inserted in the center of the cake comes out fairly clean, 25 to 30 minutes. Do not overcook. Cool the layers on a wire rack, then unmold.

7. Make the frosting: Cut the tomato in half, and place it in a blender. Blend until smooth. Strain the purée through a sieve. Measure off 4½ tablespoons of the strained purée, and set it aside.

8. Beat the butter in a large bowl until light. Add the egg yolks, one at a time, beating thoroughly after each addition. Add the reserved tomato purée and the cognac. Slowly beat in the confectioner's sugar. Spread the icing over the bottom layer, then place the second layer over it. Ice the top and sides of the cake. Keep the cake in a cool place, but do not refrigerate.

Serves 8 to 10

Note: This icing contains raw eggs. Recently some uncooked eggs have been a source of salmonella, a serious infection. If you are unsure of the quality of the eggs you buy, avoid recipes using them raw.

TOO TALL GREENE'S REAL SHORT RECIPES

*L*uckier than most Americans, I have never consciously been the object of any active form of discrimination against my race, religion, sex, or lifestyle. And, even putting inalienable rights to one side, that is a dispensation not to be taken lightly.

However, of late I have noticed a rather curious attitude (frankly I am reluctant to call it a full-fledged prejudice) toward a segment of society of which I am a member. Namely: the *tall*! Now, I must explain flat out that I am a man of not inconsiderable size (six feet, four inches high in my socks), and I take any new sling or arrow directed at the heighted as an act of outrageous aggression.

To get this beef down to basics, I am speaking of the recent (nationwide) decision on the part of the telephone company to rescale all pedestal-type public pay phones on streets, along highways, in airport terminals, and you name it, to a size (fifty-four inches from the ground) that happily accommodates a munchkin, perhaps, but gives a guy of my longitude the bends when he has to dial a number.

The act of what appears to be "dimensional discrimination" on the part of Ma Bell, I am reasonably informed by the public relations department of that company, is actually a mandatory compliance with a federal statute. The law demands equal rights for handicapped users. God bless the law, I say. But how about a compromise: Why not a brace of equal phones of unequal heights at every installation?

"That is just not feasible," says a spokesman for the phone company. "Besides, smaller telephone accommodations in public places reduce the possibility of vandalism." Except from some outraged incredible hulk like me!

I suppose I wouldn't be so bitter about abbreviated public facilities if I were also not faced with the ongoing problems of a like nature in the private sector as well. I refer to diminished legroom in most theater seats (at escalated ticket prices, yet), as well as a raft of highly reduced berths in airplanes, buses, and what most tall men laugh at when referred to as "intermediate-size" cars.

There *is* a ray of light at the end of the tunnel . . . for Greene, at least. According to recent medical statistics, as I grow older I can expect to shrink at least half an inch per decade after age fifty. I can hardly wait!

To honor the new "short chic" that is on the way—when in the words of T. S. Eliot, "I grow old . . . and wear the bottoms of my trousers rolled," I have unearthed some truncated recipes.

Each of the following "short" dishes is long in savor but may be prepared in less than twenty minutes. Even by a tall chef!

BOURBON
STEAK

ᗩᗩᗩ

*T*his example of short-order cookery is tenderly delicious, and not truly pricey since a small amount goes a long way.

1 to 1¼ pounds rib-eye or
    sirloin steak
2 tablespoons plus 1 teaspoon
    unsalted butter
2 teaspoons olive oil
1 shallot, minced
1 clove garlic, minced
1½ teaspoons Dijon mustard
¼ cup strong homemade beef
    stock or canned broth
    (see Note)

Dash of hot pepper sauce
3 tablespoons bourbon
Salt and freshly ground black
    pepper
1 tablespoon chopped fresh
    chives

1. Cut the meat into thin slices. Pound the slices between 2 sheets of waxed paper (or in a large reclosable plastic bag) until about ⅛ inch thick. Pat dry.

2. Heat 1 tablespoon of the butter with the oil in a large heavy skillet until smoking hot. Quickly sauté the meat, about 20 seconds per side, adding the remaining 1 tablespoon butter as needed. Transfer the pieces to a plate as they are browned.

3. Reduce the heat to low, and add the 1 teaspoon butter to the skillet. Sauté the shallot for 1 minute. Add the garlic, and cook until golden,

3 minutes. Whisk in the mustard, beef stock, hot pepper sauce, and bourbon. Cook over medium heat until slightly thickened, about 5 minutes.
Return the meat to the skillet, and toss briefly to warm through. Add salt
and pepper to taste, sprinkle with the chives, and serve.

Serves 4 to 6

Note: To make strong stock, simmer ½ cup until reduced by half.

D I L L E D   C A R R O T S

illed Carrots (quick-cooked) are of Norwegian stripe: blanched,
then sautéed in cream and broth till tender, the sauce finally
reduced until the carrots turn pure gold!

4 large carrots	*¼ cup heavy or whipping*
2 tablespoons unsalted butter	*cream*
3 tablespoons very strong	*¼ cup chopped fresh dill*
homemade chicken stock	*Salt and freshly ground black*
or canned broth (see Note)	*pepper*

1. Peel the carrots and cut them into thin sticks about ¼ inch wide and
3 inches long. Cook them in boiling salted water for 2 minutes. Rinse
under cold running water, and drain.

2. Melt the butter in a large saucepan over medium heat. Add the carrots and stock; stir well to coat the carrots. Add 3 tablespoons of the
cream. Cook over high heat, stirring constantly, until the mixture begins

to thicken, 3 to 4 minutes. Then reduce the heat and add the dill. Toss well. Stir in the remaining 1 tablespoon cream, add salt and pepper to taste, and serve.

Serves 4 to 6

Note: To make very strong stock or broth, simmer ½ cup until reduced to 3 tablespoons.

STRIPED ORANGES

O ranges and cream (both slightly frozen) are a felicitous amalgam. What gives them majesty is a swirl of hasty-tasty chocolate sauce.

2 seedless oranges, peeled
    and sliced
3 tablespoons hazelnut
    liqueur
¼ cup plus 2 tablespoons
    heavy or whipping cream

4 ounces (4 squares) sweet
    baking chocolate, broken
1 tablespoon unsalted butter
2 tablespoons milk

1. Arrange the orange slices on a serving plate. Sprinkle them with the hazelnut liqueur and ¼ cup cream. Place the plate in the freezer for at least 1 minute but no more than 4.

2. Meanwhile, combine the remaining 2 tablespoons cream with the chocolate, butter, and milk in the top of a double boiler. Cook over hot water, stirring occasionally, until smooth, about 4 minutes. Let stand over hot water until ready to serve.

3. Just before serving, remove the plate from the freezer, and dribble the chocolate sauce over the orange slices.

Serves 4

HARD TIMES AT LUNCHTIME

*T*he worst part of childhood, in retrospect at least, was hating every single thing I was given to eat. And while I certainly predated the Dr. Spock generation, who had the option of free choice at the high chair, nothing that was ever placed before me as a youngster received a gracious nod of approval. I ate out of duress, clearly and simply. As a matter of fact, one of the very first words I managed to pronounce—or so it was always alleged by my parents—was "Yuck!" Spoken loud and clear in reaction to a bowl of steaming farina.

The most awful foods I remember from my formative years were not cereals, however. They were school lunches. You know the kind—what kids even today refer to as "the brown-bag grab-bag," a snack composed of whatever comestible is closest at hand in the fridge or pantry by a rattled parent on a rainy morning. My mother's specialty was soggy sardine sandwiches, a repast that instantly betrayed its incriminating evidence to everyone in my immediate circle. No matter how carefully the sliced bread was wrapped, telltale oil stains were manifest on the sack's surface by the time I entered the classroom. And to this very day, the smell of sardines (along with the aroma of drying rubbers and galoshes) makes me unaccountably queasy.

Fifty years ago, kids had a sneaky practice: swapping lunches. That is, they traded one of their tuna fish or ham sandwiches for someone else's peanut butter or cream cheese and jelly. As I recall, there was always a taker for my second sandwich, even if it was composed of odd ingredients like cold fried egg and bacon. But no one, resolutely, ever made a bid for my sardines. So the second half of my midday repast inevitably went into the trash bin untasted, while I returned to class rejected and ravenous.

I know the grass is always greener across the way, but I must also admit I hankered after more salubrious school fare for years until, as a teenager, I retired my mother from the role of lunch-maker and prepared my own. To her very evident relief, for she would give me an unsolicited dime every time I wrapped up the paper sack—to assuage parental guilt, I suspect.

When I became master of the brown bag, its contents instantly turned golden, for my preference then (and now) in sandwich fillings was unflaggingly the same: egg salad.

Though nutritionists may look askance, eggs have always been my favorite fast food. And over the years I have developed a remarkable repertoire for converting them into sandwich upholstery; some so salutory I often skip the bread and serve the salad on lettuce alone. Have the following formulas as evidence—each worth two caviar sandwiches in trade, at least in my opinion!

A D U L T   E G G   S A L A D

el call this egg salad "adult" because kids have a tendency to stick up their noses at such odd *groceria* as shiitake mushrooms and sopressata. But you will not, I promise.

1 tablespoon unsalted butter
1 large shallot, quartered
1 large wild mushroom
    (shiitake, crimini, porcini),
    cap and stem coarsely
    chopped
1 tablespoon minced Italian
    hard salami, such as
    sopressata, (about 1
    ounce)

6 hard-cooked eggs, chopped
1 tablespoon mayonnaise
1 teaspoon chopped fresh
    chives or scallion (green
    onion) tops
Salt and freshly ground black
    pepper

1. Melt the butter in a small skillet over medium-low heat. Add the shallot and mushroom; cook until golden, about 5 minutes. Remove them from the skillet and finely chop. Sauté the minced salami in the same skillet until crisp, about 5 minutes

2. In a medium-size bowl, combine the eggs, shallot, mushroom, salami, and any residual drippings from the skillet. Add the mayonnaise and chives. Mix well. (The salad will be relatively dry.) Add salt and pepper to taste.

Makes about 3½ cups (enough for 4 sandwiches)

EGG SALAD NICOISE

❧

learned to make this egg mixture when I lived in the South of France—five miles out of Nice, to be precise. In Eze we made the dressing with crème fraîche, Pernod, and softened butter, but sour cream is quite an acceptable stand-in at home.

6 hard-cooked eggs, chopped
1 cup minced fresh fennel
1 teaspoon minced fresh
    chives or scallion (green
    onion) tops
½ tablespoon sour cream
2 tablespoons unsalted
    butter, at room
    temperature

1 tablespoon Pernod
2 tablespoons sliced black
    olives (I prefer Niçoise
    style)
2 tablespoons chopped fennel
    fronds
Salt and freshly ground black
    pepper

1. In a medium-size bowl, combine the eggs, fennel, and chives.

2. In a small bowl, combine the sour cream, butter, and Pernod. Mix well, and add to the egg mixture. Mix gently, and stir in the olives, fennel fronds, and salt and pepper to taste.

Makes about 3½ cups (enough for 4 sandwiches)

EGG SALAD, RANCHERO STYLE

his egg salad recipe was invented in Texas by the lady who was my daily escort on a media tour in Dallas. She knew from my schedule that lunch was not on the agenda, and provided sandwiches of pepper-egg salad instead. A wonderful notion, you'll agree.

1 medium-size red bell pepper
1 jalapeño pepper
6 hard-cooked eggs, chopped
½ teaspoon anchovy paste
1 scallion (green onion),
    trimmed and minced

2½ tablespoons mayonnaise
1 teaspoon chopped fresh
    coriander (Chinese
    parsley)

1. Roast both the peppers over a flame (or broil in an oven) until the skins are blackened. Carefully wrap in a paper towel, and place in a plastic bag until cool. Rub off the charred skins. Core, devein, and finely chop.

2. In a medium-size bowl, combine the peppers with the eggs, anchovy paste, scallion, mayonnaise, and coriander. Mix thoroughly.

Makes about 3½ cups (enough for 4 sandwiches)

FOWL PLAY

ost working folk (and that includes three-quarters of the general population) are faced with the prospect of making dinner when they come home from the office every night.

Luckier than most, I've had a longtime reprieve from such last-minute K.P. assignments, largely due to the fact that I not only worked at home but cooked there as well. And, more to the point, did both in my own sweet time!

But no longer. Several months ago, out of sheer physical discomfort, my two associates and I were forced to move our working quarters from my relatively small apartment to more spacious quarters four subway stops away. So, while I no longer write a column with a cake baking and a capon roasting just an arm's length away, nor have two telephones and a trio of electric typewriters clanging inches from my ear, I have inherited another problem: making dinner (like everybody else) when I finally commute home after 6 P.M.

Of a necessity, most of the meals I prepare these days are quick-cooked—though never, I must make clear, "fast foods" in the accepted sense. The collation at my table is dependent on several shortcuts, however. Like leftovers. I always make an extra portion of a fresh vegetable I am cooking so the residual can be tossed into the next day's salad bowl with other greens. I also keep a healthy stock of fresh pasta in the freezer for instant complex-carbohydrate collaboration. And though it may seem like a lazy man's trick, I always keep a jar of homemade vinaigrette dressing in the fridge, to be replenished once a week.

However, real mealtime magic (in my book) lies in having a few terrific recipes for chicken breasts. For that simple ingredient is a staple I can always count on finding at the supermarket, no matter how late I arrive home.

The watchwords for chicken breast-cooking in my lexicon are *sauté* and *poach*. Do not overcook the meat; it is usually done when it is firmly springy to the finger, when a fork produces golden juices only.

Aside from a good recipe that will turn a slice of white meat into a *poulet du jour* in forty-five minutes or less, the chicken cooker always needs a good sharp knife. Get into the habit of boning a breast (and cutting up an entire bird) by yourself. It's a heck of lot less stressful on the purse strings, and with very little practice you will find yourself approximating costlier cuts (like veal for scaloppine) by halving a boneless chicken or turkey breast. Merely place the breast on a wooden surface, skin side up, and make a series of horizontal slices ½ to ¼ inch thick. Then, whack the dickens out of each piece (under a heavy-duty plastic bag) with the bottom surface of the nearest fry pan.

SIMONE'S BRANDIED CHICKEN BREASTS

〰

Walter's Market, once a Greenwich Village landmark on the corner of Greenwich Avenue and Jane Street, was a butcher shop of the highest quality. It sadly closed its doors in the 1970s due to a high rent increase. Simone Roscam, chef-owner, was a wonderful, creative cook who displayed her talents by creating carry-out entrées tucked in among the steaks and chops. One of my favorites is the chicken dish that follows.

2 whole chicken breasts, boned and halved but not skinned
4 slices prosciutto
3 tablespoons plus 1 teaspoon unsalted butter
1 cup finely chopped onion
2 cloves garlic, minced
¼ cup finely chopped fresh parsley
1 teaspoon chopped fresh basil, or ¼ teaspoon dried

¼ teaspoon chopped fresh thyme, or a pinch of dried
Salt and freshly ground black pepper
¼ cup cognac, warmed
⅓ cup cold water
1 teaspoon all-purpose flour
Chopped fresh parsley, for garnish

1. Preheat the oven to 350° F.

2. Lay the chicken breasts flat, skin side down, on a work surface. Cover each breast piece with a slice of prosciutto.

3. Melt 1 tablespoon of the butter in a medium-size saucepan over medium-low heat. Add the onion and cook until wilted but not browned,

4 minutes. Stir in the garlic; cook 2 minutes longer. Then stir in the parsley, basil, and thyme; remove the pan from the heat. Spread the mixture evenly over the prosciutto slices.

4. Roll up the breasts as tightly as possible, and tie them in three places with string. Sprinkle with salt and pepper to taste.

5. Melt 2 tablespoons butter in a large skillet over medium heat. Sauté the breasts until golden brown all over, about 3 minutes per side. Reduce the heat to low, and pour the warmed cognac over the breasts. Very carefully ignite the cognac (the flame will be quite high). Turn the chicken breasts until the flames subside. Transfer the breasts to a baking dish. Stir the water into the pan juices, and pour over the chicken. Bake, basting frequently, for 30 minutes.

6. Before serving, pour the cooking juices from the chicken into a small saucepan. Mix the flour with the remaining 1 teaspoon butter until smooth; stir into the juices. Cook over medium heat until slightly thickened, 4 to 5 minutes. Pour the sauce over the chicken, sprinkle with parlsey, and serve.

Serves 2 to 4

S U P R E M E S   D E
V O L A I L L E ,   D E N V E R
S T Y L E

An East/West variant on a French classic, the following dish is the handiwork of chef Kevin Dowling of the Plum Tree Restaurant in Denver, Colorado. The chicken's flavor is dependent upon fresh ingredients and good strong stock.

4 thin slices fresh ginger
Salt
2 whole chicken breasts,
    skinned, boned, and
    halved
Freshly ground black
    pepper
¼ cup all-purpose flour
2 to 3 tablespoons unsalted
    butter
2 scallions (green onions),
    trimmed and thinly
    sliced

1 small clove garlic,
    minced
3 ounces shiitake
    mushrooms, sliced
16 snow peas
1 tablespoon soy sauce
¼ cup rich homemade beef or
    veal stock (see Note)
1 teaspoon sesame seeds
2 tablespoons white wine
    (optional)

1. Preheat the oven to 350° F.

2. Sprinkle the ginger slices with salt, and let them stand for 10 minutes. Then wipe off the salt.

3. Sprinkle the chicken breasts with salt and pepper to taste. Dredge them in the flour, shaking off any excess. Heat the butter in a heavy skillet over medium-high heat. Sauté the chicken breasts until lightly golden, about 3 minutes per side. Transfer the chicken to a baking dish, and place in the oven.

4. Add the scallions to the skillet; add the ginger slices and the garlic. Cook over high heat for 2 minutes. Add the mushrooms and cook for another 2 minutes. Then add the snow peas and soy sauce, and cook 2 minutes longer.

5. Reduce the heat to medium and add the stock to the skillet; return the chicken breasts. Sprinkle with the sesame seeds, and cook for about 1 minute. Add the wine if the sauce seems too thick. Serve immediately.

Serves 2 to 4

Note: To make strong stock or broth, simmer ¾ cup until reduced to ¼ cup.

TORTE VS. TART, A RESOLUTION

*L*ong, long ago, before I seriously thought of staking a claim at the stove, I had a problem of acute culinary semantics—one that stayed with me for years. I never knew the difference between a *tarte* and a *torte*.

You may laugh, but as an adolescent I would become absolutely tongue-tied at a bakery counter when the decision had to be made, never certain whether the confection I was about to select was one or the other!

My father, a dessert lover in the extreme, was sanguine on the subject. In our one and only "man-to-man" talk, he bypassed the issue entirely, responding gravely to my query that an "addiction to *tarts* was a weakness that a strong man simply had to overcome if he wanted to maintain a normal home life." His oblique references mystified me entirely. "*Torts,* on quite the other hand," he explained, "are a fact of life. Particularly if a man is in business." My father, a member of the board of aldermen for years, was touchy about any litigious stain on an otherwise unblemished reputation.

This conversation took place when I was a late teenager, about to leave home for college. I certainly knew as much about sex as my Victorian parent, but our chat left me more dubious than ever about baked goods!

How I first came to know the distinction between these two pastries I cannot exactly recall, but it was certainly a way back. Paula Peck, in her excellent (if out of print) primer *The Art of Fine Baking,* helped to define the characteristics: " A tart is not a pie," she reported. "It is a . . . delicate shell filled with fruit and sometimes custard. But never, as most pies are, covered by a *complete* top crust." She also unequivocally stated, "Beautiful cakes, rich with butter cream icings and liqueurs, [are known] in Vienna and Warsaw as *torten.*" Why? It was still a moot point.

It took my first cooking teacher, Dione Lucas, to dispel the variances. Dione was a lady with a masterful hand at the oven and a quick wit besides. Tired of being asked about tarts and tortes, she simplified the matter with a *bon mot.* "Tarts are usually containers, while tortes are absolute containments!" Dione declared. And further amplified the matter by producing a torte on the spot. From that day forward, I never had a problem distinguishing either again, for Dione Lucas's formula was printed on my brain pan (and tastebuds) ever after.

"You see," she demonstrated to the class, "a torte may be made of grated nuts or ground bread crumbs, but the essential ingredients never vary: butter, sugar, and eggs. Many, many eggs. Whipped to a fare-thee-well!" Dione always murmured as she worked in the kitchen, and her litany that day closed the subject once and for all: "A torte is, as you can see, not a tart. It also has nothing whatsoever in common with a *tortilla,* a *tortellini,* or a *biscuit tortoni,* either!"

The following tortes, devised of nuts, sugar, and eggs (as prescribed by Dione Lucas), compound the culinary confusion by being baked in tender crusts. I guess you could call them *tartortes* if you wish. Unconventional, both are merely unforgettable dessert experiences.

EXTRAORDINARY LINZERTORTE

♥♪♫

FOR THE PASTRY
6¾ ounces blanched almonds
1½ cups all-purpose flour
¾ cup sugar
Finely grated zest of 2 lemons
¼ teaspoon ground cinnamon
½ teaspoon ground allspice
½ cup (1 stick) unsalted
   butter, cut into bits
3 egg yolks
2 teaspoons water
   (approximately)

FOR THE ALMOND PASTE
5 ounces blanched almonds
½ cup sugar
1 egg, lightly beaten

FOR THE FINAL ASSEMBLY
10 ounces raspberry
   preserves
1 tablespoon Grand Marnier
½ teaspoon grated orange zest
1 egg yolk
2 teaspoons water

1. Preheat the oven to 375° F.

2. Prepare the pastry: Place the almonds in a food processor, and process until finely ground. Add the flour, sugar, lemon zest, cinnamon, and allspice. Process briefly. Add the butter and process until mixed. Add the egg yolks and water, and process until a soft dough is formed. Add more water if necessary. Knead the dough briefly on a lightly floured board.

3. Remove slightly more than half the dough. Wrap the smaller portion, and place it in the freezer. Roll out the larger portion between sheets of waxed paper to form an 11-inch round, and line a 9-inch loose-bottom tart pan with it, pressing the dough against the sides and bottom with your fingers.

4. Make the almond paste: Wipe out the processor bowl, and add the almonds and sugar. Process until finely ground. Add the beaten egg, and process until a smooth paste is formed. Carefully spread the mixture over the bottom of the tart shell.

5. Make the filling: Combine the raspberry preserves with the Grand

Marnier and orange zest in a medium-size bowl. Spoon evenly over the almond paste in the shell.

6. Remove the chilled dough from the freezer, and roll it out between layers of waxed paper until thin. Remove the top layer of waxed paper. Using scissors, cut the dough into strips about 1 inch wide, cutting through the paper with the scissors. Pick up the pastry strips, one at a time, and flip them over on top of the torte to form a lattice pattern. Peel off the waxed paper as you place each strip on the torte. (You can arrange the strips on the diagonal to form a diamond pattern.) Press the edges of the strips into the shell.

7. Combine the egg yolk and water in a small bowl, and blend well. Brush this glaze over the pastry strips. Bake for 10 minutes. Then reduce the heat to 350° F., and bake 20 minutes longer. Cool on a wire rack. Remove the outside ring from the pan before the torte has completely cooled.

Serves 8 to 10

MACADAMIA NUT TORTE

9 tablespoons unsalted
    butter, chilled and cut into
    bits
1 cup plus 2 tablespoons all-
    purpose flour
1 egg yolk
1½ tablespoons cold water
    (approximately)

2 eggs
1 cup plus 2 tablespoons
    sugar
1 teaspoon vanilla extract
1 teaspoon finely grated
    orange zest
1 cup finely chopped
    macadamia nuts

1. Preheat the oven to 350° F. Lightly grease a 9-inch quiche pan.

2. In a large bowl, blend the butter, flour, and egg yolk with a pastry blender until the mixture has the texture of coarse crumbs. Add just enough cold water to form a dough. Knead the dough briefly on a lightly floured board. Cover, and refrigerate for 1 hour.

3. Stir the eggs and sugar together in a medium bowl for 20 minutes; do not beat (use the lowest speed of an electric mixer). Add the vanilla, orange zest, and nuts.

4. Roll out a little more than half the dough between sheets of waxed paper to form an 11-inch round. Line the bottom and sides of the prepared pan with it; trim the edges. Fill with the macadamia mixture. Roll out the remaining dough, and place it over the filling, pressing the edges into the sides of the pan. Cut a small hole in the center of the pastry. Bake for 30 minutes. Cool on a wire rack and serve slightly warm or at room temperature.

Serves 10

SERVING THE BEST FOR LAST

A week or so ago, I was forced to think seriously about mortality. My own! For, quite irrationally, I found myself stopped dead, that is stalled in the center of an extremely volatile thoroughfare—midway, I might add, through a highly illegal U-turn—while a steady stream of oncoming traffic careened past one side of the yellow line and a large and ominously red truck barreled down the other.

They say your entire life passes before your eyes when you are in danger of imminent annihilation. That is a highly poetic notion, but speaking for myself, I can not altogether attest to its accuracy. With sudden death a viable possibility, all I could think about was the pair of weekend guests on their long day's journey from the city for a night or two in the country.

Who would cook dinner for them, I wondered. Particularly if the supply of groceries I had purchased only moments before *smashed* along with me. And, more pertinently, if the comestibles survived and I did not, how would they possibly be able to eat dinner without a serious case of indigestion afterward?

Luckily, these queries all turned out to be academic. Somebody up there obviously likes cooks, because the truck in question—going well beyond the speed limit—managed to brake and come to a whining halt a scant half foot from my tight-shut eyes. But still close enough for both drivers to hear each other's sighs of relief.

The reason how and why I came to be an unmoving object in a highway of irresistible forces is relatively unimportant to this tale. But the truth is, on my way home from a supermarket I realized that I'd left a full billfold on a shopping cart in the parking lot, and in panic turned the car around to retrieve it. Aside from the fact that the money was still there, I came home richer by far. For you see, I had been given the gift of another chance, and all at once it seemed terribly important to make the most of it.

Not exactly born-again, let's say merely that my option was renewed. For starters, I finished a long and difficult piece that I had procrastinated about writing for a month. Then, the dinner I cooked for my friends was the best thing produced at my range in eons. Even the prospect of losing at "Trivial Pursuit" afterward seemed relatively trivial in the scheme of things.

A few days after this incident, another food writer called. She was doing a survey and wanted to know what I would choose to eat for my "last meal on earth." Without hesitation, I elected the simplest and homeliest dishes I could name, food that is easy to prepare and a blessing to consume. Like the following . . .

POT-ROASTED CHICKEN WITH RICE

❧❧❧

Childhood favorites are on my agenda for a last meal on earth. This wonderful chicken dish (simmered in a pot with rice) is a version of a meal my grandmother prepared whenever one of her brood looked "peaked." Her prescription always set them straight!

1 chicken (4 pounds)
4 sprigs fresh parsley
2 fresh sage leaves, or a pinch of dried
1 large clove garlic, bruised
1½ tablespoons olive oil
1 tablespoon unsalted butter
1 medium-size onion, finely chopped
½ to 1 teaspoon minced fresh hot red pepper

1 slice hard Italian salami or sopressata, ¼ inch thick, chopped
2 cups homemade chicken stock or canned broth
½ cup dry white wine
1 cup rice
Chopped fresh parsley, for garnish

1. Rinse and pat the chicken dry with paper towels. Stuff the cavity with the parsley sprigs and sage. Sew and truss. Rub the chicken with the bruised garlic. Then mince the garlic and set it aside.

2. Heat the oil in a large saucepan or Dutch oven over medium-high heat. Add the chicken and brown well on all sides, about 8 minutes.

3. Remove the chicken from the pan, and wipe out the pan. Add the butter, and cook the onion over medium-low heat for 1 minute. Add the reserved garlic and the red pepper; cook 4 minutes longer. Stir in the salami.

4. Return the chicken to the pot, breast side up. Pour the stock and wine over the chicken, and heat to boiling. Reduce the heat, cover, and simmer for 1 hour.

5. Add the rice, stirring it in around the chicken. Continue to cook, covered, until all the liquid has been absorbed by the rice, about 20 minutes.

6. To serve, carve the chicken and place the pieces on a warmed platter. Surround with the rice, and sprinkle with chopped parsley.

Serves 4

CHOCOLATE CREAM

𝓝 ot pudding, and far from mousse or soufflé, this comfort food is an unctuous blend of cream and chocolate that is literally to die (or in my case to live) over!

5 egg yolks	1 ounce (1 square) unsweetened
½ cup sugar	baking chocolate, chopped
1 cup milk	1 envelope unflavored gelatin
3 ounces (3 squares)	1 tablespoon cold water
semisweet baking	1½ cups heavy or whipping
chocolate, chopped	cream

1. Beat the egg yolks with the sugar in a large bowl until light and fluffy. Set aside.

2. Heat the milk to a low simmer in a heavy saucepan over low heat. Add both chocolates; stir until melted and smooth.

3. Soften the gelatin in the cold water, about 1 minute. Slowly add it to the hot chocolate mixture. Stir until dissolved. Remove the pan from the heat.

4. Slowly add the hot chocolate mixture to the egg yolks, and stir until smooth. Place the bowl over ice, and continue to stir until the mixture begins to thicken, 6 to 8 minutes.

5. Beat 1 cup of the cream until stiff. Fold the whipped cream into the chocolate mixture, and pour into a 6-cup mold. Cover and chill until set, about 3 hours, or overnight.

6. To unmold the cream, heat 1 inch of water in a skillet. Dip a sharp knife into the water, and run it around the edges of the mold. Then place the mold in the water for about 5 seconds, and invert it onto a platter. Rechill for at least 30 minutes. Whip the remaining ½ cup cream, and using a pastry tube, pipe a decorative pattern over the top of the chocolate mold.

Serves 6 to 8

A MARRIAGE THAT SHOULD'VE

GONE TO POT

arriage is a private affair, at least until it becomes public. Which is another way of saying—gone to pot!

In the past six months, four pair of my very close friends have announced their intention to split and, in passing, render marriage vows null and void. Which should not have come as the surprise it did, considering the fact that recent survey figures indicate the average tenure of a U.S. marriage in the eventful 1980s to be a scant nine years. And (here's even more dispiriting news) that a full third of the population—mainly those in the western states—do not remain in tandem longer than thirty-six months!

Since it is my dear friends who are separating, I take the loss rather more personally than I do the national average. And while I would not presume to expose these intimates' psychological or (heaven forfend) sexual incompatabilities in a food column, particularly when Ann Landers and cohorts are only pages away, I do believe most of these marriages could be saved with a little kitchen therapy.

What (you may ask yourself) is that darn fool, Bert Greene, saying? Well, starting with the premise that food is love, after all, he is suggesting that the fragile bonds of matrimony might just possibly be recemented with the application of a little old-fashioned "togetherness."

Take the case of two bespoke friends. An extremely amicable pair (on the surface at least), they have never agreed on what to eat or, more pertinently, what to serve at their table in ten years of marriage. He always cooks steak or lamb chops on the outdoor grill (even in December), even though his wife, who is a nominal vegetarian, eschews all red meat entirely. She, on quite the other hand, always prepares a wet, ill-seasoned salad and toasted garlic bread as adjuncts to his culinary pyrotechnics—though he publicly confides that garlic gives him a migraine and that the salad is like eating "wet wash"!

On one occasion (after several strong helpings of Scotch on the rocks), he supplicated me to give his spouse a lesson in drying greens and whisking together a tolerable vinaigrette.

"Lord knows," he sighed, *sotto voce,* "she has all your cookbooks. But they don't do her a damn bit of good because she never reads the recipes right!"

He *does,* however, and my advice to these friends (publicly) is to get it together. To physically join each other in the business of preparing a meal, from scratch, in concert—hand in hand, arm in arm, and spoon in bowl!

Men are essentially romantics at the stove. They become as excited as lovers when they attempt extravagant culinary feats. Women are somewhat more practical, governors and guides who temper their enthusiasms with realism and judgment. They make wonderful kitchen teammates. And I know that if my chums could manage to declare an emotional truce for the time it takes to perform a bit of serious cooking, they just might discover at the chopping board, food processor, and range the seemingly lost sense of compatibility that once took them to the bed.

And, with any luck, the feeling of mutuality might send them back in that direction once again!

What follows is a wonderfully complicated dish—Dr. Greene's very American version of a Greek classic—that just happens to be designed for four pairs of hands. Loving hands!

LAMB AND MACARONI PASTITSIO

1 pound macaroni (3½-inch tubular preferred)

4 eggs, separated

4 tablespoons (½ stick) unsalted butter, melted

8 ounces freshly grated Parmesan cheese

2 tablespoons olive oil

1 large onion, finely chopped

1 small clove garlic, minced

1 can (14 ounces) Italian-style tomatoes, drained and coarsely chopped

2 medium-size fresh tomatoes, seeded and coarsely chopped

Pinch of sugar

½ cinnamon stick (2 inches)

1¼ to 1½ pounds cooked lamb, ground

1 teaspoon Dijon mustard

½ cup dried bread crumbs

2 tablespoons unsalted butter

3 tablespoons all-purpose flour

1½ cups homemade chicken stock or canned broth, heated

½ cup heavy or whipping cream

⅛ teaspoon freshly grated nutmeg

Salt and freshly ground black pepper

1. Preheat the oven to 350° F.

2. Cook the macaroni in a large pot of boiling salted water until tender but not soft, about 12 to 13 minutes. Rinse under cold running water, and drain thoroughly. Transfer to a large bowl.

3. Beat the egg whites until stiff but not dry. Set them aside.

4. Pour the melted butter over the macaroni, and toss to coat it well. Sprinkle ½ cup of the cheese over the macaroni; toss again. Fold in the egg whites. Set aside.

5. Heat the oil in the same large pot over medium heat. Add the onion, and cook 1 minute. Add the garlic; cook 2 minutes longer. Stir in the canned and fresh tomatoes. Sprinkle with the sugar, and add the cinnamon stick. Stir in the lamb and mustard. Cook until all the liquid has evaporated, 15 to 20 minutes.

6. Remove the pot from the heat, and allow the mixture to cool slightly. Remove the cinnamon stick. Stir in ½ cup of the cheese and ¼ cup of the bread crumbs. Mix thoroughly, and transfer to a large bowl. Wipe out the pot.

7. Melt the 2 tablespoons butter in the same large pot over medium-low heat. Add the flour; cook, stirring constantly, for 2 minutes. Whisk in the chicken stock, and bring to a boil. Add the cream and nutmeg, and cook until thickened, 6 to 8 minutes. Season with salt and pepper to taste, and remove from the heat.

8. Lightly beat the egg yolks in a small bowl. Whisk in ¼ cup of the sauce. Then whisk the egg yolk mixture back into the sauce, and set it aside.

9. Butter a large ovenproof lasagne pan or 3-quart baking dish. Sprinkle the dish with 2 tablespoons of the bread crumbs and 1 tablespoon cheese. Spoon half the macaroni into the dish to form a layer. Add the lamb mixture to form the next layer. Top with the remaining macaroni. Pour the sauce over the top, and sprinkle evenly with the remaining cheese and 2 tablespoons bread crumbs. Bake for 30 minutes. Allow the pastitsio to rest for 10 minutes before serving.

Serves 8

DON'T KEEP YOUR DIET A SECRET

Recently I gave a small dinner party that altered forevermore my perceptions of the role a host and a guest play at such functions—for it was a case of true trauma at the table!

Of the four invited guests, two were old friends whose eating habits I knew fairly well. The other couple were friends of theirs, people I'd met socially and wanted to know better. Actually the evening promised to be fun—until a pre-dinner toast was proposed.

"Here's to the dish that's roasting in the oven," one of the four declared with an appreciative sniff. "What is it?"
"Vegetable-stuffed roast chicken wrapped in pancetta," I replied proudly. "A good Italian friend gave me the recipe a while back."

Everyone gave a slight sigh of anticipation, *except* one of the newcomers to my table.

"I'm sorry," he stated flatly. "Isn't pancetta Italian smoked bacon? I don't eat pork products."
"Well," I found myself stammering. "Bacon merely wraps the fowl—it could be lifted off your piece, I suppose."

The gentleman shook his head. "If the chicken was cooked with bacon, I can't eat it."

Of course it had been, so it looked like slim pickings for his dinner, until I went to the fridge and discovered a leg of leftover turkey I'd been planning to feed the dog.

Everyone else was rapturously vocal about the main course, and while the odd-man-out was polite about his, I must admit the incident created a pall that dampened the evening's good spirits. At least for me.

Washing dishes after the party, I came to the conclusion that the problem of food prejudices, religious dietary principles, and even allergies is a responsibility that belongs to a guest rather than a host. A diner-out with culinary restrictions should either alert the party-giver as to their nature when the original invitation is extended or keep quiet about them when dinner is served.

Speaking for myself, I am not overly fond of kidneys. I clearly recall an evening at a French family's table when kidneys in mustard sauce was the only offering aside from bread and salad. If memory serves, I went heavy on the greens, ate a minimum of kidneys, and camouflaged the rest under a large crust of bread. I'm sure that did not fool my hostess, but at least it spared her feelings in public.

Taking up the cudgels of *guest responsibility* has given me a brand-new insight into my friends' discretion.

After I told this tale with some heat, a longtime chum placed his arm about my shoulder when I invited him to brunch. "Bert, I never wanted to tell you this before," he confessed, "but I am seriously allergic to shellfish. So put your money where your mouth is, if you were planning to serve those famous Down East Lobster Cakes of yours!"

If you think I resented his candor, you're mistaken. I relished it!

What follows are recipes for the two dishes that caused me hostly distress. Serve them without a jot of concern—after a frank discussion with your guests—because both are wonderful.

311

DOWN EAST LOBSTER CAKES

ᗜ᭣ᗯ

*L*obster cakes are a very special Maine dispensation, bringing joy to all except allergic diners. If your guest suffers the malady, consider flaked cooked monkfish as a stand-in for the lobster. Or if you do better with crab, try the crab cakes on page 185. These are just a slight variation of them.

1 pound flaked cooked lobster
  meat
1 cup fresh bread crumbs
⅓ cup milk (approximately)
1 egg, lightly beaten
¼ cup mayonnaise
½ teaspoon baking powder
2 tablespoons finely chopped
  fresh parsley
1 teaspoon minced fresh
  basil, or a pinch of dried

2 tablespoons minced
  scallion (green onion)
  (optional)
½ teaspoon salt
¼ teaspoon freshly ground
  white pepper
All-purpose flour, for dusting
4 tablespoons unsalted butter
  or vegetable oil
Tartar sauce

1. Place the lobster meat in a large bowl, and cover it with the bread crumbs. Moisten the crumbs with the milk.

2. Combine the beaten egg and mayonnaise in a small bowl; stir well. Add the baking powder, parsley, basil, scallions, salt, and white pepper; mix thoroughly. Pour the mixture over the lobster, and toss lightly until well mixed. Form into 10 large patties, adding more milk if needed. Place on a plate, cover, and refrigerate for at least 1 hour.

3. Dust the lobster cakes lightly with flour. Melt 2 tablespoons butter or heat 2 tablespoons oil in a large skillet over medium heat. Sauté the lobster cakes until golden, 2 to 3 minutes per side. Add more butter or oil as needed. Drain on paper towels. Serve with tartar sauce.

Serves 4 or 5

PANCETTA-CLOAKED ROAST CHICKEN

✂

 he party-dampening roast chicken, crammed with veggies and cloaked with Italian-style bacon, is a wonderfully satisfying dish. If pancetta is hard to come by, substitute smoky ham or Canadian bacon—though it still will be no-no to guests with religious shibboleths.

8 tablespoons (1 stick) unsalted butter
1 large onion, chopped
2 medium-size potatoes, cut into ¼-inch cubes
2 medium-size carrots, cut into ¼-inch cubes
1 medium-size zucchini, cut into ¼-inch cubes
¼ cup chopped fresh parsley
1 tablespoon soy sauce
½ teaspoon salt
¼ teaspoon freshly ground black pepper
2 chickens (about 2½ pounds each)

1 clove garlic, bruised
4 slices pancetta (Italian smoked bacon), about ⅛ inch thick
1 cup homemade chicken stock or canned broth
1 tablespoon plus 1 teaspoon all purpose flour
1 cup heavy or whipping cream
2 teaspoons strong brewed coffee
Chopped fresh parsley, for garnish

1. Preheat the oven to 375° F.

2. Melt 4 tablespoons of the butter in a large heavy skillet, and cook the onion over medium-low heat for 5 minutes. Stir in the potatoes, carrots, and zucchini; cook for 2 minutes. Add the parsley, soy sauce, salt, and pepper. Toss well, and remove the skillet from the heat.

3. Rub each chicken well, inside and out, with the bruised garlic; discard the garlic. Spoon half the vegetable stuffing into each chicken, and truss the chickens. Place the chickens on a rack in a roasting pan, and spread 1 tablespoon butter over each one. Place 2 strips of pancetta over each breast. Pour the stock around the chickens. Bake, basting every 20 minutes with the pan juices, until the chickens are tender, about 1½ hours. Remove the trussing; place the chickens on a platter, and keep warm.

4. Degrease the pan juices. Melt the remaining 2 tablespoons butter in a medium-size saucepan over medium-low heat. Whisk in the flour and cook, stirring constantly, for 2 minutes. Add the pan juices and cream. Increase the heat slightly, and simmer until thickened, 4 to 5 minutes. Then stir in the coffee. Season to taste with salt and pepper.

5. To serve, spoon ¼ cup of the sauce over the chickens, and sprinkle them with parsley. Pass the remaining sauce.

Serves 4 to 6

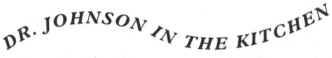

R are books are not exactly my cup of tea. However, a friend who is a serious collector of antique printed matter recently permitted me to have a squint at one of his newest (which is to say oldest) acquisitions. And I must report that a single glance blew my twentieth-century mind.

The volumes were two enormous, yellowed folio editions of Dr. Samuel Johnson's *Dictionary*. The first great English dictionary of the meaning and derivation of words, this book, printed in 1755, predated Webster by seventy-five years and the *Oxford English Dictionary* by over a century.

For a hundred years, Dr. Johnson's formidable tome was the supreme arbiter of the English language. So it was quite an eye-opener to me—riffling through a dozen or so pages at random—to realize how the sense of words still very much in use in 1988 has drastically altered from their original meanings back in 1788.

Speaking as a food writer and stovetop jockey, almost all the words I logged were recipe terms or in some odd way related to the ordering, preparation, or serving of meals. But I tell you here and now, I don't think I would have survived long in yesterday's kitchens; language alone would have done me in. If you don't think that's true, have a clutch of examples from the dictionary—and think again.

In Dr. Johnson's day, if a cook used a *whisk*, it wasn't to stir a sauce; whisks were leather whips that were kept in the kitchen to lash the scullery boy when he grew lax.

To *wallop*, on the other hand, meant to bring something to the boil. Preferably in a *skillet*, which was the eighteenth-century term for a kettle.

If a *quick* chicken was requested, it came live rather than cooked. If a steak was served *rear*, you sent it back to the cook—because rear meant sodden and rotten food. However, a *tidy* dish was always a well-seasoned one, while a *tasty* dish was one that was totally tasteless.

The kitchen worker who *faltered* was the poor soul responsible for cleaning and washing the dishes. He was probably lucky to have a *job*. However, he didn't talk about it because any job was considered to be low, mean, piddling work, in the kitchen or out.

When buying foodstuffs, the request for a *barnacle* usually produced a fowl. (The call for a *fowl* produced a dueling weapon!) *Grass-goods* were salad greens, and *hard-goods* were root vegetables, and *candy* was anything coated with aspic or meat jelly.

Macaroni was a derogatory term for the lace furbelows and flounces on menswear at the time, and *macaroons* were the rude and coarse fellows who wore them. But the most pejorative kitchen term in Dr. Johnson's lexicon was *house-wife,* for that was an epithet applied to a woman of very low character. Obviously, no longer the case!

Words do change, obviously, but many dishes prepared and consumed almost 300 years ago still come to the table in reasonably the same form. For instance, Dr. Johnson's *Dictionary* limns a *smashed potato* as a porringer of cooked skinned tubers beaten with a spoon and knife till light and greasy. *Green pease* were advised to be stirred as little as possible to avoid *shriving* and were seasoned with only *sprynge leafs.* The dictum on *pole beans* is that they be cooked when the pod is no more than a thumb's length and that the dish be very *tidy.* Here are a few veggies that seem to be just what the doctor ordered.

S U P E R - C R E A M Y
M A S H E D   P O T A T O E S

3 large baking potatoes
(about 2½ pounds)
4½ tablespoons unsalted
butter, at room
temperature

6 tablespoons heavy or
whipping cream
Salt
Chopped fresh parsley for
garnish (optional)

1. Peel, cube, and cook the potatoes in boiling salted water until tender but not mushy, about 20 minutes. Drain the potatoes, and wipe out the pot with a damp paper towel.

2. Force the potatoes through a ricer back into the hot pot.

3. Place the pot over low heat, and using a wooden spoon, beat in the butter and cream. The potatoes should be light and fluffy. Add salt to taste and sprinkle with parsley if desired.

Serves 4

WILTED PEAS AND LETTUCE

1 cup heavy or whipping
   cream
2 cups fresh peas, blanched;
   or frozen, thawed
1 cup torn Bibb, Boston, or
   romaine lettuce leaves

2 tablespoons finely chopped
   fresh chives or scallion
   (green onion) tops
Salt and freshly ground black
   pepper

Bring the cream to a boil in a medium-size skillet. Reduce the heat and simmer until the cream is reduced by half, about 12 minutes. Stir in the peas and lettuce. Toss until the lettuce is just wilted, about 3 minutes. Add the chives and salt and pepper to taste, and serve.

Serves 4

OUT-OF-SEASON GREEN BEANS

1 pound green beans, halved
   lengthwise
2 tablespoons unsalted
   butter
1 large shallot, minced
½ teaspoon beef bouillon
   powder

1 small tomato, peeled,
   seeded, and chopped
Salt and freshly ground black
   pepper
Chopped fresh parsley, for
   garnish

1. Cook the beans in boiling salted water until almost tender, about 3 minutes. Rinse under cold running water and drain.

2. Melt the butter in a large saucepan over medium-low heat. Add the shallot and cook 3 minutes. Toss in the beans, bouillon powder, and tomato. Cook, tossing constantly, over medium heat until warmed through. Add salt and pepper to taste, sprinkle with parsley, and serve.

Serves 4

MY LATE, GREAT CAREER

Whenever I am asked why I left the catering business, I give an involuntary shudder. If I can bear it, I impart the following tale.

A decade or so ago, when I was younger and in the business of cooking for others, I was summoned to a pre-party interview with a much-publicized heiress. A woman of impeccable hauteur and no manners at all, she whistled loudly, like a truck driver, as she studied the estimate submitted, holding it at arm's length like a notice of quarantine.

"Wow! You are so expensive. I really don't know if I can afford your services. But [as I was about to rise] you are *very highly recommended*. So I guess we'll chance it. You will come in and do the main course and dessert," she determined. "I'll take care of the rest of the meal."

As I watched, she produced a blue pencil.

"No one eats hors d'oeuvres these days—they are just a waste of your time and *my money*," she said, crossing them off the menu.
"I always do the fish course myself. I am actually rather famous for my salmon mousse. And it makes less work for you!"

She studied the list again, with pencil poised.

"No soup. No bread and butter. And no cheese and fruit. Too much food deadens a good party, anyway. Agreed?"

Agreed. With pain in my pocketbook, I took my leave. Aside from the hostess's frugality, there were other drawbacks to this event. It took place in Connecticut, which meant long-distance transportation of food and personnel. The hostess also bred Siamese cats for a hobby, and there were always dozens of them underfoot.

The day of the party, everything was prepared—even the tables set—before the lady appeared, martini in hand, with a trail of adoring, enigmatic cats in her wake.

"It looks quite nice," she announced, poking a finger into various skillets and pans. "So I guess we're all set."
"Except for your mousse."
"My what?"
"The fish course. The one you are famous for!"
"My God!" She groaned. "I knew I forgot something."

As I watched, she advanced to the freezer with a cleaver, cats parting before her like the Red Sea. With much hacking and swearing, she eventually produced from its depths a copper mold swathed in layers of ice and plastic wrap.

"I made this last year when salmon was cheap. Or maybe the year before. Do you think it's any good?"

Together we sniffed the frosty gray salvage.

"It doesn't smell rancid," I offered.
"Well, that's always a good sign. Let's unmold it and cover it with mayonnaise. Perhaps a little parsley and dill . . ."

She placed the empty copper form on the kitchen floor, where a small Siamese was asleep. "Have a taste, darling," she cooed as the kitten surveyed the cold metal with her tongue.

"It's perfectly fine," she announced to me. "She likes it! Everyone knows cats never eat *anything* that isn't perfectly good for them!"

The party started on a high note. Guests, accustomed to her Spartan fare, relished the first course. Plates were scraped clean when they returned to the kitchen.

The hostess was in fine fettle, full of compliments, sailing into the kitchen to order more wine. "So far everything is divine. Divine," she murmured as she inspected a sauce I was about to flambé. As I lit a match, she shepherded a clutch of cats to the safety of the back porch—and promptly shrieked in horror.

"Oh my God! It killed her," she screamed. "The mousse killed the cat!"

The kitchen staff and I were galvanized by her cries. There outside the door lay a very small and inert Siamese kitten, unmistakably stretched in *rigor mortis*.

"Oh my God," she repeated to herself as the realization finally hit home. "It will kill them all!"

Racing to the kitchen phone, with some assistance, she dialed the emergency clinic of the nearest hospital. A doctor there determined that all the guests must have their stomachs pumped at once. An ambulance was being sent immediately.

"Make it a large one!" she groaned.

That party ended this caterer's career on a high note as well. The ultrasonic wail of a police siren and the sight of two ambulances filled with guests in formal gowns and tuxedos haunt my dreams to this very day.

I suspect I do not have to report that the bill for this event was never fully paid, as recrimination for being part of a forever maligned social event. But the worst blow occurred a year after, when a lawyer called to negotiate a settlement out of court.

"The funniest thing about that disastrous dinner party is probably something you don't know," he allowed after some parrying back and forth about costs. "The cat didn't die of tainted mousse at all. It was run over in the driveway by one of the guests' chauffeurs. He hadn't wanted to spoil the party, so he left the poor thing on the back porch instead. We didn't actually find out the truth until, oh, a week or so later. But that's how these things go, y'know . . ."

Indeed I do. Then and now!

MILLIONAIRE'S POUND CAKE

he following recipe is *not* for fish mousse. A pound cake, it is a residual of my catering days. The recipe was passed on to me by an inordinately lovely and generous client from Texas, who thought it rightfully belonged in my repository.

2 cups (4 sticks) unsalted
   butter, at room
   temperature
4 cups sugar
6 large eggs

¾ cup milk
4 cups cake flour
1 tablespoon vanilla extract
½ teaspoon almond extract
½ cup fresh lemon juice

1. Preheat the oven to 325° F. Grease and flour a 10-inch Bundt pan.

2. Beat the butter in the large bowl of an electric mixer until light. Beat in 3 cups of the sugar until light and fluffy. Then add the eggs, one at a time, beating thoroughly after each addition.

3. Stir the milk into the batter in three parts, alternating with three parts flour. Stir in both extracts, and mix well.

4. Pour the batter into the prepared Bundt pan and bake until a toothpick inserted in the center comes out clean, about 1 hour. Cool it on a wire rack for 5 minutes.

5. Combine the remaining 1 cup sugar with the lemon juice in a small saucepan. Heat over medium heat until the sugar has dissolved, 2 to 3 minutes. Spoon over the cake. Let the cake stand until cool before unmolding.

Serves 12 or more

INDEX

K, L

Kansas City, Mo., 179-80

Lace cakes, Southern, 11-12

Lamb:
and macaroni pastitsio, 308-9
shanks Provençale, 278-79

Lasagne straordinarie, 135-37

Latkes:
Myra's potato, 52-53
traditional meat sauce for, 53

Leftovers, 244-45

Lemon:
angel cake, 94
and caramel souf-flé, 149-50
yogurt cake, 43-44

Lettuce, wilted peas and, 317-18

Linzertorte, extra-ordinary, 299-300

Lobster cakes, Down East, 312

Louisiana cookery:
jambalaya dressing, 85-86
see also New Orleans cookery

Lovenjoy, Sadie, 129

Lucas, Dione, 130-32, 162, 241-42, 298

Lunch fare, 288-89
frittatas, 189-93
New England "pannycakes," 219

pipérade, 193-94
un-grandmotherly scrambled eggs, 27-28
see also Sandwiches

M

Macadamia nut torte, 300-301

Macaroni and lamb pastitsio, 308-9

McSweeney, Eugene, 65-67

Marital problems, kitchen therapy for, 306-8

Marmalade, pineap-ple-apricot, 90

Marshall, Raymond, 236

Meat loafs:
cold jellied, with whipped-cream horseradish dressing, 119-20
spicy Texas, 80-81

Meat sauce for latkes, traditional, 53

Melon:
mêlée, 124
vinaigrette, 125

Millionaire's pound cake, 322-23

Minced beef Dijon-style, 226

Mrs. Pendleberry's unforgettable coconut cake, 106-8

Moravian orange bread, 81-82

Moss, Katharine, 232

Muffins, English, 181-82

Mushroom:
beef, barley, and tomato soup, 28-29
omelet, Dione Lucas's, 242-43
strudel, Black Forest, 273-74

Mustard, 224-25
baked shrimp, 227-28

My mother's choco-late icing, 36-37

My mother's old-fashioned yellow cake, 35-36

Myra's ham, 51-52

Myra's potato latkes, 52-53

N

National Beef Cook-Off, 228-33

New England "pan-nycakes," 219

Newman, Paul, 122-23

New Orleans cookery, 125-27
avocados vinai-grette, 129-30
country captain, 127-29
praline cakes with caramel syrup, 59-60

New potatoes in white wine, 165-66

Veal:
- balls, bean soup with, 74-75
- and cherry stew, 254-55
- in green sauce, 202-3

Vietnamese cookery, 174-75
- chicken steamed with ham and vegetables, 177-78
- nuoc mam, 178
- tomatoes stuffed with pork, 175-76

Vinaigrette:
- dressing, 147
- melon, 125
- sauce, simple, 171

W

Wafers:
- coconut, 108-9
- slow-cooked spinach tart, 168-69

Waffles, 8-10
- country, 10-11

Welsh rarebit, 5, 6

Whipped-cream horseradish dressing, 120

Whole-wheat batter bread, 209

Wilted peas and lettuce, 317-18

Wolfert, Paula, 139

Woodward, Joanne, 122-23

Y

Yellow cake, my mother's old-fashioned, 35-36

Yogurt lemon cake, 43-44

Z

Zasu Pitts's Chocolate Fudge, 62

Zasu Pitts's Panocha, 63

Zoe Chase (New York), 113-15

Zucchini:
- and tomato salad, cold, 265
- tousled, 24-25